ECONOMY AND SOCIETY

ECONOMY AND SOCIETY

A Study in the Integration of Economic and Social Theory

by

TALCOTT PARSONS

and

NEIL J. SMELSER

THE FREE PRESS, *New York*

First published in the United States of America in 1956 by
The Free Press, A Corporation

Printed in the United States of America

Collier-Macmillan Canada, Ltd., Toronto, Ontario

First Free Press Paperback Edition 1965
Reprinted by arrangement with Routledge and
Kegan Paul Ltd., London.

Second printing February 1969

DEDICATED

To the Memory of

ALFRED MARSHALL

and

MAX WEBER

Two great pioneers

in the

integration of economic

and sociological theory

CONTENTS

Chapter I

THE PROBLEM: CURRENT SOCIOLOGICAL THEORY AND SOME CENTRAL CONCEPTS OF ECONOMICS

Chapter III

THE INSTITUTIONAL STRUCTURE OF THE ECONOMY

Chapter VI

CONCLUSION: ECONOMIC THEORY AND THE GENERAL THEORY OF SOCIAL SYSTEM

TABLE OF FIGURES

PREFACE

This volume is designed as a contribution to the synthesis of theory in economics and sociology. We believe that the degree of separation between these two disciplines—separation emphasized by intellectual traditions and present institutional arrangements—arbitrarily conceals a degree of intrinsic intimacy between them which must be brought to the attention of the respective professional groups.

We dedicate the book to the memory of two great figures in the recent history of social science, one identified with each of the two disciplines. The work of Marshall and Weber, considered together, constituted a level of rapprochement between economics and sociology which has not been matched since. From a somewhat different point of view Pareto also made a notable attempt at synthesis which has greatly influenced our thinking. It seemed as though the theory of economic equilibrium he took over from Walras and developed was about to merge into a general theory of social systems. But the initiative of these men failed to gain momentum. Indeed, we feel that there has been, if anything, a retrogression rather than an advance in the intervening half century.

Why has such a promising start failed to lead to further developments? On the side of economics, we might suggest three barriers. First, economists have become increasingly preoccupied with the great potentialities of the technical apparatus of economic theory (to which Marshall himself made such a major contribution). Second, the pressing problems of public policy have required immediate contributions from economists; under such pressure, exploration of theoretical side-roads to neighbouring disciplines seemed inappropriate. Finally, the elementary level of sociological theory itself—including the fact that most of the best sociological theory has remained until recently in languages other than English—for a long time provided little to which economists could turn.

For the sociological tradition, a major isolating factor has been a revolt, perhaps, against the subtle ways in which the "ideology" of economic thinking has permeated the wider intellectual atmosphere. Furthermore, neither substantive concepts nor methods of analysis derived from economics have seemed appropriate for the more immediate purposes of sociological theory. Sociology had to find a footing on its own, as it were, before it could profit from its sister discipline.

In the American case, disillusion with the abortive institutionalist movement undoubtedly exaggerated the distance between the two disciplines. The combination of (to us) not very good sociology and a negative attitude toward economic and almost any other theory made this movement a poor entering wedge for exploring interdisciplinary relations on a theoretical level. In Great Britain a comparable role has been played by the negative attitude toward any sociology except that of primitive peoples in whom the economist has not interested himself traditionally. Perhaps also the atmosphere of general scepticism toward highly generalized theory, prevalent in both countries, has played a part.

Whatever the determining factors of their separation, we feel it is necessary for the future of both disciplines to re-establish interest in the borderline relations; we offer this volume as a contribution. We hope that there will be much substantive criticism of our exposition. We also hope, however, that serious criticisms can be separated from those which derive from the unfortunate fact that few persons competent in sociological theory have any working knowledge of economics, and conversely, that few economists have much knowledge of sociology. In the nature of the case, we have had to introduce both technical sociology and technical economics. Except for the rare individual who is competent in both, there will be difficult passages. We can only plead, therefore, that with tolerance and care in working through unfamiliar materials, both the economist and the sociologist may be rewarded with insights which are not accessible within the confines of either discipline taken alone.

This volume originated when, for the fall of 1953, the senior author was invited to deliver the Marshall Lectures at the University of Cambridge on the "Integration of Economic and

Sociological Theory." Years before he had dealt with problems in this field—as documented in *The Structure of Social Action* and in various papers—but in the meantime had turned to other areas. This invitation provided a welcome occasion to return to an old interest, to acquaint himself with many important developments in economics in the interim, and to relate them to changes in his own field. The time limit for this task was grossly insufficient, however, and the lectures as delivered (in November 1953) represented an incomplete and in other ways inadequate treatment of the problem. It was clear that publication in the original form was inadvisable.

At the time of the Marshall Lectures the junior author was in the last year of a Rhodes Scholarship in Philosophy, Politics, and Economics at Oxford, with emphasis on economics; he had previously been a student of sociology at Harvard. We established contact immediately and carried on a series of discussions in Europe during the academic year 1953–54. When both of us returned to Harvard for the year 1954–55, these discussions ripened into the collaboration of which this book is the product.

The first three chapters follow, in a broad way, the outline of the subject-matter of the three Marshall lectures. But practically none of the actual exposition contained in the lectures survives. The material has been reworked entirely in the light of many recent theoretical developments. The subject-matter of Chapters IV and V was not treated at all in the lectures. Chapter IV reaches to levels of technicality in economic analysis for which the senior author felt entirely incompetent at the time of the lectures. Chapter V, though more sociological than economic on the whole, deals with a subject which was omitted from the lectures both because of lack of space and for lack of assurance in mode of attack. We include these chapters both because of the addition of reinforcement to the original one-man working force and because of the further development of thinking which more than two years of collaborative work have made possible.

The senior author wishes at this time to record his gratitude to the academic community at Cambridge for its cordiality in connection with the Marshall Lectures and more generally in connection with his tenure as Visiting Professor of Social

Theory during 1953–54. In particular, Professor Austin Robinson, who presided at the lectures, and Mr. Harry Johnson, now Professor at the University of Manchester, who subjected the manuscript to a most helpful critical analysis, may be singled out. In less specific ways, Professor Meyer Fortes, Professor M. Postan, Dr. Richard Stone, Mr. Bryant King and Mr. Noel Annan were particularly stimulating influences. Of other British colleagues Professor Raymond Firth also helpfully criticized the manuscript of the lectures and suggested the title which has been adopted for the book.[1] It also seems appropriate to acknowledge—albeit belatedly—a very warm welcome which the senior author received in Cambridge long ago in 1930, when he was working on a study of Marshall's sociological ideas which eventually appeared in two articles in the *Quarterly Journal of Economics*, and later as Chapter IV of *The Structure of Social Action*. The late Mrs. Marshall was particularly considerate and helpful on that occasion.

The junior author thanks Mr. William R. Moffat of Harvard University for a patient and detailed criticism of the Marshall Lectures; his clarification of the Keynesian position relative to the boundary processes was the germ of an extensive revision of material which now appears in the second chapter. Mr. Alain Enthoven of the Massachusetts Institute of Technology read the economic material on the trade cycle which appears in Chapter IV and suggested the elimination of several inelegancies. More generally, gratitude is due to Mr. G. D. N. Worswick, Fellow of Magdalen College, Oxford, who tutored the junior author through two years of economics. He insisted on the mastery of economic subject-matter as such, but welcomed suggestions and interpretations from a sociologist temporarily on leave from his training.

During the course of the academic year 1954–55, the theoretical developments incorporated in Chapters II and III were

[1] We are conscious that this title is an almost literal translation of Max Weber's *Wirtschaft und Gesellschaft*, but, in spite of the difference in scale and comprehensiveness, we respectfully hope it is worthy to stand in a line of succession to such a work. We also have inadvertently used the same title as Professor Wilbert E. Moore in his excellent pamphlet (Doubleday series, 1955). It was decided upon independently of any knowledge of Professor Moore's enterprise.

greatly facilitated in weekly discussions in an informal seminar of graduate students in the Harvard Social Relations Department on the classification of occupational types. Besides the authors, members of this group were Miss Christine Kayser, Messrs. Robert W. Avery, Jesse R. Pitts, Howard E. Roseborough, and for a period Dr. Frank E. Jones. In connection with matters of economic sociology, Messrs. Pitts and Roseborough have been especially helpful. During the fall term the foundations for the theoretical material in Chapter II were formulated and discussed extensively in a graduate Seminar on The Theory of Social Systems.

In the later stages several economists subjected the manuscript to a critical reading. We are particularly grateful to Professor Bert F. Hoselitz of the University of Chicago who undertook an unusually thorough and penetrating critical commentary which has stimulated extensive revisions. Others whose criticisms have been extremely helpful are Mr. Chester I. Barnard, Dr. Alfred Conrad of Northwestern University, Professor James Duesenberry of Harvard, Professor Marion J. Levy of Princeton, Mr. Henry Rosovsky of Harvard, Professor W. W. Rostow of the Massachusetts Institute of Technology, and Dr. Francis X. Sutton of the Ford Foundation. Convergence on the same themes by several of these critics was particularly helpful in guiding our revisions. None of them, however, bears responsibility for the views we have finally expressed. We have accepted many suggestions but also have rejected some, and bear sole responsibility for the result.

Mrs. Dorinthe Burkholder Sacks, with the assistance of Mrs. Anna Connors, has performed with great effectiveness the difficult task of processing the manuscript through several stages of revisions.

T. P.
N. J. S.

CAMBRIDGE, MASSACHUSETTS
January 1956

ECONOMY AND SOCIETY

CHAPTER I

THE PROBLEM: CURRENT SOCIOLOGICAL THEORY AND SOME CENTRAL CONCEPTS OF ECONOMICS

THE PROBLEM

We would like to take as our point of departure the view, common among economists, that the science of economics deals with one major "aspect" of social life. Even such an apparently simple notion bristles with questions: how is this economic aspect to be defined? What other aspects are there? How are they related to the economic and to each other? In the economic literature one frequently encounters such words as "psychological," "social" and "political"—to say nothing of "physical"—which are used to refer to these "non-economic" aspects of social life. But one seldom finds serious attempts to define these concepts rigorously. They are used mainly as tags to indicate that the "economic" territory has boundaries and that something lies beyond them. Of course, this lack of precision is understandable; it is not the primary business of the economist to explore the areas beyond the economic boundary.

The lectures on which this book is based were addressed to an audience composed mainly of economists. To a large body of opinion, it seems anomalous to speak to economists on non-economic matters, since among the social sciences economics above all is believed to be a science sufficient unto itself. We wish to attempt to dispel this belief and to demonstrate that economics must lean on the other social sciences, both on the theoretical and empirical levels, as they also must lean on it.

On the *theoretical* level economists agree fairly well that economic theory is an abstract theoretical scheme which by itself is adequate to solve some empirical problems, but only under carefully defined conditions. Economists define these conditions as postulates and parameters, and spell out limitations to be observed in their application. For certain kinds of analysis, however, economists disagree among themselves as to the appropriate assumptions and parameters. We hope, first, to show that such disagreements arise from a selective use by different economists of concepts on the theoretical borderline of economics. More importantly, we hope to demonstrate that these postulates and parameters possess more than economic significance; they articulate with other parts of the theory of social systems in theoretically specific ways. If this can be done, the problems concerning the limitations of economic theory—problems which derive from its abstract character—can be given more specific solutions than is now possible.

On the *empirical* level, the view that economic theory is abstract implies that empirical phenomena must be considered to be resultants of economic and non-economic factors. Following this thesis, we will attack the following sorts of problems. What specific factors are the important ones in different types of empirical phenomena? Given the fact that the relation between economic and non-economic is not uniform in all cases, is there any theoretical approach by means of which we can differentiate, classify and analyse these non-economic factors further?

A few examples may be in order. Schumpeter and Keynes both addressed themselves to problems of the stability and instability—in different respects, of course—of a free enterprise or capitalist economy.[1] Each held that relative stability is possible under certain conditions, but each devoted a major part of his analysis to sources of possible instability. The questions which interest us are, first, whether in these analyses some of the conditions of stability and instability can be assigned theoretical meanings in *other* than strictly economic terms and, second, whether these non-economic meanings can be formulated in a way that is empirically and theoretically useful to the economist.

[1] Keynes, J. M., *General Theory of Employment, Interest, and Money*, 1936, pp. 249 ff. Schumpeter, J. A., *The Theory of Economic Development*, translated by Redvers Opie, 1934.

One way to attack these questions is to isolate the non-economic aspects of the processes which impinge on the economy. Schumpeter, for instance, centered on entrepreneurial innovation.[1] He emphasized that this is only partly an economic process; the entrepreneur is not simply *homo economicus*, the embodiment of economic rationality. In one of his incarnations the entrepreneur is the would-be founder of a family "dynasty," the prestige of which extends far beyond his own lifetime. Keynes analysed instabilities in employment and income, and in this connection he utilized concepts such as the "stickiness of money wages" and the "marginal propensity to consume."[2] What is the status of these concepts from the point of view of other aspects of the social system? Can the sociologist say anything about their probable empirical validity? Can he analyse their non-economic implications?

A related set of problems concerns the character of market relationships, which economists have analysed in certain respects with great persistence and acumen. For certain theoretical purposes economists view markets as differing along the dimension of degree of control over output and prices by firms. At the ends of the dimension are a perfectly free market and a completely monopolistic market, respectively, with varying degrees of imperfection between these two extremes.[3] We want to emphasize that the imperfection of markets differs not only in degree *but in sociological type*. The market for consumers' goods differs from that for labour, and both differ from that for capital funds. These markets differ in type primarily because the different markets connect the economy with *different* sectors of the society: these connections enforce qualitatively different limitations on the respective market conditions.

As another example we might note the sharply defined difference of emphasis between the analytical economist and the economic historian. This difference stems largely from the fact that the economic historian deals with processes of change

[1] Schumpeter, J. A., *op. cit.*, pp. 90–93.

[2] Keynes, J. M., *op cit.*, Chaps. 2, 8, 9, 19.

[3] Stigler, G. J., *Theory of Price* (Revised ed., 1952), Chaps. 12, 13; Chamberlin, E. H., *The Theory of Monopolistic Competition* (6th ed; 1948), pp. 204 ff.

where some of the parameters which are most important to the economic theorist cannot be presumed to be constant. Above all, he deals with changes in the institutional structure of the economy. For instance, in the present state of development of economics, the economic theorist as such can tell us little about the reasons for the change from an "entrepreneur-controlled" type of big business in the United States to a "management-controlled" type during the last fifty years. Yet surely this type of problem is economically relevant. Toward the end of this volume we shall explore some possibilities of establishing continuity between the "theoretical" and "historical" branches of economics, particularly in connection with the problems of economic fluctuations and economic growth.

With respect to the empirical application of economic theory, one crucial question is the comparative one, i.e., how far the problem of such application is similar in different types of social structure in different times and places. We cannot hope, within the limitations of this study, to develop a full analysis of comparative social structure with reference to economics. But we will try to define, with occasional illustrations from societies other than our own, the nature of the problem and its bearing on the abstractness of economic theory.

Our first obligation is, therefore, to present an account of the nature of the boundary between the territories of economics and sociology as it looks from the sociological side. There should be considerable gain from exploring the boundary between these two contiguous areas. But can we proceed even further? Can these two areas be more accurately placed, not only relative to each other, but to still other territories? Can one, indeed, attempt to sketch in crude outline a "Columbian" map of the social world, on which all the main land masses can be located relative to each other?

We believe it possible to make the "Columbian" attempt now, on the basis of the outline of a *general* theory of social systems within the "action" frame of reference. If this theory is applicable, there should be a *determinate* number of aspects of human society—of which the economic is one—distinguished on a cognate level of abstraction.

We must emphasize the word "outline" when we refer to a general theory of social systems. It is a theory in the process of development which has not yet evolved to a desirable level of refinement and elegance or of empirical validation. None the less, tools adequate for the present purpose are available. The origins of the general theory of action lie deep in the history of Western social thought, but the turn of the century brought a critical development which we associate above all with the work of Max Weber in Germany, Emile Durkheim in France, and Vilfredo Pareto, as sociologist rather than economist, in Italy and Switzerland. Freud made a critical psychological contribution. Though no other individual was of the same stature, important contributions were made by the early American sociologists, especially Cooley, G. H. Mead, and W. I. Thomas, and by the social anthropologists in several countries, but notably Boas and Kroeber in the United States and Malinowski and Radcliffe-Brown in England.[1]

THE PROGRAMME

Let us return to the problem of the abstractness of economic theory. How is economic theory's relation to the non-economic aspects of social life to be formulated? We would like to distinguish between two ways of defining the problem which differ in their theoretical consequences. The senior author held the first of these in an earlier phase of his concern with the problem some years ago.[2] This view grew out of the "institutionalist dilemma" as it was posed by the institutionalist movement in American economics as that developed in the 1920's and early 1930's. This movement—of which Veblen's negative critique was the Bible[3]—boiled down to a view that traditional economic theory, say from Adam Smith to Marshall, should be

[1] The annotated bibliography at the end of the book will give the reader unfamiliar with sociological theory and its history some guides to the relevant literature. We will, for purposes of this discussion, use the terms "theory of action" and "general theory of social systems" interchangeably unless otherwise specified. Since the former includes personality theory and certain aspects of the theory of culture, it is broader than the latter, which can be considered a major branch of it.

[2] Treated at length in Parsons, T., *The Structure of Social Action*, 1937, especially in Chap. IV on Marshall and Chaps. V–VII on Pareto.

[3] "The Preconceptions of Economic Science," in *The Place of Science in Modern Civilization*, 1919.

discarded because *by itself* it fails to explain adequately a large proportion of the concrete facts of economic life. Economic theory must give way to a complete theory of social development in which the "economic aspect" loses its theoretical specificity altogether.

The only alternative to such a conclusion which seemed adequate at that time was stated most cogently by Pareto.[1] Its essence is that economic theory as an abstract system dealt with *some* of the *variables* which determine concrete social behaviour in the "economic" as in other spheres. Economic theory therefore must be supplemented by one or more distinct abstract theoretical schemes dealing with the *other significant variables.* Pareto himself formulated these other variables as "residues," "derivations," and the division of society into unequal classes. These *plus* the economic variables are the variables of his general sociology.[2]

Our view now is distinctly different; the possibility of its application did not occur to us until quite recently.[3] Economic theory should, according to this view, be regarded as the theory of typical processes in the "economy," which is a sub-system differentiated from other sub-systems of a society. The specifically economic aspect of the theory of social systems, therefore, is a *special case* of the general theory of the social system. If this is true, we must clarify the position in which this special case stands relative to other possible special cases, in order to "locate" economic theory in relation to other branches of theory. But the *basic* variables operative in all the special cases are the variables of a more general theory. The peculiarity of economic theory, therefore, is *not* the separate class of variables it employs but the *parameters* which distinguish the special case or class of cases we call economic in the use of the general variables of social theory from the other important types of special case.[4]

[1] Cf. *The Mind and Society*, 1935, Vol. I, Chap. I, esp. Sec. 34.

[2] Cf. Pareto, *op. cit.*, Vol. IV, Chap. XII, esp. Secs. 2079 ff.

[3] The original suggestion is owed to Professor W. W. Rostow of the Massachusetts Institute of Technology (personal discussion).

[4] We have already noted (p. 2) that empirically most so-called "economic" processes must be regarded as resultants of economic and non-economic factors. In the cases which are most favourable empirically to "purely economic" analysis, the phenomena are always a resultant of the

In order to establish this conception of the relation between economic and non-economic theory and to obtain significant results from it, we must set a number of tasks. First, it is necessary to demonstrate that there *is* a general conceptual scheme available under which we may regard economic theory (in its main system of categories) as a special case. Second, we must show that economic theory can be derived from the general theory by introducing the appropriate logical restrictions. Third, it is necessary to show that economic theory does not stand alone, but is one of a family of special cases on a cognate level. Finally, we must show that systematic analysis of the *relations* between the economic and certain of the non-economic cases illuminates the boundaries of the economic field.

During the course of this general programme we will consider two questions implicit in the above. In what way is economic theory comparable and related logically to the general theory? How is it comparable and related logically to the other cognate branches of the general theory?

To accomplish these tasks, we will first introduce a sketch of the general theory—the "theory of social systems." We will then attempt to show that, when this theory is compared with certain important categories of economic theory, direct correspondence between their logical structures obtains. Beyond this, we will try to establish that economic theory deals with a special class of social system—an economy in the sense we will define—which is conceivable empirically as a differentiated sub-system of a more inclusive social system—a society in the usual sociological sense.[1]

In the second chapter we will construct a theoretical foundation for interpreting problems of dynamic analysis in economics by attempting to place the economy in *systematic* relation to the cognate sub-systems of the society. We should then be able to

operation of the *general variables of systems of social action* and of parameters specifically relevant to the economic case. In cases less favourable to purely economic analysis, the phenomena are a result of *the same variables* and of *other* parameters less relevant to the economic case. Thus, in the strictest sense of general theory, it is incorrect to speak of "economic variables." It is, however, correct to speak of economic "factors" as resultants of the general variables and specific economically relevant parameters.

[1] Cf. Parsons, T., *The Social System*, 1951, Chap. I, p. 19, for a sociological discussion of a "society."

designate the economy's principal boundaries and to analyse processes of boundary interchange *between* the economy and other sub-systems. We will then turn to the relevance of this boundary analysis to strictly economic interpretations of certain dynamic problems, especially those of the classical economists, Keynes and Schumpeter.

In the third chapter we will analyse the institutional structure of the economy in a sociological sense and will attempt to relate this analysis to the structure of markets and to the problem of economic rationality.

The fourth chapter will begin with a formal discussion of several models of the trade cycle, with particular attention to certain areas of indeterminancy of economic analysis. From this starting-point we will turn to the *internal* differentiation of the economy, the internal boundary processes, the regulation of these processes, and the ensuing internal market structure. Then we will return to the model of the trade cycle and comment substantively on the noted areas of indeterminacy.

In the fifth chapter we will discuss, in a preliminary way, the processes which accompany change in the institutional structure itself. This field is of particular interest to the economic historian, and of limited interest to growth theorists.

SOME CONGRUENCES BETWEEN ECONOMIC AND SOCIOLOGICAL THEORY

A. *Between Categories*

A social system is the system generated by any process of *interaction*, on the socio-cultural level, between two or more "actors." The actor is either a concrete human individual (a person) or a collectivity of which a plurality of persons are members. A person or a collectivity participates in a given system of interaction not usually with its whole individual or collective "nature" or set of motives or interests, but only with that sector relevant to this specific interaction system. Sociologically we call such a sector a *role*. Typical examples of sociological roles are those of husband, businessman, voter, etc.; an individual may be an incumbent of all these roles at once.

A society is the theoretically limiting case of the social system which, in its sub-systems, comprises *all* the important roles of the persons and collectivities composing its population. This is a limiting concept, only approximated, for example, by a modern national society. A society in the theoretical or the empirical sense is a network of differentiated sub-systems in very complex relation to each other.

Social interaction is the process by which the "behaviour" or change of state of members in a social system influences (*a*) the state of the system and (*b*) each other's states and relations. Every concrete act thus originates in a unit (member) and has effects on the state of the system and its other component units. Hence these units constitute a system in the scientific sense that a change of state of any one will effect changes in the states of one or more others and thus of the system as a whole.

We may now note a first case of matching between the general paradigm of a social system and the frame of reference of economic theory. In the process of interaction, an act analysed in terms of its direct meaning for the functioning of the system, as a "contribution" to its maintenance or task performance, is called a *performance*.[1] On the other hand, an act analysed in terms of its effect on the state of the actor toward whom it is oriented (and thus only indirectly, through his probable future action, on the state of the system) is called a *sanction*. This is an analytical distinction. Every *concrete* act has both a performance aspect and a sanction aspect. But in the analysis of any particular process in a system the distinction—in terms of the relative primacy of one of these two aspects—is of the first importance.

We wish to suggest that the economists' distinction between short-term supply and demand is a special case of this distinction between performance and sanction in the general theory of social interaction. Supply is the "production" of utility or economic value; each act of the supplier is interpreted by the economist in terms of its contribution to the functioning of the economy or one of its sub-systems, e.g., the production of a particular class of goods or services. Demand is the disposition to "pay," in a process of market exchange, for the

[1] Cf. Parsons, T., Bales, R. F., and Shils, E. A., *Working Papers in the Theory of Action*, 1953, Chap. V, Sec. V.

availability of such goods and services. The economist interprets the *significance* of any given state of demand in terms of its bearing on the disposition of the relevant supplying agencies to produce in the future. Thus only indirectly does the state of demand bear on the performance of function in the economy.

The respects in which supply and demand constitute a special case of the performance-sanction schema will be investigated presently in the light of terms such as "production of income" or "economic value" as the criteria of contribution to the functioning of the economy. In the meantime we might point to a further fit between the supply-demand and performance-sanction frames of reference. The economist formulates conditions of supply and conditions of demand in terms of schedules which represent functional relations between quantity and price. Perhaps the most fundamental theorems of economic analysis are those governing the slopes of supply and demand curves: a theoretical supply curve must always slope upward, i.e., the greater the amount supplied, the higher the price; and a demand curve must always slope downward, i.e., the greater the amount demanded, the lower the price offered.[1]

The same logic applies to the performance-sanction relationship in all social interaction. The *amount* of performance contribution is a function of the expectation (and in the long run, receipt) of sanction, or as psychologists would put it, of "reward." Conversely, amount of sanction or reward is a function of amount of performance contribution. The conceptual structure is identical. The difference lies only in the specific types of performance and sanction which are economically significant, namely of "production" and "money returns," or in this general sense, of "profit."[2]

[1] Cf. Schumpeter, J. A., "The Instability of Capitalism," *Economic Journal*, Sept. 1928, reprinted in *Readings in Economic Analysis*, ed. R. V. Clemence, 1950. Schumpeter points out that the alleged "exceptions" to these generalizations must be referred to empirical discontinuities in the data of an economic system. They have empirical consequences, but they are not reasons for altering the fundamental theory. They concern, in our terminology, non-economic factors.

[2] The economic generalization about the slopes of supply and demand curves (the only significant meaning of the expression "the law of supply and demand") and what psychologists call the "law of effect" are two different special cases of the same fundamental generalization about action,

A second parallel between the schema of interaction and economic usage concerns the classification of objects. The familiar economic distinction between "goods," "services," and a less precise third category concerning "technique," "knowledge," "the arts," etc., is a resultant of two fundamental cross-cutting distinctions in the general theory of social interaction. The first of these distinctions is among physical, social and cultural objects; the second is between quality and performance.

All action takes place in a situation which consists in (*a*) "physical" objects, which do not interact reciprocally with the actor; (*b*) "social" objects, or other actors to which the actor orients his action and with whom he interacts reciprocally; and (*c*) "cultural" objects, or "information," which is a special kind of generalization of the meaning of physical and social objects. Only interacting actors constitute a social system. Physical objects, either in their "intrinsic" significance, or as symbols which control access to and use of information, are always part of the situation of particular actors and of social systems.[1]

The economic classification of commodities as either "goods" or "services" is a special case of the general distinction between physical and social objects. A "good" in the economic sense is a physical object which is demanded because it is held to be want-satisfying. A "service" is a performance by one or more actors, also having economic value; there is no intervention of physical objects on other than symbolic levels. The third category—"cultural objects"—also appears in economic theory, especially in connection with the significance of information in economic processes and in connection with such concepts as the

namely, the "law of equivalence of action and reaction" (cf. *Working Papers*, Chap. III). It should be noted that our remarks are limited to short-term supply and demand curves. Long-term supply curves can be horizontal or they may even slope downward. This qualification, however, has its parallel in the other social sciences. In psychology, for instance, the "law of effect" depends strictly upon timing, and cannot be said to be the only significant principle of learning. Furthermore, in the general theory of action, the "law of equivalence of action and reaction" is not the only principle governing the relationship between performance and sanction. Indeed, it often is not strictly applicable to longer-term processes.

[1] Cf. Parsons and Shils, eds., *Toward A General Theory of Action*, 1951, pp. 64–67.

"state of the arts." On the whole, however, there has been a lack of clarity in dealing with this class of objects both in economics and in the general theory of action.

The gross classification of goods as a special case of physical objects and services as a special case of social objects is, however, not sufficiently precise for many purposes. In certain cases, e.g., slavery, social objects may up to a point be treated as goods. To account for such cases, we introduce the distinction between performance and quality, which is an assessment of the significance of objects and events according to "whether or not the object . . . is considered to be a performance of a social object, or significant as the consequence of a performance and hence as an expression of the intentions of the actor concerned."[1] If this condition is fulfilled, then the significance of the object is as performance; if not, its significance is as quality. An actor's age is a quality, his achievement on an examination a performance.

Applied to the goods-services distinction, a good is an object or event of economic value which is significant as quality; a service is an object or event of economic value which is significant as performance. Of course, this distinction overlaps with that between physical and social objects, since only social objects can perform and have intentions. Yet it differs in so far as it permits the assessment of those aspects of social objects defined as goods or qualities. Thus, in the slavery example, the significance of buying and selling slaves in the market is as "goods," i.e., independent of their performance; on the other hand, the working contribution of slaves on a plantation is still a "service," i.e., performance in its economic significance. Conversely, economists often speak of physical goods as performing "services" over time. This usage is acceptable in calling attention to the fact that such goods are not utilized all at once but are the source of a "flow" of utility. In the sense in which we have spoken of services as pertaining to social objects above, however, physical goods do not perform services since their utilization is not part of a reciprocal interplay on the action level between *actors*. It is this interactive interplay which makes process in the economy that of a *social* system.

[1] Parsons, Bales, and Shils, *Working Papers in the Theory of Action*, p. 81.

We might merely mention a third point of matching between economics and the general theory. In any balancing of performances and sanctions, there is a "something" which each party values and which depends upon the action of the other. This parallels the economic frame of reference in the discussion of the phenomenon of exchange. Supply and demand makes empirical sense because each party supplies some wanted, desired, or valued thing to the other. In Professor Knight's terms,[1] there is "mutual advantage" in exchange. In the typical economic case the supplier offers and the consumer receives goods and services and the consumer offers and the supplier receives money income. We will discuss the mechanisms which regulate exchange relations in Chapter III. For the present we merely point out that the conceptual structure in economics which defines the elements involved in an exchange transaction can be generalized to all cases of performance-sanction balancing.

B. *Between System Types*

So far we have treated parallels between economic and sociological theory only on the elementary level of logically equivalent concepts. To push the parallels further, we must develop the concept of a *system* of interacting units. Most economists' statements of the scope of economics explicitly include the notion of system. A classical illustration is Marshall's delineation of economics as concerned with those aspects of men's attitudes and activities which are subject to measurement in terms of money. A more recent authoritative statement is Harrod's: "The method of procedure is to take certain elements of the situation as given—namely the preference lists of individuals[2] for goods and services, the terms on which they are willing to contribute their assistance in production and the current state of technology—and to take other elements as unknown, namely the prices of all commodities which will be produced and of factors which will be employed, and the precise methods of production among the variety of those technically possible which will be used. If the elements taken

[1] Knight, Frank H., "Ethics of Competition," Chap. II in the volume of essays under that title, 1935.

[2] (Can we not say "actors," individual or collective?—Authors.)

as known were in fact known, it would be possible to write down a number of equations expressing some of the unknowns as functions of the others. The object of this procedure would be to provide means of showing how changes in the fundamental data, desires, etc., will govern the course of events."[1]

Harrod, like Marshall, is referring to a conceptual scheme's scope of relevance. At the same time he is isolating the particular type of empirical system analysable in terms of this scheme. This system, the economy, is the set of relations of units of social interaction *in so far as*—within the limits of the "givens"—their interaction determines prices, quantities, and methods of production.

To elucidate the meaning of this conception it will be necessary to elucidate certain fundamental conceptions of the theory of social systems. The whole society is in one sense part of the economy, in that all of its units, individual and collective, *participate in* the economy. Thus households, universities, hospitals, units of government, churches, etc., are *in* the economy. But *no* concrete unit participates *only* in the economy. Hence no concrete unit is "purely economic." This fact is clear in the case of persons who, as family members, for example, are involved in many non-economic activities and functions. But it is equally true of collectivities such as the business firm. Economic considerations may be primary for the firm, but the latter clearly has, for example, "political" aspects as well.

In interpreting the above propositions the critical problem concerns the relations between the most general concepts of *social system* and the more specific concept of a *collectivity*. A social system, we have said, is *any* system generated by the interaction of two or more behaving units. The basic criterion for establishing the existence of such a system is the existence of meaningful interdependence between the actions of the units (interaction). Thus the consequences of actions by any one unit can be traced through the system; ultimately these consequences "feed back" to the units initiating the change.

[1] Cf. Marshall, Alfred, *Principles of Economics*, Book I, Chap. II, p. 15 (8th ed., 1925); Harrod, R. F., "Scope and Method of Economics," *Economic Journal*, Sept. 1938, reprinted in Clemence, ed., *Readings in Economic Analysis, op. cit.*

All this is implied by the notion of interdependence. In this most general sense we propose to treat the economy as a social system.

A collectivity, on the other hand, is a *special type* of social system which is characterized by the capacity for "action in concert." This implies the mobilization of the collectivity's resources to attain specific and usually explicit goals; it also implies the formalization of decision-making processes on behalf of the collectivity as a whole. This explicitness applies both to the legitimation of the rights of specific units to make such decisions and the obligations of other units to accept and act upon the implications of these decisions. The formal organization (e.g., a bureaucracy in the widest sense) is the prototype of such a system.

It follows that the economy as we conceive it is *not* a collectivity, even though every concrete social system has an economic aspect. For reasons we will set forth in the next chapter, it is, in its "developed" sense, a sub-system of the total society.[1] As a social sub-system, the economy is differentiated on the basis of *functions* in the society. As such it consists of modes of orientation of actors and their relation to the orientations of other actors through a process of mutually oriented decision. A collectivity, on the other hand, is never unifunctional but always multifunctional. For this reason the economy cannot be a collectivity. Certain concrete acts and certain collectivities (e.g., the business firm) may have *primarily* economic functions, to be sure. But a collectivity's primary function never exhausts its functional significance in the larger system in which it is a concrete unit.

The concept of the functional differentiation of a social system and the concept of a collectivity thus *in principle* cut

[1] Cf. Parsons and Shils, "Values, Motives and Systems of Action," Chap. III of Part II of *Toward a General Theory of Action*. Where, however, economic goals are explicitly paramount in the action (as distinguished from values—cf. below, pp. 20–29 and 175–87) of a total society, we conceive the economy to be subordinated to the political or some other non-economic aspect of that society. The modern theory of a "free enterprise" economy in which the economy is subject to controls but not to any centralized "direction" is, with certain qualifications, in accord with our conception of the economy as a sub-system highly differentiated from other cognate sub-systems of the society.

across each other. Both are types of organization in terms of social sub-systems, but they must not be identified with each other. In considering the relation of the economy to the total society—hence the empirical applicability of economic theory—we must investigate *both* the "pure theory" of an economy *and* the ways in which the economy is involved in the structure of collectivities in the society.

Societies differ from each other in the degree to which the collectivities of which they are composed are differentiated in terms of functional primacy. For instance, in our society the bulk (but not all) of economic production is carried on in the functionally specialized organizations we call firms, which are sharply differentiated from the households of which "workers" in the firms are members. In classical peasant agriculture, on the other hand, the household and the productive unit are a single undifferentiated collectivity. Further, societies will differ in the degree of elaboration of the system of economically differentiated units and in the mode of relation of these units to other functional exigencies of the society. We shall have occasion to illustrate and expand these ranges of variation below.

In the light of these considerations we must now turn to two general questions concerning the relation between the conceptual status of a social system and that of the economy.

What are the most important features of a social system by means of which we may define the cognate features of an economy? In what respects is an economy, considered as a differentiated sub-system of a society, differentiated from other cognate (i.e., functional) sub-systems of the same society?

According to the general theory, process in any social system is subject to four independent functional imperatives or "problems" which must be met adequately if equilibrium and/or continuing existence of the system is to be maintained.[1]

A social system is always characterized by an institutionalized value system. The social system's first functional imperative is to maintain the integrity of that value system and its institutionalization. This process of maintenance means stabilization against pressures to change the value system, pressures which spring from two primary sources: (1) Cultural sources of

[1] Cf. *Working Papers in the Theory of Action, op. cit.*, Chaps. III and V.

change. Certain imperatives of cultural consistency may mean that cultural changes taking place *outside* the value system relevant to the social system in question (e.g., changes in the belief system) may generate pressures to change important values *within* the social system. The tendency to stabilize the system in the face of pressures to change institutionalized values through cultural channels may be called the "pattern maintenance" function. (2) Motivational sources of change. Motivational "tensions," arising from "strains" in any part of the social situation or from organic or other intra-personal sources, may threaten individual motivation to conformity with institutionalized role expectations. Stabilization against this potential source of change may be called "tension management." The first functional imperative, therefore, is "pattern maintenance and tension management" relative to the stability of the institutionalized value system.

Every social system functions in a situation defined as external to it. The processes of interchange between system and situation are the foci of the second and third major functional imperatives of the system.

The first interchange concerns the situation's significance as a source of consummatory goal gratification or attainment. A goal state, for an individual actor or for a social system, is a *relation* between the system of reference and one or more situational objects which (given the value system and its institutionalization) maximizes the stability of the system. Other things equal, such a state, once present, tends to be maintained, and if absent, tends to be "sought" by the action of one or more units of the system. The latter case is necessary because only in limiting cases are processes in the situation closely "synchronized" with processes in the system of action; hence the system must "seek" goal states by controlling elements of the situation.[1] Goal states may be negative, i.e., noxious situational conditions, or positive, i.e., a maximization of favourable or "gratifying" conditions.

The second interchange deals with the problem of controlling

[1] The supply of oxygen in accordance with the biological need for air is an example of high synchronization between system process and situation; the supply of food is an example of a situational process relatively unsynchronized with organic needs.

the environment for purposes of attaining goal states. Since relations to the situation are problematical, there arises a *generalized* interest in establishing and improving control over the situation in various respects. Of course the pursuit of particular goal states involves such control. A different order of problem is involved, however, in the generalization of facilities for a variety of system and sub-system goals, and in activity specialized to produce such facilities. When a social system has only a simply defined goal, the provision of facilities or the "adaptive" functions is simply an undifferentiated aspect of the process of goal attainment. But in complex systems with a plurality of goals and sub-goals the differentiation between goal attainment and adaptive processes is often very clear.

Whatever the interacting units in a system process—motivational units of personality (need dispositions), roles of individual persons in a social system, or roles of collectivities in a more macroscopic social system—the actions of the units may be mutually supportive and hence beneficial to the functioning of the system; but also they may be mutually obstructive and conflictful. The fourth functional imperative for a social system is to "maintain solidarity" in the relations between the units in the interest of effective functioning; this is the imperative of system integration.

The four fundamental system problems under which a system of action, in particular a social system, operates are thus (latent) pattern maintenance (including tension management), goal attainment, adaptation, and integration. Their gross relations to each other are schematically represented in Figure 1.

Any system of action can be described and its processes analysed in terms of these four fundamental categories. The aim of analysing a system is to assess the effects of changes in the data of the system, the situation and the properties of its units, on changes in the state of the system and the states of its component units; statements about the effects on the system and its units are framed in terms of these four dimensions. For instance, we say a system "adapts" to certain situational disturbances. Furthermore, if these categories formulate "directions" in which process can move, certain constraints prevent processes from moving equally in all directions at once, at least unless very specific conditions are fulfilled. Indeed, the idea of system itself implies such constraints.

Now we may specify the relations between this conceptual scheme and some fundamental economic concepts on a level where the economy is treated as a system. We will deal first with the concepts of production and utility, then with the factors of production and shares of income, and finally with the concept of cost. Throughout this discussion we will be using the above outline of a social system *to refer to two different system levels.* The first system reference is that to an *economy* as such; thus we will ask what is meant by the goal orientation of an economy as a system, by its adaptive imperatives, by its integration and its value pattern. The second system reference is to the *society,* of which the economy is a differentiated

FIGURE 1

THE FUNCTIONAL IMPERATIVES OF A SYSTEM OF ACTION*

A Adaptive Instrumental Object Manipulation	*G* Instrumental-Expressive Consummatory Performance and Gratification
L Latent-Receptive Meaning Integration and Energy Regulation Tension build-up and drain-off	*I* Integrative-Expressive Sign Manipulation

KEY

1. *A* – Adaptation
2. *G* – Goal Gratification
3. *I* – Integration
4. *L* – Latent-Pattern Maintenance and Tension Management

* Adapted from Figure 2, p. 182, in *Working Papers, op. cit.* The above figure deals with the "functional imperatives" aspect of the system of action; that in the *Working Papers* deals with the "phase movement" aspect. Cf. Chap. IV, pp. 242–45.

sub-system. The basic categories—goal attainment, adaptation, integration, and pattern maintenance—are, of course, the same as for the economy, but their specific references (empirical content) are different.

We wish to suggest that the two systems in question, the society and the economy, articulate in the following way: the economy is that sub-system of a society which is differentiated with primary reference to the *adaptive* function of the society as a whole. This proposition is very important indeed; we will return to it again and again. It is what we mean by the assertion that an economy is a *functional* sub-system of a society.

Economists seem to agree that the paramount goal of economic activity—and hence of an economy as a system—is best defined as "production." But what is meant by production? Production of what? For a long time it seemed plausible to define production in physical terms: production of commodities and services, of numbers of automobiles, of tons of coal, of woman-hours of domestic service. This idea has proved to be entirely inadequate. On two grounds economists have been forced to seek a reference different from physical products. First, physical units must be given a "meaning" or "economic significance"; and second, qualitatively different physical units, such as tons and hours, must be rendered quantitatively comparable. The agreed reference for economists has been, in the first instance, to "consumers' wants." A good or service has economic value or significance in so far as it is a means to "want satisfaction." In this sense it has utility and added utility (i.e., income) constitutes an addition to the "wealth" of the community.

Maximizing utility or the economic value of the total available means to want satisfaction therefore defines the system goal of an economy. A goal state has been defined above as a satisfactory *relation* between the state of a system and relevant objects in the external situation. For the economy this relation is some optimum between the state of the economy, in the sense of the productive achievements of its members, and the individual and collective members of society, *in their roles as consumers*. Though largely the same concrete persons occupy consumers' roles and producers' roles respectively, these roles belong in different systems. We define the former as outside the economy, the latter as inside.[1]

To summarize: the concept of production defines the goal orientation of the economy as a sub-system of the society. Production is of utility, or of goods and services in so far as they satisfy wants. Wealth is defined as the aggregate economic value of such goods and services at any given time. Income is defined as the flow of command over such values per unit of time.

If this is acceptable, then what is the significance of "want satisfaction" from the standpoint of the society as a total social system? According to the general theory, the goal of a differentiated sub-system "contributes" to the functioning of its larger system. We have defined the economy's contribution as specialization in the solution[2] of the adaptive problem of the larger system. This adaptive function now may be more closely defined. Negatively it implies the minimization of subjection to control by the exigencies of the external situation (e.g., floods, famines, shortages, etc.). Positively it implies the possession of a maximum of fluid disposable resources as means to attain *any* goals valued by the system or its sub-units. The general concept for these disposable resources is wealth from a static point of view and income from the point of view of rate of flow.

In defining production, utility, wealth and income, the focal point of reference is for us the *society* as a system. The role of producer is *internal* to the economy as a sub-system of the society; that of consumer is *external* to the economy in the sense that it pertains to one or more *other* sub-systems of the society But the functional *significance* of these concepts is evaluated in terms of the *institutionalized value system* of the total society, and only as mediated through this, in terms of its sub-systems including individual personalities. From our point of view, therefore, utility or the satisfaction of wants should not be

[1] This duality (in this respect) of system membership for the same concrete individuals illustrates the central point that a social system does not comprise the *total* action of concrete persons and collectivities, but only their actions *in specific roles*. The precise sense in which we consider consumers external to the economy is outlined in Chap. II, pp. 53–55 and 70–72.

[2] This is always only relatively satisfactory.

defined in relation to "the individual" but in relation to the society. Its significance for the individual is a function of the kind of society in question and the place of individuals in it. There is no reason, moreover, to assume that this function is the same for all societies.

We repeat: the goal of the economy is not simply the production of income for the utility of an aggregate of individuals. It is the maximization of production relative to the whole complex of institutionalized value-systems and functions of the society and its sub-systems. As a matter of fact, if we view the goal of the economy as defined strictly by socially structured goals, it becomes inappropriate even to refer to utility at this level in terms of individual preference lists or indifference curves. This view of utility also means that, in formulating concepts of social utility or utility in a social context, it is not necessary even to consider the time-honoured economic problems of the interpersonal comparability of utility, the cardinal and/or ordinal measurement of utility, etc. Since the individual is not the defining unit for the maximization of utility, it is inappropriate to refer to the measurability of utility *among* individuals. Therefore, it is correct to speak, with only apparent paradox, of the "maximization of utility" in a social context without at the same time making *any* statements about the interpersonal measurability of utility. The theoretical occasion for drawing such comparisons in the traditional sense does not arise at all, since the categories of wealth, utility, and income are states or properties of social systems and their units and do not apply to the personality of the individual except *through* the social system.

Utility, then, is the *economic value* of physical, social or cultural objects in accord with their *significance as facilities* for solving the adaptive problems of social systems. Wealth is the aggregate of this value for a given social system at a given time (Adam Smith was correct to speak of the *wealth of nations* rather than their individual members). Income is the *rate* of production or reception of such value for a period of time.

Economic valuation is a mechanism by which particularized significances of specific resources for individuals and collectivities are *generalized* in terms of their significance to the system as a whole. This generalized reference is not a "result of" certain properties of individuals' wealth or income but is the central defining characteristic of income or wealth. To be sure, individuals have wealth or income as "shares" of societal wealth or income, but it does not follow that the wealth of a society is an aggregate of the *independently given* wealth of its members.

The relation between this social aspect of income and wealth on the one hand and individual motivation on the other can be analysed adequately in terms of modern personality theory, most of which has developed since economic theory became crystallized along these lines. The essence of this personality theory is that economic values, which form the basis of the meaning of wealth and income to the individual, are internalized in the process of socialization. They are social values which become part of the personality in its development, not "propensities" of the individual which determine social processes. We will treat this problem in detail in Chapter III.

We realize that this position runs counter to what is probably the dominant strand of at least the English-speaking tradition of economics.[1] We feel that the prominence of this "individualistic" strain in the treatment of want-satisfaction and utility is a relic of the historical association of economic theory with utilitarian philosophy and psychology. If pushed to its extreme, it leads to a type of psychological and sociological atomism: this position has been set forth perhaps most conspicuously by Robbins.[2] But in more moderate form it permeates the work of such authors as Pareto,[3] Hicks,[4] and certain welfare economists.[5]

[1] This, incidentally, seems to be the only critical point in this chapter at which we are forced to enter directly into the internal controversies of economics.

[2] Robbins, L., *The Nature and Significance of Economic Science* (2nd ed., 1948). Robbins refuses to admit that even the individual has an integrated system of goals or wants—he is motivated by an unorganized plurality of "conflicting psychological pulls" (p. 34). Taking this position precludes recognizing any higher order social integration of goals or values. Cf. Parsons, "Some Reflections on 'The Nature and Significance of Economics,'" *Quarterly Journal of Economics*, May 1934.

[3] Cf. *The Mind and Society*, *op. cit.*, Vol. IV, Chap. XIII, Secs. 2111–2146. Pareto distinguishes between several types of utility to individuals and

For continuation and Notes 4 and 5, see page 24.

Our view accords with that of Marshall (in his treatment of the relation of wants and activities) as it links directly with that of Weber and Durkheim. In addition to its other merits, Marshall's contribution seems altogether to avoid what many economists conclude to be an insoluble problem: the comparison of individual preference lists *assumed in advance* to be independent of each other. We will try to show that for purposes of the theory of the economy of a social system this assumption is both unnecessary and contrary to fact.

Finally, our emphasis is associated with a shift in perspective in the definition of wealth. The earlier emphasis was on physical consumers' goods and their "hedonistic" consumption values. The later emerging emphasis has been on the *generalizing* of wealth as purchasing power, hence on its relation to productivity and to the control of behaviour. Wealth is not so much an inventory of commodities as an instrumentality for achieving goals and inducing the co-operation of actors in that achievement. This shift of emphasis in our opinion prepares the way for a genuine integration of economic and sociological theory which has been blocked by the remnants of utilitarianism.

To return to our main analysis: we regard the transition from production to consumption as a "boundary process" between the economy and other parts of the society. When the process of production is completed the economy has "done its job." The product is put at the disposal of other sub-systems for

several types to collectivities. Furthermore, he distinguishes between ophelimity *of* a collectivity (which does not exist because individual ophelimities cannot be compared) and ophelimity *for* a collectivity (which is determined independently of the comparison between ophelimities of different individuals). While Pareto's subtle discussion of these distinctions shows that he was aware of the significance of several system-levels as reference-points for discussion of welfare and utility, we feel our conception of utility goes well beyond Pareto in so far as we *exclude* (not merely consider impossible to solve) the problem of interpersonal comparison of individual ophelimities.

[4] Hicks, J. R., *Value and Capital* (2nd ed., 1946). While Hicks and other indifference curve analysts do not necessarily subscribe to such a doctrinaire atomistic position as Robbins', their starting-point is individual preference lists, and few systematic attempts are made to tie this set of schedules to the social system.

[5] Cf. for example, Pigou, A. C., *The Economics of Welfare* (4th ed., 1952). Cf. below, pp. 30–32.

whatever uses may be relevant. Consumption in the broadest sense is thus *any* use to which economically valuable goods and services are put, other than as means of production in the economic sense.

The lines along which we might push this conception of boundary process further are suggested by the consequence of the fact that the economy is confronted by all the essential functional problems of any social system. So far we have dealt only with the boundary process which involves the economy's primary output of or production of consumable goods and services (the attainment of its goal as a system).

But the economy has adaptive needs of its own. In order to produce, it must acquire disposable resources for productive purposes. If wealth is the stock and income the flow of resources at the disposal of the society, there should be a corresponding body of disposable resources available to the economy for its own specialized uses. We suggest that the concept of capital as ordinarily used by economists constitutes precisely this stock or flow of resources available for production.[1]

In essential respects the resources available for economically productive and non-productive uses are interchangeable. For the economy the functional problem is the process of determination of the proportion of the society's resources to be made available for economic production. There is a boundary process concerned with the determination of this share. More particularly, there is an input of capital into the economy and a return to those who decide to relinquish resources they control from alternative uses. This boundary involves the adaptive processes of the economy itself; it concerns the capital market and the relations between capital, interest and related phenomena.

Another boundary of the economy concerns disposable resources, the supply of which is not contingent on short-term economic sanctions. This boundary is of a different order

[1] The definition of capital as "producers' wealth" as opposed to "consumers' wealth" definitely implies this distinction. In another context, the fact that "capital" as a term is applied both to liquid funds and to "physical stock" refers to the fact that commitment of resources to actual production may vary in degree. For discussion of the various levels of commitment of capital resources, cf. Chaps. III and IV below.

from the two mentioned above. The inputs include "physical" resources in the traditional economic sense of land factors; it also includes two other categories. The first is "cultural" objects, in so far as they are available for economic production without specific cost. This would include "the state of the arts," commonly held technology, intuitive knowledge of market conditions and "business experience," etc. The second involves human services for productive purposes in so far as there is an underlying commitment to work independent of current economic sanctions. Examples of this category are both an underlying commitment to work and differentials in ability which give rise to the "rent of ability."[1] These three factors within limits, therefore, behave like land in the physical sense; hence it is legitimate to group them together as "land" for economic analysis.

According to the general theory of social systems, the "land" elements are *governed* by an institutionalized system of values; hence they are most closely associated with the pattern-maintenance sub-system of the economy. Such values will, within limits, be acted upon wherever appropriate, independent of cost. Their availability marks a third boundary process of the economy.

A fourth boundary concerns the integration of the economy. Integration refers to the ways in which available resources are combined in the productive process. The conception of organization as a factor of production by Marshall is appropriate; this is the locus of the entrepreneurial function as developed by Schumpeter and his followers.[2] In its economic context integration refers to the long-term apportioning of men and machines, in accordance with production opportunities.

We have omitted the input of labour into the economy, that factor most directly related to the output of goods and services for consumption. This is the contribution of the worker which is sensitive to short-term economic sanctions (payment of wages, etc.). There are thus two distinct components in human services. The first is the underlying willingness to work; the

[1] This rent is often referred to as one sort of quasi-rent. Marshall, *Principles*, *op. cit.*, pp. 425 ff.

[2] Cf. *Principles*, *op. cit.*, Book IV, pp. 138–139; *The Theory of Economic Development*, *op. cit.*, Chap. II.

second the response to the specific rate of remuneration and conditions of employment.

In the next chapter we will carry the analysis of these boundary processes of the economy and their input-output relations further than we have been able to in this introductory discussion. At the present stage, however, we suggest an important conclusion. If the view of the economy as a differentiated sub-system of the total society is accepted as a point of departure, then such a sub-system is subject to *particular and determinate* types of boundary interchange with the rest of society and with the physical environment. The economic categories —factors of production on the one hand and shares of income on the other—can be identified as the appropriate inputs and outputs, respectively, over these boundaries.

In interpreting this conclusion, we do not identify the boundaries of the economy with any particular "organizational" features of any particular society. In very highly differentiated cases, some of the boundaries may coincide approximately with specific concrete markets such as the market for consumers' goods and the labour market in our society. In a peasant society, on the other hand, the boundary between production and consumption lies to a large extent within the same household, regarded as a collectivity. This view is, of course, not new; economists have long been aware that the factors of production cannot be identified with concrete organizations or groups in any simple way and that organizational arrangements vary from one society to another.

Assuming these qualifications, we treat *labour* (as a factor) as the input of human service into the economy in so far as it is contingent on short-term economic sanctions. This is balanced by *wages*, or "consumers' income" (not goods and services). *Capital* is treated as the input of fluid resources into the economy: this input is contingent on decisions between productive and consumption uses. It is balanced by a category of income which traditionally has been called *interest*.[1] The third input are those factors available for production, but not contingent on immediate economic remuneration. These factors fall into three sub-classes—physical resources, cultural resources and

[1] We will raise certain questions about this category in Chap. II.

social resources—which we group under *land*. These are balanced by various kinds of *rents*. Finally, there is the factor of *organization* balanced by *profit* in the technical sense.[1]

Among the input-output items in the "rent" category are certain human factors. We think it is legitimate to identify these, at least in part, with what Marshall discussed under the heading of "activities" as distinguished from "wants" as the subject-matter of economics. As is well known, Marshall insisted that the "science of wants" could only be half of economics; the other half is the "science of activities." With respect to the orientation of human behaviour, it is clear that he referred to those respects in which men were devoted to productive functions without specific relation to short-term economic reward; because "work, in its best sense, the healthy energetic exercise of faculties is the aim of life, is life itself." We agree that this is true, in so far as work is not in the usual sense "economically motivated" but is an expression of internalized values. Thus Marshall's theory of activities falls naturally into place, instead of being an anomalous "foreign body" in the corpus of economic theory.[2]

The striking fact, in sum, is the correspondence—category for category—between the established economic classifications of the factors of production and the shares of income and a classification of the input-output categories of social systems which was arrived at in work on the level of general theory independently, without the economic categories in mind at all. Whether this correspondence is genuine or spurious can best be evaluated only after we have used it to interpret various

[1] These identifications deal only with the monetary rewards for the factors of production. The relations between money income and real income will be discussed in Chap. II, pp. 70 ff.

[2] Cf. Pigou, A. C., ed., *Memorials of Alfred Marshall*, 1925, p. 115, and Parsons, *Structure of Social Action*, Chap. IV. This, it will be noted, is a revision of the view put forward in the senior author's earlier study of Marshall. May we again call attention to the resemblance between Marshall's empirical views in this field and those of Max Weber in connection with his study of the relation between Protestantism and capitalism—despite all the difference of perspective of these two writers. In view of the interpretation of the place of economic rationality as the "value system" of the economy (Chaps. III and V, below), this coincidence will take on special significance.

substantive propositions of economic theory and to explore the relations between the economy and the rest of society more thoroughly.

THE PROBLEM OF COST

Finally, we might note two problems of economic analysis which follow from the conception of the economy as a differentiated sub-system: the problem of cost and the problem of welfare. The goal of the economy is production on behalf of the society as a system. From the point of view of the society, the cost of a given level of income or national product is the total input from other sub-systems of the society of factors of production necessary to achieve this level. This cost must be measured in relation to the *social* (not merely economic) value of the product, i.e., it must be assessed in terms of its alternative *non-economic* uses. This aspect of cost is what economists have ordinarily discussed under the heading "real costs." The cost of capital investment for national defence in terms of consumption and the cost of labour service in terms of "leisure" are obvious examples of real cost. In the case of rent factors, the use of a body of scientifically trained personnel for economic production entails the loss of their services for "pure" scientific research, which is a non-economic function.

The problem of cost can be viewed, however, not only in terms of cost to the society, but also to the economy or one of its units. In this case the shares of income rather than the factors of production are the costs. The shares of income are the "price," payment of which is necessary to secure the services of the factors of production. Economists have treated this range of costs as "money costs."

Society institutionalizes the availability of certain "land" factors, so that only the distribution of income to the owners or controllers of these factors is problematical. On the other hand, the input of other factors into the economy is contingent on current economic sanctions. The empirical line between these two types of factors is not an intrinsic one, but depends upon the time range under consideration, as Marshall made abundantly clear. In the short run many factors behave as rent factors; in the longer run they may be contingent on economic returns. Marshall called the rewards for such factors "quasi-rent." The analytical distinction between the two orders of factor, however, is fundamental.

Such a perspective underlies the economists' distinction between money cost and real cost. We have not yet discussed the place of money in the functioning of an economy; we will postpone this discussion to the following chapters where we consider mechanisms of economic adjustment. But, following Marshall's definition of the scope of economics, we might conclude that "measurement in terms of money" is the perspective which is characteristic of the internal processes of the economy as a system. When the point of reference is shifted to the society as a whole, however, some other standard—to which money values and costs are themselves relative—must be introduced. This, it seems to us, is why economists have not been able completely to ignore the problem of real costs.

What applies to the economy as a system, of course, applies to any sub-system within it. Thus a firm, for instance, treats its cost problems from the same sort of perspective. What is most important to us is the distinction of the meaning of cost from two different system references—first the society as a system, second the economy. The indispensability of this distinction follows from the conception of the economy as a differentiated sub-system of the society as a system.

THE PROBLEM OF WELFARE

In quite a different area of economic inquiry—welfare economics—certain issues can be reduced to the attempt to establish points of articulation between the economy and some other system. In our terms, most of welfare economics has dealt with: (1) the bearing of changes in economic variables on changes in the overall gratification-deprivation balance in the personality system—the problem of individual satisfaction or happiness, and (2) the bearing of changes in economic variables on changes in the welfare of the community—the problem of the social optimum. Such concerns require a clear conceptualization of the economy as a system, the personality (individual) as a system, and the community (society) as a system, and some statement of the principles by which the gratification-deprivation equilibria of each are defined and related to each other. In economics the definition of economic welfare is usually a direct translation from the scope of economic activity in general[1] into some version of gratification-deprivation significance. Thus Pigou, in an early formulation, defines economic welfare as "that part of social welfare which can be brought directly or indirectly into relation with the measuring rod of money."[2] Little defines economic welfare (for both the individual and the community) as changes in well-being brought about by a change in goods or services directly or indirectly obtainable by money, together with the amount and kind of work which people do.[3] Even at this stage—prior to consideration of the personality system and other societal sub-systems—certain logical difficulties arise, particularly in connection with the comparability of welfare among societies with differing value systems and differing levels of differentiation of a monetized economy.[4]

More serious theoretical problems arise in connection with the translation of changes in economic welfare into overall gratification-deprivation significances (general welfare, happiness, satisfaction) for the individual and for society. For Pigou the translation was fairly simple: individual happiness is the sum of satisfactions and community happiness is the sum of individual happinesses. Indifference-curves analysis avoids the problem of simple additivity and emphasizes the highest ordinal level of satisfaction. Of either formulation of individual and community satisfaction, however, one might ask: does an increase (cardinal or ordinal) in economic welfare mean an increase in individual happiness?[5] Does the sum of increases of individual happinesses increase community happiness? Does the gain of one person's economic welfare mean the loss of economic welfare—or even happiness—for another whose economic welfare does not change?

1 Cf. the definitions of Marshall and Harrod above, pp. 13–14.

2 Pigou, A. C., *The Economics of Welfare*, *op. cit.*, p. 11.

3 Little, I. M. D., *Critique of Welfare Economics*, 1950, p. 6.

4 For a detailed logical examination of some of these difficulties, cf. Frankel, S. H., *The Economic Impact on Underdeveloped Countries*, 1953, esp. Chap. III.

5 As Little puts it: Does position on a higher behaviour-line (in indifference-curve terms) entail an increase in welfare? *Op. cit.*, Chap. III.

These are typical issues of the theory of welfare economics. Without pursuing the actual technical controversies which have mushroomed about these issues, we might suggest, on the basis of our conception of utility, wealth and income (and, of course, welfare), why the field of welfare economics has tended to be relatively barren both theoretically and as a guide to policy. As we have emphasized, the starting-point for the definitions of utility and welfare is the economic significance of objects as facilities for solving adaptive problems of social systems. Only through the institutionalized value system of the society and its various functional sub-systems which develop in accord with specific exigencies is concrete meaning given to the concept of welfare. It follows that to define economic, much less social welfare in terms of some aggregate of allegedly independent individual welfare functions or in terms of some elaborate system of comparison of individual functions is theoretically untenable. Since the development of individual motivation is, in the relevant respects, conceived as a process of the internalization of social norms and not as the independently given basis of social processes and social values, such issues as the assessment of independent preference lists, their representation in ordinal and/or cardinal form, their relation to community welfare, etc., are theoretically meaningless because they start from an inappropriate theoretical base.

We do not mean to imply that all economists accept the sort of results that welfare economics has produced. On the contrary, certain of its critics—Little, Samuelson, and others—have convincingly rejected such views on logical grounds. But because they have not attempted *systematically* to relate the relevant social systems and sub-systems, they have been able to say few positive things about the problems of utility and welfare. We believe that the approach we suggest permits positive statements about utility and welfare without generating the theoretical embarrassment which welfare economics often creates.[1]

By now we have spaded up enough of the ground of theoretical economics to establish the presumption that economic theory is a special case of a more general theory. A

[1] For a critique of "the desire for happiness" as a driving force in social change, cf. Chap. V, pp. 290–91.

crucial field for strengthening this presumption concerns the boundary processes between the economy and other sub-systems. We will devote the next chapter to these processes.

TECHNICAL NOTE

Readers who are familiar with the previous theoretical work of the senior author and various of his collaborators may be concerned with the relationship between the approach developed in this and the following chapters and this previous work. In particular, questions are likely to be raised concerning the relations between the classification of four general functional problems of systems of action, which we have related to the economic classifications of the factors of production and the shares of income, and the scheme of "pattern variables" which has figured prominently in previous publications.

The most general statement of the theoretical position which is a starting-point for the analysis presented in this study is formulated in *Working Papers in the Theory of Action*, by Parsons, Bales, and Shils (1953), especially Chapters III and V. In the first of these chapters the pattern-variable scheme was related systematically to a scheme of four "system problems" of action (including, of course, social) systems, first explicitly formulated by Bales (*Interaction Process Analysis*, 1950, Chapter II). This classification was for Bales the logical basis from which he derived his scheme of "interaction categories" which have served as the theoretical and operational core of his programme of analysis of interaction in small groups.

The scheme of pattern variables originated in an attempt to classify modes of orientation in social roles in order to connect role structure with an analysis of values as institutionalized in social systems. The starting-point was Toennies' famous distinction between *Gemeinschaft and Gesellschaft* as types of social relationship. Gradually it became clear that this dichotomy concealed a number of independently variable distinctions. The empirical starting-point of the pattern-variable classification was the problem of assessing the relation between the professional practitioner and his client or patient. By the criterion of universalism as distinguished from particularism—a criterion in the medical case associated with the application of scientific knowledge and with the universalism of rights to medical care—the professional relationship was one of *Gesellschaft*, whereas *Gemeinschaft*, in which Toennies included the family, is clearly particularistic. By virtue of the canon that the "welfare of the patient" should come ahead of the self-interest of the doctor, this case was clearly one of *Gemeinschaft*.

On this kind of basis, four independently variable dichotomies were distinguished, and for a considerable time used in comparative analyses of social structure.[1] The four were (1) self-interest vs. "disinterestedness" (later changed to self-orientation vs. collectivity-orientation), (2) universalism vs. particularism, (3) functional specificity vs. functional diffuseness, and (4) affectivity vs. affective neutrality. The first concerned the structure of the "market" relation in terms of the extent to which pursuit of "advantage" took precedence over the performance of "service." This was essentially the problem of self-interest in the traditional sense of economic theory; in its sociological application it raised the question of the range of social relations to which this conception was applicable. The second dichotomy concerned the criteria of eligibility for certain services in a functional role. The criterion of eligibility for the services of a physician, for instance, was to be sick, which is defined as an objectively determinable condition which "might happen to anyone." On the other hand, the obligations of kinship applied only to persons standing in a particular pre-existing relationship to the actor. "Ego's son," for example, is to be treated by ego, as "his father," quite differently from other boys of his age, ability and other characteristics. The third dichotomy concerned the basis of interest in an object or scope of the definition of an obligation. In most occupational roles in our society, the specific function which the incumbent performs is the basis of his interest in the role. Thus, a patient is important to a doctor in the context of "health," but the patient's morals, or even his financial condition, are not of the same order of concern to his physician. On the other hand, an object, e.g., a person, may be of interest

[1] Three of the four were outlined and illustrated in the paper "The Professions and Social Structure," *Essays in Sociological Theory* (Revised ed., 1954), Chap. II.

in a diffuse, non-specific way in a role-relationship. This is generally true in kinship and friendship relations. The fourth dichotomy, that between affectivity and affective neutrality, concerned the type of attitude which was considered appropriate toward the object. This is a matter of whether it is held to be legitimate to have a positively "emotional" attitude, which is not merely permitted but expected in most kinship relations, or in friendship, but is not appropriate in most occupational roles. The physician, for instance, is expected to treat the patient in a "job" context and not to become too "emotionally involved" with him as a person.

This scheme, consisting of four dichotomous concept-pairs, and applying mainly to the classification of social role-relationships, remained substantially unchanged for several years. In connection with a general collaborative review of the theory of action,[1] however, the scheme was revised considerably and extended in relevance. It became clear that the classification had roots not only in the structure of social systems, but could be generalized to the theory of action, including personality systems and certain aspects of culture. This point need not directly concern us further here, however.

The revision of the content of the scheme involved the addition of a fifth dichotomy, proposed by Linton as the distinction between ascription and achievement, which has been widely used in sociological and anthropological analyses. Later, this was altered to the quality-performance distinction, on the grounds that ascription-achievement was too specifically oriented to social system problems of a certain type.

Furthermore, a determinate order among the different category components emerged. Of the five pairs thus far formulated, two, universalism-particularism and quality-performance, concerned criteria for the categorization of objects, whereas two others, specificity-diffuseness and neutrality-affectivity, concerned the definition of attitude toward objects. This basic distinction formalized that which was implicit in the general frame of reference of action, namely, the distinction between those elements pertaining to the *situation* of action, and those pertaining to *orientation* of actors toward that situation. Though all action is relational and hence involves

[1] Cf. Parsons and Shils, eds., *Towards a General Theory of Action*, *op. cit.*

both these references, the stress can be placed either on the situational or the orientational pole of the relationship.

This left the fifth pair, self- vs. collectivity-orientation, in a special position. In the course of time it became apparent that the categories of this pair were not significant as defining characteristics of one specific system of action; rather they defined the relations between two systems placed in a hierarchical order. Self-orientation defined a state of relative independence from involvement of the lower-order in the higher-order system, leaving the norms and values of the latter in a regulatory, i.e., limit-setting, relation to the relevant courses of action. Collectivity-orientation on the other hand defined a state of positive membership whereby the norms and values of the higher-order system are positively prescriptive for the action of the lower.

This addition to and rearrangement of the pattern-variable scheme focused attention on the four pairs grouped as attitudinal and object-categorizing, respectively. Since a system of action was held to be a system of relations between actor and situation, it seemed reasonable to use this arrangement as a basis for attempting to establish connections across the attitude-object line. From this perspective the following set of correspondences emerged: specificity-universalism, diffuseness-particularism, neutrality-quality and affectivity-performance. It was then discovered that these correspondences converged logically with Bales' fourfold classification of the functional problems of systems of action. In the terminology finally adopted, the adaptive problem was defined from the attitudinal point of view in terms of specificity, from the object-categorization point of view in terms of universalism; the goal-attainment problem from the attitudinal point of view in terms of affectivity, from that of object-categorization in terms of performance; the integrative problem from the attitudinal point of view in terms of diffuseness, from the object-categorization point of view in terms of particularism; finally, the pattern-maintenance and tension-management problem from the attitudinal point of view in terms of affective neutrality, from the object-categorization point of view in terms of quality.[1]

[1] This new viewpoint was first stated in *Working Papers in the Theory of Action*, *op. cit.*, Chap. III, and further developed in Chap. V.

When the pattern variables were seen in this perspective and thus related to the functional system problems, the scheme seemed to possess the characteristics of a space which, because of its logical structure, had four dimensions. Ever since this formulation became consolidated we have been dealing with these four, plus the factor of relative importance or "weight" of a unit in a system, as the basic variables of a system. The distinction between the attitudinal and the object-categorization aspects of the four dimensions has not, however, ceased to be important. It has been used above all to differentiate perspectives of reference relative to different aspects of the functioning of a system. For example, the object-categorization version is appropriate to the definition of performances in an interaction process, whereas the attitudinal version is appropriate to the formulation of sanctions.

In general terms this four-dimensional scheme had been used, prior to the present work, in the analysis of processes of input into and output from a system of action over its boundaries, with special reference to the significance of the categories of rewards and facilities. (Cf. *Working Papers in the Theory of Action*, Chapter V, Sec. vi.) This analysis was applied by Bales and others to the phase-movements of processes in small group interaction, and, in a general way, to the process of socialization in relation to the development of personality. (Cf. Parsons, Bales, *et al.*, *Family, Socialization and Interaction Process*, esp. Chapter IV.) The same dimensional scheme was also used to analyse the main trends of functional differentiation in a system of action, first by Bales with reference to the small group (*Working Papers*, Chapter IV), and later with reference to the family and to the development of personality (*Family Socialization and Interaction Process*, Chapters I–IV).

The main methodological procedure of the present work is based on these developments. We feel that it is fruitful to treat the system-function (pattern-variable) scheme as the main frame of reference for analysing the structural differentiation of the large-scale society. The primary basis of this differentiation is the process of meeting the functional exigencies of a system in relation to its situation. In this sense we propose that an economy, as this concept has been defined in economic theory, can be treated as that functionally differentiated sub-system of a society which is specialized to meet adaptive exigencies.

We have then used this conception of the economy as a differentiated sub-system (analogous to a differentiated role in small-scale systems) to attempt to relate the economy systematically to the other cognate sub-systems of the same society. This is achieved by analysing input-output processes on the sub-system level, which are at the same time processes of exchange between sub-systems. Thus the identification of the traditional economic classifications of the factors of production and the shares of income with our own classification of system problems constitutes the theoretical focus for the main logical structure of our analysis.

CHAPTER II

THE ECONOMY AS A SOCIAL SYSTEM

In the last chapter we took two steps toward demonstrating our principal thesis that economic theory is a special case of the general theory of social systems. (1) We attempted to show logical parallels between the categories of the general theory of social interaction and some central economic concepts. We chose three examples: the supply-demand schema as an instance of the performance-sanction paradigm, the goods-services classification as a case of the distinctions between physical and social objects and between qualities and performances, and the similar sociological and economic conceptions of the mutual advantage in exchange. (2) We introduced the general concept of *social system* and showed that the concept of an economy—as defined by Harrod, for instance—can be treated as a social system.[1] Specifically, the economy can be regarded first as

[1] We do not wish to claim that the conception of the economy as a social system is entirely original with us. The closest approaches to it will probably be found in the Marx, Sombart, Weber line of continental European students of "capitalism." The first two of these writers do not, we feel, adequately distinguish economy and polity (which will be discussed, pp. 47–48) especially with reference to the problems we will treat below (pp. 56–64) in connection with the input of capital as a factor of production. Weber probably came closest to our conception of any previous writer, especially in his clear distinction between "economic action" and "economically relevant action," the former belonging to the economy as a system, the latter not (cf. Weber, *Theory of Social and Economic Organization*, Chap. II, Sec. 1; see also 1st German Edition, Pt. II, Chap. I, pp. 181–183). He defines an economy (*Wirtschaft*) as "an autocephalous system of economic action." It is, we believe, much more difficult to find precursors of this view in the English-language literature though we think at times Marshall came close to it. It seems likely that this possibility of theoretical development has been mainly blocked by the (often implicit) assumptions of utilitarian individualism which we criticized in the last chapter.

meeting the *adaptive* exigencies of the society as a whole by means of the production of utility, and second as having goal-attainment, adaptive, integrative and pattern-maintenance exigencies of its own. In the latter connection we suggested treating the factors of production and shares of income as classes of input into and output from the economy, respectively, corresponding to the four fundamental system problems. Furthermore, we noted that the economic distinction between real and monetary cost refers to evaluations of inputs into the economy, first from the standpoint of the society and second from that of the economy. And finally, we tried to make clear, though without extensive development, that the ways in which the conception of the economy as a social system can be spelled out empirically depend on variations in the concrete structures of different societies, on their levels of general social differentiation and the more specific ways in which the economy is conceived to fit with the other aspects of the total society.

Now we must further develop the theme of the economy as a social system and its relation to its situation—including the rest of society. Then we should be able to relate the general theory of social interaction not only to frames of reference and concepts of economic theory, but more importantly, to some central dynamic propositions of economic theory. As in the first chapter, we will incorporate some propositions about the general nature of social systems without providing full justifications for them here.[1]

As we have noted, a social system tends to differentiate with respect to all four of the basic functional dimensions. Before we discuss these dimensions extensively, we must clarify the special status of the economy's value pattern and the processes of pattern maintenance. One aspect of the value pattern concerns the modes in which it is incorporated into *institutions*, the primary function of which is to regulate certain classes of activity. This is what we mean by "institutionalized" value patterns. We will inquire into the institutional structure of the economy in some detail in the next chapter, when we examine the institutions which govern most closely

[1] We will refer the reader to such justifications as the analysis proceeds, however.

the exchanges between the economy and the other sectors of society.

But another context in which the institutionalization of value patterns is important for the economy *as a system* concerns the economy's own pattern-maintenance exigencies. For the economy the most important implication of the institutionalization of its value pattern is a relatively stable pattern of *control* over the "rent factors" in the productive process. This means that (1) on the cultural and social levels a given "state of the arts" and organization of the social system in non-economic respects, (2) on the physical level a given supply of physical resources, and (3) on the motivational level a given set of commitments to productive functions are given (within limits) independently of changes in the current level and patterns of sanctions (prices).

These "givens" are a society's *economic commitments*. From a sociological point of view these commitments reflect the direct implications of the societal value system for the performance of the adaptive or economic function. On the one hand, they specify the relative importance of economic production compared to other social system goals; on the other hand, they imply the segregation of certain of the society's resources for economic production.[1]

To say that these social commitments are in a certain sense "given" is not to say that they operate without the mediation of "mechanisms." In the utilization of rent factors, however, the mechanisms operating are of a *different* character from those operating in the other boundary processes of the economy. This proposition is a special statement of the sociological principle that "pattern-maintenance" functions are in some sense qualitatively different from other performance-sanction interaction systems. The difference in the economic case lies in the segregation of these commitments from the operation of ordinary price mechanisms, i.e., the insulation of supply from fluctuations of demand. This is what the term "commitment" implies. At the same time, once the commitment is made,

[1] These resources include, of course, the physical, cultural and organizational components we have mentioned; they also include that aspect of concrete labour services which Marshall referred to as involving the "science of activities" as distinguished from that of "wants."

the specific allocation of the "given" elements within the economy *does* become an integral part of ordinary economic processes. This system of economic commitments is, therefore, *interdependent* with the differentiated sub-systems of the economy.[1]

These institutionalized value commitments guarantee the availability of a certain quota of resources for economic production. In this way, however, only the pattern-maintenance exigencies of the economy are met. As a system, it still faces goal-attainment, adaptive and integrative exigencies. As we have defined it, the *goal* of the economy is to provide goods and services for consumption. If the wants relative to these goods and services were quantitatively and qualitatively stable, and if the conditions of production were completely determined by the above "givens," then production processes could be completely routinized. Production would be a function of two sets of "givens": the commitments on the resource side, and the schedules of wants. Once an allocation of resources relative to the wants had been established, there would be no need for *economic* analysis.[2]

But in fact both the state of demand and conditions of production change continuously, and adjustments must be made within the limits left open by the institutionalized commitments. Relative to the body of given commitments, therefore, a set of processes in the economy differentiates in order to accommodate specific expected consumers' demand for particular quantities of particular goods and services. This differentiated aspect of the economy—which includes sales and distribution—is the "production" sub-system in a narrower sense. Within this sub-system the *goal* of the economy is implemented. This implementation involves continuous mutual adjustment between changing states of demand and changing processes of production. The latter depend partly upon the demand conditions, but partly upon

[1] For an analysis of this interdependence, cf. the discussion of the internal boundaries of the economy in Chap. IV.

[2] An approximation to such a state of affairs does, in fact, exist in highly traditional "underdeveloped" economies; this is the primary reason why economic theory is not very helpful in the study of such cases. See, for instance, Firth, R., *Primitive Polynesian Economy*, 1939.

changes originating in the conditions of production themselves.

Next, the *adaptive* specialization of the economy concerns the allocation of consumable resources between ultimate consumption and further productive use. It is impossible to assume that from the point of view of the economy this allocation will automatically be stable. Specialization therefore develops in this area of investment for productive purposes; the distinctive exigency to be adapted to is the need for procurement of capital funds.

Finally, the area of *integration* of the economy itself is not inherently stable. New opportunities arise, and changes in the situation force internal changes. Hence there is specialization in the adjustment of the organization of the factors of production. The entrepreneur is the specialist in this area.

These four—economic commitments, production-distribution, provision of capital, and entrepreneurship—are the primary *functional* bases of differentiation of the economy as a system. They are schematically represented in Figure 2. We will develop them further in connection with institutional structure in the next chapter, with economic fluctuations in Chapter IV, and with economic development in Chapter V.

By themselves, these functional bases are not adequate to account for the *concrete structure*—the firms, banks, plants, etc.—of the economy. For this purpose we must consider, besides the value system and the functional bases, at least two other sets of exigencies: (1) adaptive exigencies to which concrete units in the economy are subjected; (2) integrative exigencies, or the consequences of the fact that the economy must be integrated on an institutional level, both within itself and with the non-economic sub-systems of the society. The second set is the subject-matter for the next chapter. We will discuss the first set briefly here.

The adaptive exigencies confronting concrete economic structures may be classified according to our four-problem scheme: (1) in connection with the land factors—physical, cultural, and motivational commitments—certain non-economic conditions operate as adaptive exigencies; (2) in connection with the economy's production sub-system, conditions governing labour supply and demand for consumption goods are adaptive exigencies; (3) at the capital boundary non-economic conditions of capital supply and various political regulations upon capitalization are exigencies; and (4) in the case of the entrepreneurial function, the conditions on which entrepreneurial service is available to the economy and the forms of the "profit motive" among actual and potential entrepreneurs are adaptive exigencies.

FIGURE 2

FUNCTIONAL DIFFERENTIATION OF THE ECONOMY AS A SYSTEM*

A		G
	Capitalization and Investment Sub-system.	Production Sub-system—including Distribution and Sales.
	Economic Commitments: Physical, Cultural and Motivational Resources.	Organizational Sub-system: Entrepreneurial Function.
L		I

* Adapted from Figure 1, Chapter I.

Exigencies such as these, in manifold combination, account for the modes and levels of *segmentation* of the economy, i.e., its division into *concrete* units of organization such as firms and the aggregation of firms to form industries. They are also relevant to the relation between size of firm and form of business organization, problems of location of industry, and similar questions.

We may distinguish two main aspects of these adaptive exigencies. The first is *technological and ecological*, referring to supply and location of natural resources, size and geographical distribution of the population, etc., in relation to the technical problems of organizing production. The second aspect is *socio-cultural*, which deal with non-economic aspects of the social system and its culture. Under this heading are many elements of the motivation to productive work, consumers' wants, attitudes toward risk, control of economic enterprise, definition of the entrepreneurial and managerial roles, etc.

The differentiation of the economy by industries derives primarily from one complex of these exigencies. On the socio-cultural side is the specific composition of consumers' wants; on the technological side are the requirements for materials and labour for the process of production itself.[1]

Segmentation into firms and plant units involves other combinations of the exigencies. Within the determinants of any particular firm or plant, we may isolate three sets of conditions: (1) Market conditions at the consumers' end—the market or markets for the particular products, actual want structure and purchasing power of consumers, accessibility of markets, retail outlets, etc. (2) Market conditions at the producers' end—access to materials, labour supply, capital funds, etc. (3) Complex social exigencies in the actual organization of production—the technological conditions determining the economies of scale, the conditions of the organization of labour and its effective supervision, etc.

The productive organization, e.g., a plant, is a *concrete* social system in itself. Its *goal* is defined by its place in the economy, but it is not only an economic entity. It has a political system with loyalties and institutionalized authority; it is subject to internal integrative exigencies like any other social system, and it must have its own institutionalized values and cultural tradition. Therefore, the general type of analysis by means of which we treat the economy as a social system can be repeated on the appropriate levels for each of its concrete units.[2] It goes almost without saying that at these levels the most important ranges of variation in concrete forms of economic organization are found. The economic historian and the

[1] Some industries, e.g., iron and steel, are of course derivative in that they do not produce consumers' goods but rather producers' goods.

[2] Perhaps the most extensive recent analysis of the factors in the adaptive structuring of the units of the economy is found in P. Sargant Florence, *The Logic of British and American Industry*, 1953.

student of comparative problems must therefore devote particularly intensive attention to this problem area.

The concrete structure of the economy thus presents many challenges for sociological analysis. It is not, however, possible to develop them here. What follows is confined to the primary *functional* differentiation within the economy and between the economy and other social sub-systems. This differentiation is closely related to what we have called boundary processes. We have referred to these processes in connection with the classifications of the factors of production and the shares of income, but we have not yet examined the boundaries from all sides. That is to say, we have not attempted a direct analysis of the *structure of the situation* in which the economy functions. We must now turn to this task.

THE FUNCTIONAL DIFFERENTIATION OF SOCIETY

As we have pointed out repeatedly, the economy is a sub-system of a larger system—the society; furthermore, the economy is differentiated from other sub-systems on a primary-function level. These other sub-systems are the most essential part of the situation in which the economy functions. Before approaching the intensive analysis of the boundaries of the economy and the interchanges over them, we must lay the theoretical foundation for this analysis by considering the structure of society as a whole.

We must ask the reader's patient attention to this theoretical material for the next twenty or thirty pages. It will not be easy reading. A theory of social systems is abstract in its own right; when this is applied to the relations between the economy and other social systems, reasoning becomes compounded in its complexity. We feel it worth while to generalize these relations as far as possible, however, both to develop general theory and to provide the reader with the widest possible scope for interpreting our subsequent analyses.

Any social system must, as a condition of equilibrium, reach a relatively satisfactory solution of the four basic system problems. Maximization with respect to all four—and probably any two—at once is impossible. Put in a slightly different way, the social system is subject to these four dimensions as primary functional exigencies.[1]

The general paradigm of these four system problems is presented in Figure 1 in Chapter I, p. 19. We have used this paradigm to analyse the four factors of production and the four shares of income; we will use it in Chapters III and IV to analyse market structure and the internal differentiation of the economy. Now, however, we wish to apply it to the structural differentiation of the society as a whole.

Our most general proposition is that total societies *tend* to differentiate into sub-systems (social structures) which are specialized in each of the four primary functions. Where concrete structures cannot be identified, as is often the case, it is still often possible to isolate types of processes which are thus specialized.

The economy is the primary sub-system specialized in relation to the *adaptive* function of a society. If this proposition is correct, three other cognate sub-systems in a differentiated society should correspond to the other three functional problems. The sub-system goal of each of the three should be defined as a primary *contribution* to the appropriate functional need of the total society. For instance, the goal of the economy is the production of income which is at the disposal of the society.[2] In these terms, the other three societal sub-systems cognate with the economy are: (1) a goal-attainment sub-system, (2) an integrative sub-system, and (3) a pattern-maintenance and tension-management sub-system—all three of which possess the characteristics of social systems. Let us discuss each in turn.

The goal-attainment sub-system focuses on the political (in a broader sense) functions in a society. Since these functions are not coterminous with the governmental structure, it seems appropriate to term this sub-sector the "polity," parallel with the economy. The goal of the economy, as we have noted, is to

[1] As noted above (pp. 43–46), other secondary exigencies account for segmentation and integration of the concrete units of the social system.

[2] Secondarily, such a sub-system is then defined by *its* own adaptive exigencies, integrative exigencies, and type of institutionalized value pattern (as a specialization of the value pattern of the total society).

produce generalized facilities, as means to an indefinite number of possible uses. The important feature of this production is not only the quantity of such facilities (in a "physical" sense), but their *generalizability*, i.e., their adaptability to these various uses. The goal of the polity, however, is the *mobilization* of the necessary prerequisites for the *attainment* of given system goals of the society. Wealth is *one* of the indispensable prerequisites, but as we shall see, there are other equally important ones.

To put it in a slightly different way, the goal of the polity is to maximize the capacity of the society to attain its system goals, i.e., collective goals. We define this capacity as *power* as distinguished from wealth. We will discuss wealth as an ingredient of power presently; suffice it to say that the use of wealth for collective goals means a sacrifice of the *general* disposability of wealth, and hence its availability for other subsystems than the polity.

The polity is related to government in approximately the same way that the economy is to "business." The analytical system does not coincide with concrete organization but political goals and values tend to have primacy over others in an organ of government, much the same as economic goals and values tend to have primacy in a business organization.

For present purposes we will not analyse the internal differentiation of the polity or of the other two remaining systems. We will specify only those functions in each of these three sub-systems which impinge directly on the economy. It is possible, however, to analyse the internal differentiation of the polity, the integrative sub-system and the pattern-maintenance sub-system in much the same way as we have analysed the economy above and will analyse it further in Chapter IV.

The integrative sub-system of the society relates the cultural value-patterns to the motivational structures of individual actors in order that the larger social system can function without undue internal conflict and other failures of co-ordination. These processes maintain the institutionalization of value patterns which define the main structural outline of the society in the first instance. Sociologists refer to specialized integrative mechanisms primarily as mechanisms of social control.[1]

The integrative system of the society is the "producer" of another generalized capacity to control behaviour analogous to wealth and power. Some sociologists, notably Durkheim, refer to this capacity as "solidarity."[2] Wealth, therefore, is a generalized capacity to command goods and services, either as facilities or as reward objects for any goal or interest at any level in society. Power is the generalized capacity to mobilize the resources of the society, including wealth and other ingredients such as loyalties, "political responsibility," etc., to attain particular and more or less immediate collective goals of the system. Correspondingly, solidarity is the generalized capacity of agencies in the society to "bring into line" the behaviour of system units in accordance with the integrative needs of the system, to check or reverse disruptive tendencies to deviant behaviour, and to promote the conditions of harmonious co-operation.

Wealth or income is an output of the economy *to* other sub-systems of the society. Thus only in a secondary sense should we describe an economy as "wealthy"; the appropriate adjective is "productive." The *society* is wealthy or not wealthy. Similarly, a polity is not powerful, but a society is. The polity is more or less effective in the "production of power." Finally, the society has a high level of solidarity, but the integrative sub-system itself does not. The integrative system "contributes" solidarity to the social system. In the case of all three, "factors" analogous to the factors of production combine to produce the appropriate output or contribution; similarly, the output itself is distributed by shares among the different sub-systems of the society.

The pattern-maintenance and tension-management sub-system stands relative to the society as the land complex stands relative to the economy. At the societal level, this sub-system focuses on the institutionalized culture, which in turn centres on patterns of value orientations.[3] Such patterns are relevant

[1] Cf. Parsons, *The Social System*, Chap. VII.

[2] Another term is "cohesion."

[3] For the general theoretical background, cf. *Toward a General Theory of Action*, *The Social System*, and *Working Papers in the Theory of Action*.

to all social action. For any system, however, they are most nearly constant and relatively independent of the urgency of immediate goal needs and the exigencies of adaptive and integrative problems imposed on the system.

This relative constancy and insulation from exigencies does not mean that pattern maintenance occurs "automatically," i.e., without mechanisms. On the contrary, such patterns are institutionalized only through organization of potentially very unstable elements (in the process of socialization), and to be successful this organization requires complex "maintenance operations."

Pattern maintenance and tension management differ from the integrative problem in the sense that they focus on the *unit* of the system, not the system itself.[1] Integration is the problem of *inter*unit relationships, pattern maintenance of *intra*unit states and processes. Of course such a distinction depends on the degree of differentiation between system units. In the present context the distinction raises questions of the importance of the differentiation of the economy from other sub-systems in any given case. The differentiation is very clear in the modern industrial case. Hence it is essential to discriminate between the processes by which the basic economic commitments are *maintained* and the processes by which the boundary relations between the economy and other social sub-systems are *adjusted*. To take a specific case, a sharp fall in production occasioned by a deficit in consumer spending (a Keynesian depression) differs vastly from a fall occasioned by a breakdown in the fundamental motivation to work productively. In the latter case "pump-priming" measures are irrelevant; it is a problem of maintaining patterns of value.

The functioning of a unit in an interaction system ultimately depends on the motivation of the individual actors participating in the unit. The "tension-management" aspect of the pattern-maintenance sub-system concerns this motivation. The primary adaptive exigencies *of this sub-system* lie in those personality elements which maintain adequate motivation to conform with cultural values. The tension which is managed is indi-

[1] This is what is implied by referring to *latent* pattern maintenance and tension management. Essential *conditions* of the larger system functioning, rather than the functioning itself, are involved.

vidual motivation,[1] in actual or potential conflict with the fulfilment of behaviour expectations in institutionally defined roles. Unless controlled or managed, such tension disorganizes the relevant unit and thereby interferes with its functioning in the system.

The pattern-maintenance sub-system also has a type of "product" or contribution of generalized significance throughout the total social system. This is a type of "respect" accorded as a reward for conformity with a set of values. In cases when degrees of this respect are compared to others, we might call it *prestige*. Prestige, therefore, is the "product" of successful pattern maintenance or tension management in the interest of pattern conformity; it is a *capacity* to act in such a way as to implement the relevant system of institutionalized values.

The exact mechanisms of tension management and pattern maintenance vary from system to system. The primary function of the latency sub-system is always relative to a given superordinate system reference. It defines the conditions of stability of the units of this superordinate system, whatever the units happen to be. But the units themselves, at the next level down in an analytic breakdown, have the properties of systems. The definition of the conditions of stability therefore depend empirically on the system level in question.

THE BOUNDARIES BETWEEN THE SUB-SYSTEMS OF SOCIETY

The four primary functional sub-systems of a society—the economy, the polity, the integrative sub-system, and the pattern-maintenance and tension-management sub-system—are shown in Figure 3. In what relation do they stand to each other? As we have suggested, each constitutes part of the *situation* for each of the others. From the point of view of any one sub-system, the primary cognate *social* situation or environment consists of the other three. For the economy,

[1] It does not matter, for purposes of the present analysis, what proportion of this motivation is constitutionally given and what proportion is affected by learning.

for instance, the polity, the integrative system and the pattern-maintenance system constitute the primary social situation.

But is not the relationship between system and social situation more specific? We introduced an element of specificity in the above analysis of the economic classification of the factors of production and the shares of income, in which we tried to demonstrate that these constitute the inputs and outputs, respectively, between the economy and the rest of society. This brief statement can be developed further.

Certainly the boundaries of the economy are not completely undifferentiated with respect to the relative concentration of *types* of input and output. Labour services, for instance, do not come from the same sources as capital resources; similarly, wages are not paid to the same elements as "interest" and other capital returns. To be sure, in the history of economics, there have been difficulties in identifying the sources of the factors and the recipients of the shares as sociologically distinct "classes." That there is *some* correspondence between these economic differentiations and those of social structure, however, seems beyond doubt, though the concrete social structures vary from one society to another.

If this is true for the economy's boundaries, then it should be true for the boundaries of the other sub-systems of the society. Furthermore, there should be a cognate classification of types of input and output in each of the *other* sub-systems. This follows from the general postulate that the scheme of functional differentiation is grounded in the *general* theory of social systems and therefore applies to the economy and to its cognate sub-systems in society.

If this reasoning is accepted, what is the nature of the "matching" between inputs and outputs among the various sub-systems of the society? Let us first take the goal-attainment sub-system of the economy, i.e., the production of goods and services for the "satisfaction" of consumers' wants, as one of the economy's specialized outputs. Is it a *specialized input* into another specific sub-system of the society? Or is it simply "spread" over the whole range of boundaries of the other sub-systems? The latter assumption is altogether incompatible with a vast amount of evidence for the relatively determinate structuring of social systems. But how can we demonstrate a specific "matching"?

FIGURE 3

THE DIFFERENTIATED SUB-SYSTEMS OF SOCIETY

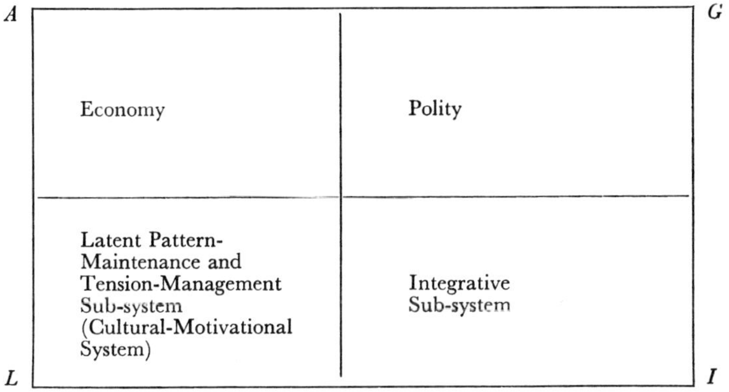

A			G
	Economy	Polity	
	Latent Pattern-Maintenance and Tension-Management Sub-system (Cultural-Motivational System)	Integrative Sub-system	
L			I

We have one obvious empirical clue at the outset. The output of consumers' goods and services from the economy is (in concrete social structure terms) primarily to the family or household; conversely the input of labour services into the economy is an input from the household.

But what is the household or family? In sociological terms, the family (in our society, specifically the nuclear family) is not simply a "random sample" of the non-economic parts of the social structure. It is specifically located in the pattern-maintenance sub-system of the society.[1] It follows that the output of the economy over its goal-attainment boundary (A_G) goes *primarily* to some branch of the pattern-maintenance sub-system, at least in the modern industrial type of society.

If this boundary identification is correct empirically, what is its theoretical rationale? Certain classical economists sensed the appropriate line of reasoning, albeit in a vague and largely untenable way. This is that the household's primary output, from the societal perspective, is the organization of human motivation. In sociological terms this involves the socialization of children and the tension management of adults, both

[1] Cf. *Working Papers*, Chap. V., Sec. viii, and Parsons, T., Bales, R. F., *et al.*, *Family, Socialization and Interaction Process*, 1955, Chap. I.

understood with reference to the central value patterns of the society.[1] The primary function (though by no means the only one) of consumers' wealth at the societal level is as an ingredient for this process. This is not merely because man, as organism, must meet biological needs: sociologically more important, it is because man, as human personality, must be provided with the symbolic media for learning and implementing values in human relations. The "style of life" of a household cannot be an abstract entity. It must have concrete content—actual premises in which everyday life is lived, the equipment of the home, clothing and many other things. Biological needs are, of course, met in this context; but they and their modes of realization occur within a cultural pattern.

Here we might note again the applicability of a distinction we believe to be fundamental to our analysis: the distinction between analytical sub-system and concrete structure of the economy. The relationship between the economy and the latent pattern-maintenance and tension-management sub-system is essentially analytical, i.e., it illustrates the crucial point of interaction between two differentiated functional sub-systems. But the economy does not "end" at the market for consumer goods. Indeed a good deal of the working capital of the economy is, even in our society, located concretely in households in the form of consumer durables in the process of depreciation. The functional differentiation of society and the concrete structure of collectivities, therefore, are overlapping classifications. As we have pointed out, our analysis deals primarily with the analytical sub-systems.

What are the reciprocal inputs from the household, i.e., labour services? Clearly they are in some sense "products" of the functioning household. It is possible, we think, to interpret them as the primary goal output of the pattern-maintenance sub-system to the economy (L_G).

The naïve economic version of this hypothesis is that the only serious function of the human services is in their contribution to the production of wealth and that socialization itself is simply a form of economic production. The alternative to this untenable interpretation is that while an aspect of the life of the household is self-sufficient and in certain respects the

[1] *Family, Socialization and Interaction Process*, Chap. I, pp. 16 ff.

household is directly integrated with "community structures," its social function *vis-à-vis* the division of labour is institutionalized as occupational roles in so far as it is institutionalized in specialized role-performance form at all.

In a highly differentiated society, the occupational role system is by no means coterminous with the economy; it extends beyond role involvements only in organizations with economic primacy (business firms). Nevertheless, occupational roles connect closely with the economy even when the organization in question is not a business firm. The basis of this connection is that occupational roles, which are always subject to the contract of employment, are subject at least to limited control by economic sanctions. Thus production of wealth has the goal primacy of occupational performance over only part of the range of occupational structure, but over the whole range labour market mechanisms control occupational performance and the allocation of personnel between occupational roles.[1] This is the sense in which labour service is always *chanelled through* the economy in the transition from household to non-household role functions in the society. Also, the terms relating to income which a household receives are always important in the contract of employment.

To sum up, the boundary relationships between the economy and the pattern-maintenance sub-system are symmetrically reciprocal; each exchanges "primary goal outputs" with the other. The household—in its occupational role aspect—institutionalizes the function of "producer" of labour service to the society via the economy. The goal of the economy is to produce income primarily for the satisfaction of consumer wants.[2]

[1] There are different *types* of markets, however. Cf. Chap. III, pp. 146 ff.

[2] It will be noted that we have been careful *not* to assert or imply that consumers are "located" only in the household or that they are in any general sense a category of individuals. The state is clearly one of the major consumers in modern societies—e.g., of military equipment. We do not think that the benefits (or costs) of this military consumption can in any sensible way be allocated among the individual members of the society. It is the government as *collectivity* which is the consumer. But in this capacity or "role" the government is acting as part of the pattern-maintenance sub-system, not of the polity, as it does in other respects.

What now is the matching at the adaptive boundary of the economy (A_A)? It will be recalled that the economy's adaptive need is for capital funds as facilities to maintain and/or increase production; clearly this means capital as a factor of production.

What, however, is the main extra-economic source of capital? It is tempting to follow certain traditions and identify the household as this source, since private individuals (in the first instance considered as members of households) are indeed important savers from private resources. It is possible to make an empirical case for the view that this is the primary source in certain societies and in certain periods. In such cases, however, we suggest that there is a relative lack of differentiation of sub-systems and their boundary relations.

To us the preferable alternative as the primary source of capital-input is the polity; hence we suggest that the economy's adaptive boundary (in the functional sense) stands *vis-à-vis* the polity. The polity as source of capital is most definitely *not*, however, simply a repository for savings which, according to some supply and demand schedule reflected by some price, permits ebbs and flows of stored liquid funds to the economy. The nature of the political input into the economy is, rather, contained in the notion of the *creation of credit*. In our technical sense, the creation of credit is primarily an *exercise of power* in that facilities necessary for pursuit of goals are restricted by means of the imposition of situational controls over the access to these facilities.[1] The decision to create credit is in the first instance a decision to make available facilities for the pursuit of economic goals; the decision not to create credit (or to reduce the volume outstanding) is a decision to restrict these facilities by direct control of the situation. Hence generalized purchasing power, introduced into the economy as capital through credit, is a form of *power* in our technical sense. The term "purchasing power" as used by economists and others is thus technically appropriate. From the economy's point of view the input is

[1] Outside the economic context, examples of the exercise of power in the sense of situational control are the control of the ownership of firearms, the restriction of geographical mobility, etc.; more generally, the political monopoly over police and military powers of coercion and control is the exercise of this type of power.

capital funds (facilities); from the societal point of view it is the use of political controls to commit purchasing power on the most generalized level to economic use to increase the *productivity* of the economy. By means of the same political controls, of course, this power can be made available for a number of alternative uses if it is not committed to the increase of economic productivity, e.g., the financing of primarily pattern-maintenance "capital" such as schools, churches, recreational facilities, etc.

It is important to note that political controls are not coterminous with governmental in this context. In our society credit creation is centred more in what in common-sense terms we think of as "economic" as opposed to "political" organizations, such as banks, even though the latter are subject to certain governmental controls. "Political" is an analytical category parallel to "economic." It does not correspond directly to concrete organizational units. Its relation to organization varies from society to society and in the same society over time.

The power to create credit is, in its political aspect, analogous to the taxation power, if we treat the latter as enforced saving imposed upon the private sectors of the community. The most notable immediate difference between the two is that the creation of credit by "political" authority accomplishes saving without directly depriving any holder of funds of his purchasing power, whereas taxing subtracts a portion of the holder's disposable wealth. We will discuss the relations between taxation and credit creation presently; at the moment we merely wish to note that both are instances of political control over the generalized facilities required for the pursuit of system-goals.

In any given society the locus of immediate control of the creation and manipulation of generalized purchasing power is problematical; often it *is* distributed among household units. The crucial element of this control, however, is the element of *generalization*, i.e., the acceptability of the relevant symbolic control mechanisms throughout the society. To insure such acceptability cannot be a function of the relatively "latent" household, but must be a function of the activity of the society's politically co-ordinating sub-system. This sub-system does not directly release specific quantities of goods and services to the economy for capitalization; rather it is the location of the mechanisms which enforce "claims" to *control* these goods and services. The "household" hypothesis cannot account for this cardinal feature of capital and credit. In other words, the supply of capital funds through credit creation does not put concrete capital goods into the economy, but puts at the disposal of economic units the *power* to command certain quantities of capital goods.[1]

The input of the control of generalized purchasing power thus meets the economy's adaptive needs in a highly differentiated society. On the presumption that generalized purchasing power is a political category, is this conception in keeping with the characteristics of the polity as a sub-system of the society? Again we will have to restrict our sociological analysis of the polity to those functions involved in the boundary-relation with the economy.

Very broadly, the control of the situation—of which control of the creation of generalized purchasing power is an important sub-type—is one of *two* primary outputs of the polity. The other, which is more immediate and crucial with respect to most societal goals, is the capacity to command support, i.e., the necessary motivational commitment of the individual and collective units of society.[2] We interpret the latter as the primary goal output of the polity. The output of situational controls over the availability of purchasing power is therefore a secondary output of the political process, just as the output of the shares of income other than wages is a secondary output of the economic process.

The output of the control of purchasing power links with one of the polity's fundamental needs, however. To produce power, it, too, must command *facilities*. One aspect of this need is to command the use of physical facilities of power. But on a more generalized level the polity also must control human behaviour

[1] *What* capital goods are purchased is a matter of intra-economic decisions, not incorporated into the external boundaries of the economy. Cf. Chap. IV pp. 210–13.

[2] In general this commitment of contingent support cannot be an occupational form of commitment, because the latter cannot be oriented so immediately to a *particular* societal goal.

in connection with these facilities. Negatively, it must prevent interference with the attainment of system goals; positively it must "induce" co-operation where positive commitments are needed.

Such adaptive needs of the polity articulate with the economy's adaptive needs for capital. Hence the adaptive boundary of the economy (A_A) is contiguous with the adaptive boundary of the polity (G_A). The flow from the polity into the economy is the creation of capital funds through credit; the reverse flow is the control of the *productivity* of the economy. This productivity is the product of the capitalization realized by using capital funds; at the same time, productivity is the basis of *one* of the primary ingredients of power. So the economy and polity stand in a reciprocally adaptive relationship to each other.

There are two primary elements of political significance in the economy's output of productivity. The first is quantitative, i.e., there is political interest in the size and capacity of the productive plant and inventory of goods available at any given time. Second, and equally important, is the element of *generalizability*, i.e., the applicability of the productive capacity to a *variety* of system goals. Thus, for example, there is a political interest both in the size of the steel and automobile manufacturing plant and its potentiality to be converted rapidly into an effective plant for the manufacture of military equipment. Productivity in its political aspect must always be assessed from both these points of view.

The *control* of economic productivity is, in the absence of salient collective system goals, often latent. In periods of domestic and international quiescence the rights and interests of the political authority in the productivity of the economy may be so seldom exercised as to appear not to exist. In periods of international tension, such as the current Cold War situation, however, explicit interest in the national productive capacity is high, and certain strategic controls over productivity are maintained. Finally in periods of acute national crisis, such as the outbreak of war, the political control of productive plant is as apparent as the political control over manpower through conscription, e.g., the executive order to stop automobile production immediately after the outbreak of hostilities between the United States and Japan. In general, therefore, the exercise of control over productivity by the polity depends upon the system goal at hand.

The above analysis of the A_A–G_A boundary interchange suggests the following implications:

(1) As we have said, the polity cannot mean "government" in the concrete sense. Sometimes, of course, important parts of the credit and capitalization function of the economy are incorporated directly into governmental agencies. This may not, however, be the most important source of capital in a "free enterprise" economy; yet our analysis applies to this case as well. Parts of the political sub-system often are *organizationally* independent of government. Central banking, for instance, while somehow involved with government, often is semi-independent and is usually "taken out of politics." A wide range of "private" agencies, e.g., insurance, which are "affected with a public interest" also have definite political components.[1] Hence our use of the concept of "political" is wider than its common-sense application. The organizational implementation of the credit-capitalization functions is important in analysing empirical monetary processes, however, and extensive historical and comparative work should prove fruitful in tracing the implications of diverse organizational arrangements for concrete economic processes.

At this point certain methodological cautions are in order. The first concerns the importance of maintaining clear relations among several system levels in analysing any specific empirical problem. Thus far we have distinguished two system levels: the functional differentiation of the society as a whole and the functional differentiation of the economy as a social system. Both these system levels bear on the assessment, explanation and prediction of economic behaviour. On the other hand, system references at such gross levels do not solve certain problems of most immediate interest to economists. To predict detailed short-term lending or investment behaviour, for instance, from the gross functional interchange between the economy and the polity is methodologically unsound; it is equally unsound to characterize the motivations or orientations of the individuals or collectivities involved in these gross functional interchanges solely on the basis of this one—or any

[1] Cf. Chap. III, pp. 162 ff.

other *one*—boundary interchange. Even though they do not solve such problems, however, the gross distinctions do bear on them. In what precise ways will become clear only after much further analysis. Suffice it to say at present that fully to characterize the related phenomena of lending, investment, and capitalization, for instance, requires reference to several interchanges at several different system-levels.[1]

Furthermore, it is incorrect, as we have pointed out repeatedly, to identify any concrete class of organizations or their orientations exclusively with any one functionally differentiated sub-system. This is particularly true at the economy-polity boundary, where the segmentation of collectivities with both political and economic involvements—banks, individuals, households, insurance companies, governmental agencies and firms themselves—is extremely complex. True, business firms have economic *primacy*, but they themselves are not the economy; government has political *primacy*, but it is not the polity. It goes without saying that the same applies to interstitial organizations. Hence it is technically incorrect to treat, e.g., insurance agencies, exclusively as political or exclusively as economic organizations, even though they are influenced by both political and economic considerations by virtue of their involvement in both sub-systems. In principle every concrete organization participates to some degree on all four functional sub-systems—the differences are those of rank-order of relative primacies.

(2) To assign the control of generalized purchasing power to the polity has important consequences for the conception of saving. By and large we consider the problem of saving to be an intra-latency problem,[2] that is to say, based primarily on the intra-system considerations governing the household and other collectivities with latency primacy. Analytically, therefore, the decision to save as such does not concern the economy *directly* at all.[3] Its most important implication for the economy is in

[1] Cf. Chap. III, pp. 123–139 and 161–169 and Chap. IV, pp. 200–02, 210–13, and 233–41.

[2] With certain exceptions, such as "public responsibility," "community spirit," etc., as bases for saving. Cf. Chap. IV, pp. 223–7.

[3] This is not to say, of course, that they are not economically relevant. Cf. Weber, *The Theory of Social and Economic Organization*, ed. T. Parsons, 1947, pp. 158 ff., for the distinction between "economic action" and "economically relevant action."

the importance of maintaining a certain level of savings in "public trust," i.e., in the hands of political agencies, from which credit can be created. This level is usually referred to as "reserves." The establishment of such a level (which may indeed be the proceeds of either saving or taxation) has necessary connection with the return of funds to the economy for purposes of investment. As we have pointed out, the decision to save does not solve the problem of surrendering funds for the function of capitalization. A second process is required, namely the expansion of the reserves by means of the credit mechanism in return for expectations of productive investment of the resulting liquid funds.

In our terms, the problem of return of capital funds to the economy involves at least two boundary processes. The decision to save itself is primarily an intra-latency process; in so far as it supplies a base for credit, it involves the boundary between the latency system and the polity.[1] The second decision, to create credit, involves the relationship between the polity and the economy. The decision processes of saving and investment, therefore, are not single or simple economic processes. So long as the requisite reserve level is maintained, in fact, it is appropriate to treat them as independent.[2]

(3) In the light of the foregoing analysis, we might re-assess the role of credit in the economy. Credit as a concrete phenomenon extends throughout the economy, even though we have located it *analytically* at the major exchange between polity and economy. This discrepancy between the credit in terms of functionally differentiated sub-systems and the credit in terms of the concrete exercise of the credit-creating power illustrates the distinction between functional sub-systems and concrete collectivities which we have emphasized again and again. For instance, we have shown that the major inputs between the economy and the latency sub-system are labour services for consumer goods; yet concretely labour permeates the whole economy and consumer's goods permeate all the

[1] In certain extreme cases this boundary is the focus of a deficit. Cf. the French experience of hoarding of gold and hard currencies instead of depositing legal tender with appropriate banking or governmental agencies.

[2] We will treat both savings and investment in greater detail in Chap. IV, pp. 221 ff.

other functional sub-systems.[1] Again, while investment and capitalization is analytically located in the adaptive sub-system of the economy, some investment goods (consumer durables) are located in households as collectivities.[2] The phenomena of credit creation illustrates, therefore, the difference between analytic categories and organizational units.

We will illustrate the role of credit in two contexts: creation of capital funds for industrial investment, and creation of consumer's credit. First let us posit as a goal for the adaptive sub-system of the economy (A_A) the maintenance and/or increase of productivity.[3] On the other hand, let us posit as a goal for the relevant latency sub-system (L_G) the maintenance and/or enhancement of a style of life in accordance with a certain income (wage level).[4] These are the respective goals of these two systems. For each system credit serves the general purpose of temporarily removing some of the contingency of the situation in which this goal is to be attained. This is accomplished by supplying a level of rewards associated with a higher level of goal-attainment than is in fact being realized at the time the credit is extended. This temporary "guarantee" of an income level (reward) is, however, *always* conditional. It is granted only if there is an expectation that some future gratification level will be higher than the present level. So long as the goal-gratification level of the borrowing sub-system in question continues to rise at a requisite rate, then credit has only a lubricative function for the system in question, in so far as it renders harmless certain situational disturbances (e.g., temporary changes in demand, indivisibility of products or factors, temporary external diseconomies, etc.). If the goal-gratification level of the borrowing system does not reach the level expected by the lender, then we are confronted with a state of discrepancy between goal-attainment and goal-expectation, and usual symptoms of disturbance and frustration may be expected to appear.

To illustrate this general statement: In the case of the input of capital funds via the A_A–G_A boundary, the expected

[1] Cf. pp. 53–57.
[2] Cf. pp. 54–56.
[3] Cf. Chap. IV, pp. 200–02 ff.
[4] Cf. Chap. III, pp. 117 ff.

goal-attainment is the maintenance and/or increase of productivity on the part of the investment-capitalization sub-system. If this goal-attainment is forthcoming,[1] then the extension of credit simply facilitates the production of productivity. But the greater the amount of credit creation, the higher the rate of growth of capital productivity required to meet the expected goal. If this requisite rate is not met, either because of the limitations of the investment process itself or because of higher requirements demanded by the relevant political authority, then the familiar consequences of economic disturbance appear: inflation, withdrawal of funds, business failure, hoarding, speculation, etc.

In the case of credit which finances consumer expenditure (consumer investment), the same balance holds. Consumer credit is an expansion of consumer purchasing power (i.e., household reward) to overcome certain situational exigencies, such as the indivisibility of consumer durables. Implied in consumer advances is a sanction that the level of borrowing will not exceed a balance struck by the following three factors: the rate of depreciation of the goods purchased, the level of the real wage rate (i.e., worker productivity), and the payments required in return for the credit creation. That is to say, if terms stiffen, if required durables depreciate too fast or if real wages decline or do not rise, then there is a discrepancy between the actual rate of goal gratification (implementation of a style of life in accordance with an income level) and the rate expected by the agencies responsible for the creation of funds. In such cases we would again expect symptoms of disturbance to arise.

To summarize, credit represents an "elasticizing" or "loosening" of economic processes by political agencies above and beyond the level permitted by self-financing. The credit mechanism renders the situation less contingent over time, allowing various economic goals and sub-goals to be attained, but only if these are attained at some minimal rate. Credit, therefore, is a conditional facilitation of goal-attainment. Or conversely, a given level of credit can be afforded only if the various goals in question are maintained and/or increased over time.

[1] The expected level of goal-attainment is usually symbolized by the interest rate. Cf. below, pp. 75–76.

Unless our analytical universe of four cognate societal sub-systems is incomplete, simple logical exhaustion locates the third open interchange between the economy and society. That is, among the "non-economic" sub-systems, the integrative is the only remaining possibility.[1]

Given this solution by theoretical exhaustion, however, is it not possible to make a substantive case for the articulation between the economy and the integrative sub-system of the society?

It is clear that the economy needs labour services, capital, and land. The need for organization is not so obvious. We rest on the authority of Marshall and Schumpeter for its importance as an independent factor of production. We have emphasized that this factor is integrative for the economy. Can we demonstrate this integrative significance? Can we treat the integrative sub-system of the society as the source of its input?

A full answer to the first question must await extensive developments in Chapter III. Organization is focused on the *combination* of the factors of production. This combination does not occur automatically: there must be some agency of combination. One major form of this agency is the institutionalization of previously determined combinations of the factors; the other form is a part of the economic process itself. Very broadly, the institution of contract constitutes the already-institutionalized elements of organization[2] and the fluid elements come to be organized in a more dynamic way.

Above and beyond this broad conceptualization, the factor of organization has been associated with the entrepreneurial function primarily by Schumpeter and his followers. The entrepreneur is responsible primarily for the input of "new combinations of the factors of production." This is an input of solidarity as we have defined the term. As noted above, solidarity or integration has both negative and positive aspects. The negative forestalls tendencies to internal conflict or

[1] Of course, we could have considered this integrative interchange first and then worked around to the economy-household boundary. Our sequence of analysis was not determined analytically. We began with the relations between "production" and "consumption" primarily because they have occupied such a central position in economic theory.

[2] Cf. Chap. III, pp. 104 ff.

disorganization. In the economy such conflict arises from disproportion in the factors of production, e.g., malemployment of one factor or another. The positive aspect of *new* combinations adds to productivity by readjusting the factors, anticipating potential demand, etc. In either case new combinations adjust proportions among the available ingredients of the productive process.

What does the economy contribute in return to the production of solidarity at the societal level? The answer is based on the fact that the outputs of the economic process (wealth and the concrete goods or services it commands) have a variety of symbolic meanings throughout the society. Distribution of wealth, for instance, raises many integrative problems. Furthermore, appropriate combinations of goods and services are necessary to symbolize a style of life adequately. In these two respects and many others the economy has integrative significance for the society. The primary output of the economy to the integrative sub-system consists therefore of those *new product combinations* which have symbolic significance in non-economic contexts.[1]

What *sub*-system of the integrative system is contiguous to the integrative boundary of the economy (A_I)?[2] We suggest that it is the integrative sub-system (I_I). We will develop the rationale for this assignment in the next chapter; by way of introduction, however, the integrative sub-system of the integrative system concerns the relation between the division of labour and the integration of society. The division of labour, because it involves specialized roles, creates a dual problem of integration: (1) communication among those with different statuses in the social system, and (2) integration of interests which are necessarily divergent to some degree. The integration at this sensitive point in the social structure—an integration primarily via the institution of contract—is the paramount focus of society's integration problem. Furthermore, the

[1] We will discuss the *content* of family style of life and its implications in Chap. IV, pp. 221–27.

[2] It will be remembered that the goal-attainment *sub*-system of the pattern-maintenance system is contiguous to the goal-attainment sub-system of the economy, and that the adaptive *sub*-system of the polity is contiguous to the adaptive sub-system of the economy (A_A).

integration of the division of labour connects closely with the economy itself. Hence, on a variety of sociological grounds we assign this type of institutionalization to the integrative sub-system of the integrative system.

We have now reviewed three of the six[1] boundary relationships that relate the four primary functional sub-systems of the society. If we are correct in this analysis, these three fit into a pattern which characterizes the social system as a whole. Figure 4 shows the entire social system and the primary boundary interchanges. The three boundary interchanges we have developed are: (1) the goal-attainment boundary of the economy *vis-à-vis* the goal-attainment boundary of the pattern-maintenance system (A_G–L_G); (2) the adaptive boundary of the economy *vis-à-vis* the adaptive boundary of the polity (A_A–G_A); and (3) the integrative boundary of the economy *vis-à-vis* the integrative boundary of the integrative sub-system (A_I–I_I). At each of these three a factor of production for the economy is exchanged primarily for an output from the economy to the appropriate sub-system.

Besides these three, we would expect cognate boundary-structures for the three remaining interchanges. That is, (1) the polity and integrative system have contiguous goal-attainment sub-systems (G_G–I_G); (2) the integrative and pattern-maintenance systems have contiguous adaptive sub-systems (I_A–L_A); and (3) the polity and pattern-maintenance systems have contiguous integrative sub-systems (G_I–L_I). After considerable study we are convinced that these three boundary relationships make good sociological sense and illuminate many problems not relevant to the present volume. We indicate them by dotted lines only, to complete the schematic outline of the major input-output categories among the major sub-systems of society.[2]

[1] The total of six is arrived at by simple arithmetical exhaustion. That is, if three of the four boundaries of four sub-systems have one interchange each with another boundary, the total is six.

[2] This is the first publication which incorporates the analysis of the boundary relations between the primary functional sub-systems of a society. It is thus not possible to refer the reader to other sources; subsequent publications by one or both of the authors should contribute to filling this gap in the not-too-distant future.

FIGURE 4

BOUNDARY INTERCHANGES BETWEEN THE PRIMARY SUB-SYSTEMS OF A SOCIETY*

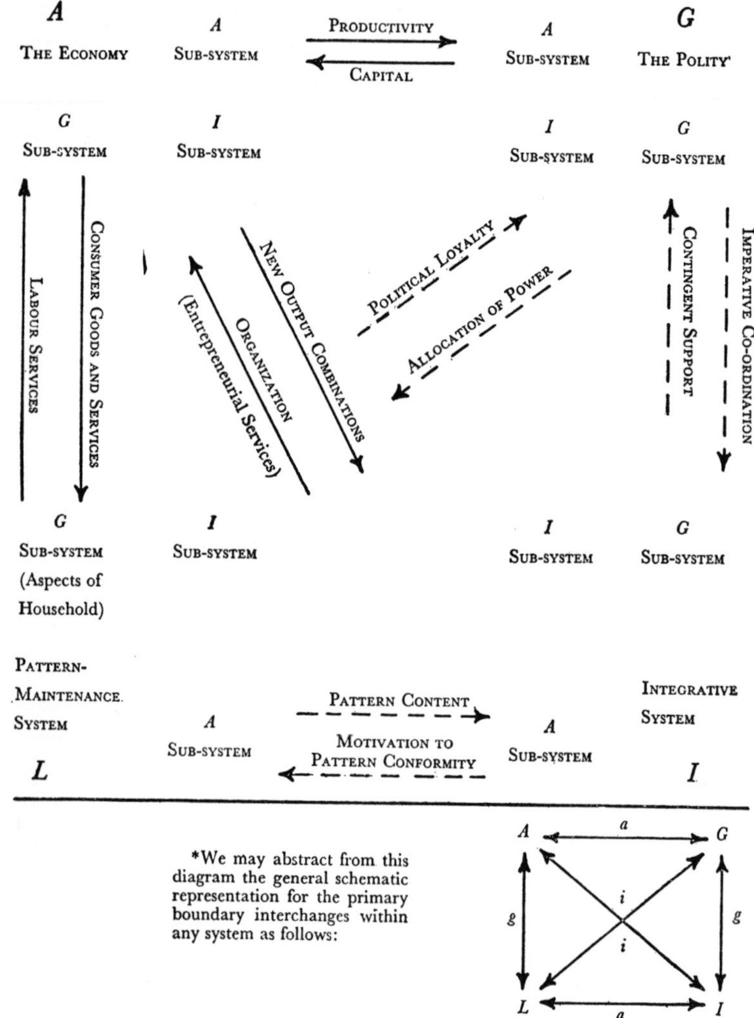

*We may abstract from this diagram the general schematic representation for the primary boundary interchanges within any system as follows:

To complete the theoretical sketch of the boundary relations we must return to the economy's latent pattern-maintenance and tension-management sub-system (A_L, which deals with "land" factors). The latency sub-system of any larger system is always a special case relative to the other three systems in the sense that it is "insulated" from sensitivity to the current performance-sanction interplay of the larger system with its cognate systems. To be sure, the latency sub-system of the society has boundary relations with the economy and the other two non-latent systems, as shown in Figure 4. But *its own* latency sub-system is not contiguous to any sub-system of any other primary system. What is the status of this "special" latency boundary?

The "special" boundary of the latency sub-system at any given system level is a *cultural* rather than an interaction boundary.[1] The latency sub-system, as we have noted, maintains value patterns. But cultural patterns are not isolated atoms, each institutionalized in connection with its own particular system or sub-system. The cultural value system of a society is more or less integrated. In particular the value patterns applicable to any given sub-system are *differentiated value sub-systems* of the general value system of the total society. The relations between these cultural sub-systems are, of course, not interactive; they include relations of consistency, level of generality, differentiation of relevant context of application, etc.

The role of the cultural value patterns is analogous to those modern machines which approximate "thinking" processes. The institutionalized value patterns are analogous to the basic "programme" or set of instructions which are "stored" in the machine's "memory." In response to more specific "information" fed in, the machine performs a series of operations to arrive at particular results. But the programme pattern cannot

[1] In no sense is the latency boundary an "external" boundary, however. This view is tempting, since land involves physical resources. But according to the general theory of action, relations to the physical environment are not the function of *any* primary sub-system of an interaction system, but are resultant functions of all of them. So far as external relations in general are specialized, of course, they belong in the adaptive and goal-attainment systems (cf. Chap. I, pp. 17–18.

be derived from the specific operational procedures or vice versa; they are analytically independent factors.

Land is a specific instance of a pattern-maintenance factor. The common denominator of the three "land" categories—physical facilities, cultural facilities and motivational commitments—is a certain order of control to which they are subject. They are committed to economic production on bases other than the operation of short-term economic sanctions. They are "fed into" the economic machine prior to current operations; consequently they must be treated as a given determinant of subsequent processes.[1]

DOUBLE INTERCHANGES AT THE BOUNDARIES

In the concrete case, the primary interchanges across each of the three open boundaries of the economy do not result from direct specific transactions;[2] there is an *intermediary mechanism* at each boundary, at least in differentiated systems.

At the A_G–L_G boundary, goods and services are sold by firms and other suppliers for money payments which are drawn from the wages of households. There are two distinct exchanges: consumers' goods for money funds and labour services for money funds. Money is thus the intervening mechanism in the overall exchange. Furthermore, the unit of the economy which receives consumers' spending is usually not the primary source of the wage income of the household. The "employing units" and the "selling units" in the economy are directly united only by the market nexus.

There are two bases for this duality of interchange. The first is the division of labour. The consuming household cannot receive its total income of goods and services from the specialized organization which employs the breadwinner. The intervening monetary mechanism renders the gains from employment effective to control the acquisition of consumption goods.

[1] Relative to these "givens," two types of processes occur in the economy: processes when the "givens" remain unchanged, and changes of the "givens" themselves. We will devote Chap. IV to the first type of change and Chap. V to the latter.

[2] E.g., labour services are not exchanged directly for consumers' goods.

The second basis is the divergence of interest arising from the fact that typical firms and typical households are primarily centred in different functional sub-systems of society and hence have different primary goals. Household members want to "live" according to a given pattern; the firm's goal is to "produce," secure rewards, and accumulate facilities to continue producing. Some mechanism must mediate between these two distinct orientations.

On the one hand, money represents the *generalization* of purchasing power to *control decisions* to exchange goods; on the other hand it symbolizes attitudes. The former is the "wealth" aspect of consumers' income, the latter the "prestige" aspect. If it cannot command goods and services money is not acceptable as wages; if it cannot symbolize prestige and mediate between detailed symbols and a broader symbolization it is not acceptable on other grounds. Only with this dual significance can money perform its *social* functions.

The duality of interchange, as shown in Figure 5, of course implies a duality of market structure for the consumers' goods

FIGURE 5

THE DOUBLE INTERCHANGE BETWEEN THE ECONOMY AND THE PATTERN-MAINTENANCE SUB-SYSTEM

A_G "*Economic*" Decisions		L_G "*Household*" Decisions
Decision to offer employment	← Labour Services	Decision to accept employment
	Wages →	
	← Consumer Spending	
Decision to produce	Consumer Goods and Services →	Decision to purchase

market and the labour market.[1] On each side of the firm-household exchange, therefore, are two independent sets of decisions. On the household side there is the decision of occupational choice and acceptance of specific employment *and* the decision to purchase kinds and quantities of goods and

[1] We will explore the structure of these two markets in Chap. III.

services. On the firm side there is the decision to offer employment in given quantities at given remuneration levels *and* the decision of how much to produce on what terms. Only through several delicate balances involving both intra-system and boundary relationships are these four sets of decisions co-ordinated.

At the adaptive boundary, the input to the economy is the creation of capital funds by the polity. Their supply results from the exercise of one power component or output type (creation of generalized facilities). This supply is used to develop the economy's productive capacity and therefore to improve its level of adaptation.

At the same time, increased productive capacity involves an output of *productivity* or increased potential for providing facilities for societal system goals. This interchange between capital funds and productivity meets the adaptive needs of both economy and polity. The economy gains production potential and the polity gains power potential. Each sacrifices current production for future gains.

In a broad sense these performances and sanctions balance in this interchange, just as labour services and consumption goods and services balance at the latency-economy boundary. But at the adaptive boundary as well the exchange is mediated by an intervening mechanism.[1] The first basis for this mechanism is again the division of labour. The polity is not one big organizational unit; it includes (as units with political functions) governmental agencies, banks, insurance companies, individuals in lending capacities, firms, political parties, etc. Because of this differentiation, some *generalized* short-term sanction is necessary to reward the individual or collectivity for discreet and immediate performances. This sanction is a "measuring rod" to co-ordinate the two larger inputs of control of purchasing power and productivity. The second basis for the intermediate mechanism is the *symbolization of attitudes* and interests which differ in the respective sub-systems. In the case of the polity, the mechanism ties in closely with attitudes toward *power* (as opposed to prestige at the A_G–L_G boundary).

[1] It will be recalled (cf. above, pp. 70–71) that the intervening mechanism at the A_G–L_G boundary involves monetary funds, in the form of consumer purchasing power and wages.

Presently we will discuss the nature of this intervening mechanism, and its mode of control. First, let us specify its form in balancing the control of productivity and the control of the creation of capital funds.

How does the polity "sanction" the production of productivity? These sanctions extend over a wide range of direct politico-legal encouragements and discouragements of the creation of productive enterprise. Concretely, these appear above all in governmental regulations and law codes. Probably the most direct sanctions are certain economic policies of the governmental authority, such as the tax exemption of ploughed-back profits, the general treatment of corporate taxes, direct subsidies, and protection of key industries by tariffs and subsidies. The primary emphasis of such sanctions is an *endorsement* of the industry or sector of the economy in question by the political authority; it is above all a guarantee that the industry or sector of the economy remains in good standing, especially with reference to its continuing contribution to the economy. One of the implications of these encouragements is that the industry or economic sector in question is adjudged a good credit risk. In return for these various encouragements, the relevant sector of the economy maintains or supplies productivity as a complex of facilities available for the pursuit of various system goals.

Certain other political policies, while not directly or predominantly encouragements to enterprise, often encourage the creation of productivity secondarily. A legal instance of such policies is the guarantee of "damages" to various enterprises in case of interference with their activity by any individual or collectivity. One aspect of fair trade, anti-trust and other attempts to regulate imperfect competition is what policy-makers consider to be encouragement of a more productive economy, even though the main focus of such attempts may be the integration of the economy itself or the regulation of the political activity of economic units, i.e., it is only partially economic in its effects.

At the second economy-polity interchange, how does the economy sanction the control over capital funds in the more immediate sense? It relinquishes to the suppliers of these funds certain *rights to intervene* by exercising control over the supply of capital funds. Sometimes these rights are restricted, e.g., the lender to an insurance company redeems his premiums only at a certain rate or at a certain time. In loans to firms various arrangements may be worked out as to the conditions of return of the principal. On the other hand, demand deposits are subject to no such restrictions; the right to intervene in the use of these funds is completely granted. The immediate interchange between polity and economy is therefore between the control of the creation of capital funds through credit and granting the suppliers of funds certain rights to intervene.

What common element (analogous to money as wage income and consumers spending at the A_G–L_G boundary) is shared by "encouragements to enterprise" and "rights to intervene" in credit supply? It seems to us that the mechanism of control is *primarily* political, i.e., the interchanges are not markets in the usual economic sense of the word. What the polity gives in encouraging enterprise and what it receives through the rights to intervene in credit is a sort of reputation, with special reference to the credit standing of the economic sector in question. For want of a better term, therefore, we will refer to the control mechanism at the boundary between polity and economy as "credit standing."

Credit standing is, strictly speaking, a form of power. It implies a *capacity to command* capital resources in exchange for securing the maintenance and/or increase of productivity by applying these resources to the productive plant rationally. To grant credit standing is indeed to encourage enterprise in so far as it places the recipient in the position to command actual purchasing power. On the other hand, to extend the corresponding rights to intervene implies that further extension of purchasing power to the recipient is controlled by the polity upon condition that certain results of the application of purchasing power be forthcoming.

If we think of the "encouragement of enterprise" as analogous to wage payments at the A_G–L_G boundary, then the encouragement of a certain economic sector is in effect to confer upon it a certain endorsement of its continuing existence by means of enhancing its credit standing. This credit standing may be "spent" by granting lenders rights to intervene in return for a supply of credit. Furthermore, like wages, the credit standing may be exhausted by means of excessive borrowing unless further encouragement is forthcoming from the relevant political agency.

We thus view this political endorsement, which we have referred to as "credit standing," as strictly analogous to money at the A_G–L_G boundary in so far as it is an intervening mechanism which in a more immediate sense controls the major outputs of polity and economy at the A_A–G_A boundary, and co-ordinates the "flows" of productivity and creation of credit, respectively. We will review the dynamics of this co-ordination briefly toward the end of the chapter when we point out formal parallels among all the external economic boundaries.

To summarize, we propose that the primary controls at the A_A–G_A boundary are political in our technical sense of the term. This is obviously a radical departure from traditional economic analysis, which has tended to treat the supply of capital funds as directly dependent, in one sense or another, on some money payment, usually interest. We wish to suggest an extensive modification of this view. What, therefore, is the role of monetary mechanisms at the double-interchange between economy and polity?

In one capacity "interest" is a direct payment, similar to wages, for the surrender of goods and services. In this capacity it is a generalized mechanism which *controls* the release of capital funds. But the monetary mechanism has a symbolic aspect as well. On the one hand it represents the degree of the creditor's *rights to intervene*, or power to control the relinquished capital funds. The high interest rate which accompanies high risk symbolizes a diminution of the owner's power to control supply by intervention if loss of funds threatens. It symbolizes the supplier's power position much as the wage level symbolizes the prestige position of the earner. On the other hand, the interest rate represents one of the primary symbolic means of encouraging or discouraging enterprise. Operating primarily through monetary policy, a change in the interest rate symbolizes political concern with the state of productivity and its changes in the economy. Raising the interest rate is a signal that productivity must increase at a sufficiently higher rate in order to justify the current level of credit; lowering the interest encourages enterprise by symbolically communicating that the rate of productivity increase need not be so high. In any case manipulating the interest rate signifies certain political attitudes toward the state of the economy.

One significant failing of economic analysis has been to treat the interest rate only in the direct payment sense. We do not wish to minimize the monetary reward aspects of the interest rate. In cases of exorbitant rates and of equal risk with unequal terms the reward is significant. Most recent empirical work has shown, however, that to treat interest simply as reward for capital supply is questionable.[1] We give the symbolic aspect more salience than is traditional. Changes in the interest rate (either fortuitous or directed by some central authority) are therefore analogous to a change of a traffic light. A rising interest rate—similar to a red or yellow flash—is less a "wage increase" and more a signal that rights to intervene are likely to be jeopardized by outright loss, by loss of value through inflation, etc.

In the case of the relation between the official bank rate and the volume of commercial credit this symbolic function is more conspicuous in Great Britain than in the United States. The virtual monopoly of commercial banking by five banks operating on a nation-wide basis means that policies of control are communicated by the requisite governmental agencies (Chancellor of the Exchequer and Bank of England) to the top management of these banks. The changed interest rate is not the cause of a policy change, but is a symbolization of it which helps in communicating its implications to a wider circle of lenders and prospective borrowers.

Besides interest, other monetary mechanisms play a special role in the interchange between control over productivity and encouragements to productivity. Often money returns to economic enterprises are directly concomitant—e.g., tax relief, "damages," subsidies, etc., further encouragement of productivity. In other cases, such as tariffs or direct control by injunctions, direct monetary reward from the polity is absent.

[1] Cf. Henderson, H. O., "The Significance of the Rate of Interest," *Oxford Economic Papers*, No. 1, October 1938, pp. 1–13; Meade, J. E., and Andrews, P. W. S., "Summary of Replies to Questions on Effects of Interest Rates," *ibid.*, pp. 14–31.

In general, however, this particular balance between encouragements to productive enterprise and productivity is not in the usual sense a market between government interest and economic interest, if a market means that the direct sanction in power of monetary purchasing power operates to determine a "price."[1] Hence the primary significance of the monetary mechanism is again symbolic. It symbolizes attitudes and policies of the polity toward the supply and control of productive capacity for the pursuit of system goals. The power exigencies of system-goal attainment—the business of the

FIGURE 6

THE DOUBLE INTERCHANGE BETWEEN THE ECONOMY AND THE POLITY

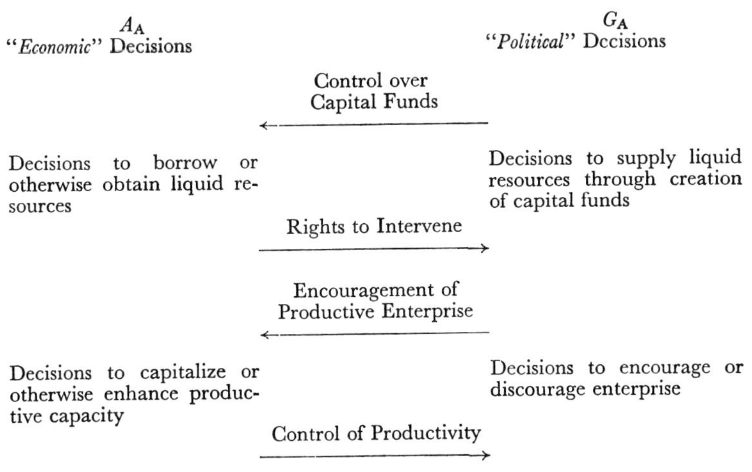

polity are so salient that the direct encouragement of enterprise overshadows the market control elements of the monetary mechanisms in this exchange.

Figure 6 shows the double interchange between economy and polity. As in the economy-household boundary, there is a duality

[1] Of course, in one sense the polity must "pay a price" to encourage productive enterprise in order to gain productivity. The *basis* of this price, however, is not the offer of purchasing power which the economy may or may not accept in return for a given increment of productivity. The order of control is different; the monetary mechanisms are a *symbol* of the encouragement or discouragement which the polity uses as sanction.

of structure in the "markets" and two partially independent sets of decisions on each side of the boundary interchange.[1]

At the economy's third open boundary, A_I–I_I, the overall exchange is between "organization" and new output combinations to the consuming public. The significance of entrepreneurial services is to adjust the proportions of the factors of production and thus integrate the functioning economy; the significance of new output combinations is integrative in so far as it impinges on the problems of the distribution of wealth and of the style-of-life symbolization with reference to the stratification of society. What is the intermediary mechanism in this exchange?

Entrepreneurial service is directly balanced by "profit," or monetary reward for introducing integrative services into the economy. Above and beyond this reward aspect, this payment symbolizes the entrepreneur's strategic position in the integrative system.[2]

The balance for new output combinations from the economy is the *demand for new product combinations*, which is analogous to consumers' demand in the short run. In one sense this demand is direct reward to the economy for producing such new combinations. It is also a symbol of the incorporation of new combinations into various style-of-life patterns relevant to the symbolization of the integration of society through stratification.

Figure 7 shows the double interchange at the A_I–I_I boundary, which we will develop further when we consider Schumpeter's treatment of the functions of the entrepreneur.

This is perhaps an appropriate place for a general summary statement of the relation between the analytical input-output categories of the economy as we have developed them and

[1] Commonly the two sets of decisions on the polity side are located in different agencies. The exchange between capital funds and rights to intervene is closely associated with banking, insurance and other fiduciary agencies, though government historically has been involved in controlling these agencies and taking a direct hand in the interchange. The balance between productivity and encouragement of productive enterprise, on the other hand, is structurally linked to the governmental and judicial elements of the polity.

[2] We investigate this position below, pp. 95–97, and in Chap. V, pp. 264 ff.

concrete social structures in our own and other societies. Our remarks also apply to the more refined analytical level of breakdown of economic processes outlined in Chapter IV below.

In our conception of the relation between economy and society, the main outline of which we have just presented, it is inherent that the analytical boundaries will correspond to the lines of differentiation between concrete roles and collectivities most closely in those societies which are in general highly differentiated and which stress the economic aspects of their structure and functioning. For this reason as well as that of the accessibility of relevant information, we have found it convenient for the most part to choose illustrations from our own society and its recent history.

FIGURE 7

THE DOUBLE INTERCHANGE BETWEEN ECONOMY AND THE INTEGRATIVE SUB-SYSTEM

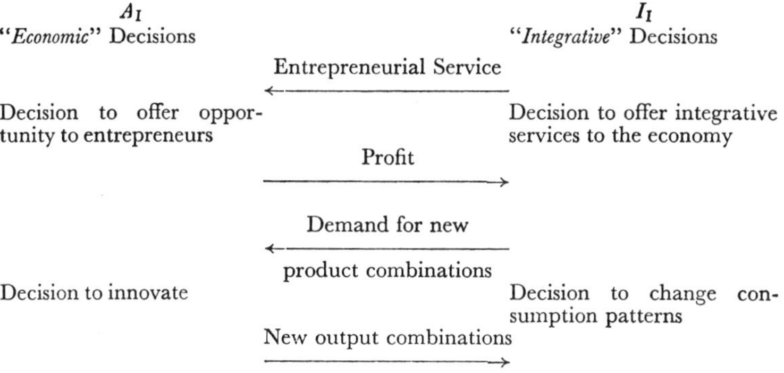

Even here, however, the lines of collectivity differentiation seldom if ever correspond *exactly* to the analytical boundary-lines between the economy and other functional sub-systems. Thus, given the high degree of differentiation in our society between occupational roles and familial roles, the line between household and firm—as mediated by the labour and consumer markets—is for many purposes a fair approximation of that between pattern-maintenance and adaptive functional sub-systems. But this organizational line is only an approximation.

For instance, durable consumers' goods in the household should be treated analytically as capital goods[1]; hence an important part of consumers' spending is analytically a process of capital investment. Correspondingly, an important part of housewives' activities within the household constitute labour services in the technical economic sense. Thus in both these respects the line between the pattern-maintenance system and economy lies *within* the household, even in our own society. By the same token the concrete role of the worker in the firm is never exclusively economic in functional significance; it involves a pattern-maintenance aspect, the preservation of which is, we will argue in the next chapter, one of the foci of the bases of trade unions in our society. It is true that the firm is characterized by the *primacy* of economic function and the household by the *primacy* of pattern-maintenance function, but this by no means implies that the firm is exclusively economic and the household totally non-economic in its significance.

Furthermore, consumption in the economic sense is by no means confined to the household in our society but is to some extent a function of *all* concrete role and collectivity units of the social structure.[2] Even business firms in our society spend part of their income for style-of-life symbols directly comparable to those of households; office buildings and their appointments, the landscaping of the grounds of industrial plants and a variety of other phenomena belong in this context. In addition governmental units, universities and other non-household organizations are important consumers in the strict economic sense.

Similar considerations apply at the other open boundaries of our economy. Even with such highly differentiated financial institutions as in our own society, the line between economy and polity does not correspond in any simple way with the concrete boundaries between concrete collectivity or role units.[3] Thus we treat the credit-creating banking organization as primarily a political unit though it is not usually an organ of government in our society. But clearly a bank has conspicuous economic aspects second in importance only to the

[1] Cf. p. 54.
[2] Cf. pp. 53–55.
[3] Cf. pp. 60–61.

political. It is thus governed to a more stringent degree by imperatives of solvency than are most households or units of government. Similarly, the large-scale self-financing of expansion by business firms means that these firms have undertaken considerable political functions. At the very least they have undertaken (usually with passive acquiescence) to withhold some of the property of the investing public from its owners in order to "plough it back." By building up their productivity, such organizations improve their credit standing. This standing may serve as a basis for seeking new funds from banks or governmental agencies or, more frequently, as the basis for justifying still further withholding of dividends from investors, thereby placing these investors (more or less involuntarily) in the role of credit-creators. The firm thus in effect borrows from its own security holders on the implicit plea that *it* has the power to convert their assets into increased productivity (hence increased capitalized value of their securities). The firm's high credit standing enables it to carry out these operations without exposing itself to unmanageable pressure for immediate dividend payments.

These imperfections of matching between the functional categories of boundary-interchange and the concrete social structure are apparent even in our own society. Similar considerations must weigh even more heavily when we analyse societies in which the level of differentiation is less advanced than in our own and/or in which the adaptive emphasis is substantially less strong.

To take an example of a less differentiated society, historically the great societies of the Oriental world have been characterized by an overwhelming majority (usually 80 per cent or more) of "peasants" in the working population engaged either in the production of food or closely related primary products such as textile fibres from the land. The typical organizational unit of such populations has been a *combination* household and productive unit in which the differentiation between occupational and familial roles does not hold. Economic considerations are certainly relevant to the analysis of behaviour in such a unit, but inevitably it is subject to constraints on giving primacy to economic considerations, constraints which the modern Western firm does not face.

An example of a fusion of economic and non-economic functions at a higher level of organization is the medieval European manor. As an economic unit it managed economic resources—the land, manpower and some capital and organization. At the same time it was a unit of formal political and military organization and of social integration by means of hereditary local ties and class status. If anything the manor's economic functions were subordinated to these latter functions as a rule. This is reflected in the marked economic "traditionalism" of medieval rural society. It is not without reason that the break-up of the manor, for instance through "enclosures," has been associated with the beginning of a new era of economic development.

Though the handicraft organization of the medieval towns was doubtless closer to economic primacy than the medieval manor on either peasant or gentry level, it was bound closely by non-economic constraints. Not only did the master craftsman himself work within his own household but his apprentices were treated virtually as adopted sons and even his journeymen were often partially integrated in a similar way. Furthermore the gild solidarity and the elaborate restrictions on competition for raw materials, labour or customers, establish beyond doubt that such craft organizations were very far from the functionally differentiated form of "business" organization, despite their elaborate "specialization."

Somewhat closer to such differentiation is the relatively recent "family business" of the type which has been particularly conspicuous in France. Here household, economic (managerial in a technical sense) and political (capital-holding) functions are fused in a single solidary kinship unit, membership in which is based on hereditary ascription (a strictly non-economic criterion) or on arranged marriage in which the probable effect on the firm's economic efficiency is scarcely the ruling consideration. Though such firms are "business" organizations producing for relatively free markets, they represent a lower level of differentiation of economic function than does modern large-scale American corporate industry.[1]

[1] Cf. Landes, David, "French Business and the Businessman: A Social and Cultural Analysis," in Earle, E. M. (ed.), *Modern France*, 1951. We are also indebted to personal discussion with Mr. Jesse R. Pitts.

As a final example, modern totalitarian societies such as Soviet Russia bring most of the economy under exceedingly stringent governmental (hence in our sense primarily political) control. At least the proximate goal, in addition to consolidating the power-position of the régime itself, is to bring about the largest scale and most rapid possible process of economic development.[1] This represents above all a fusion between economy and polity in the dominant structure of a modern socialistic state, with the political element dominant. How stable, beyond the period of "forced draft" development, such a fusion may be is a crucial question about such societies; will certain "natural" tendencies for the economy to differentiate from the polity appear or will they be inhibited?

We have cited these examples of comparative organizational and institutional arrangements involving the economy in order to outline the relation between our type of functional analysis of the economy and the more concrete and empirical analysis of social phenomena, whether or not the latter are usually defined as "economic."

We hold that our generalized theoretical scheme, for the analysis of a society and of the economy as one of its sub-systems, is *not* bound to any particular structural type of society or economy. The analytical elements we have distinguished, and others we have been unable to discuss for reasons of space, are distinguishable as elements in *any* society, indeed in any social system. These analytical elements are not, however, equally closely related to the concrete structure of collectivities and roles in all societies. In general our functional sub-system categories correspond more closely to organizationally differentiated sectors of the social structure as the society approaches greater *structural* differentiation. But even here the correspondence is only approximate. Furthermore, the categories of economic theory apply more directly to the concrete social structure of a differentiated society and its processes as adaptive or economic values approach greater primacy over others. Only in societies which meet both these criteria do many of the more technical parts of economic theory apply directly

[1] What the more ultimate goals may be, e.g., promotion of the world revolution or a maximal standard of living for all, etc., is not immediately essential for our argument.

to empirical analysis, e.g., in the analysis of price determination in specific markets.[1]

Even in such societies, as we argue throughout this volume, close application to many empirical areas such as market imperfections can be attained only by supplementing economic theory with other elements of the general theory of social systems. But as we treat societies with a lower level of structural differentiation and with less economic emphasis, economic theory alone becomes less and less satisfactory as an analytical tool. The relative importance of the non-economic parts of the theory of social systems for the empirically "economic" problem areas increases until, in the case of "primitive" economies, it becomes overwhelmingly great.

It is our contention that the line of theoretical work we are pursuing here can eventuate ultimately in a far more sophisticated classification and dynamic analysis of comparative economic institutions than is possible at present. This area of analysis would be part of a general comparative treatment of social structures and would involve, in strict theoretical terms, at least as much non-economic as economic theory. We cannot undertake this task in this volume, not because it is not urgent and challenging, but because it could not even be started without sacrificing the other goals we have set ourselves.

These goals are twofold: first to explore the *general* theoretical relations between economic theory and the general theory of social systems and certain of its non-economic branches, and second to analyse the implications of that exploration for certain controversial areas of economic doctrine. We consider this exploration as essential groundwork for the ambitious task

[1] Furthermore, as a society approaches greater and greater *structural* differentiation, i.e., as the structure of differentiated collectivities and roles approach analytical categories more and more closely, conventional economic statistics reflect the analytical categories of economics more and more closely. For instance, in a relatively structurally differentiated society, the conventionally measured national income (which is indeed a measure of transactions among differentiated roles and collectivities) approximates the economic category of "national income" relatively satisfactorily. Thus the operationalization of economic theory in highly differentiated societies is more successful because of the visibility of the transactions which comprise the data subject to statistical analysis. In less differentiated societies, the lack of demarcation between collectivities conceals more and more intra-collectivity transactions which are none the less analytically significant.

of constructing a theory of comparative economic organization. We hope to contribute modestly to the latter task in later publications, but as a whole it is sufficient to occupy a whole generation of theorists and research workers representing all the social sciences.

SOME ECONOMIC THEORIES AND THE BOUNDARY PROCESSES OF THE ECONOMY

We will deal with some familiar neo-classical doctrines (with particular, but not exclusive reference to Marshall and Pigou), some of Schumpeter's analysis, and some of Keynes'. First, we will restate these familiar doctrines in terms of our paradigm; then we will examine the points of difference among them in terms of our paradigm, with respect to both their economic and their non-economic assumptions and generalizations.

Schumpeter's exposition of the circular flow in the economy[1] is a convenient starting-point. Schumpeter regarded this as a description of an "ideal type" stable economy. His purpose was to analyse what remains when the factors associated with entrepreneurial activity are excluded; hence the relations shown in Figure 7 are not relevant to this exposition. Schumpeter also assumed that the rates of credit extension and investment remain the same; hence what we have called the adaptive boundary process (cf. Figure 6) also is stable.

The circular flow process is therefore restricted to relations between the rent factors in the economy's pattern-maintenance sub-system (A_L) and the exchange between labour and consumers' goods and services at the economy's goal-attainment boundary (A_G–L_G). On such grounds Schumpeter accepted Böhm-Bawerk's dictum that "in the last analysis" land and labour are the only factors of production. The circular flow, then, involves continuous adjustment between two sets of factors: (*a*) the "givens" of the rent complex—physical resources, the state of the arts, institutionalized motivation to production and social organization, and (*b*) the twin processes of labour recruitment and meeting consumers' demand. The rent factor supplies are not a function of conditions of short-term demand and prices. For labour supply and consumer

[1] Schumpeter, *Theory of Economic Development*, *op. cit.*, Chap. I.

demand Schumpeter assumed no pattern of cumulative instability; there are only sources of random disturbance in response to which the economy must set up adaptive equilibrating mechanisms. Given a sufficient level of competition—and certain social controls which Schumpeter did not explicitly analyse—these adaptations work out with an appropriate time lag; for such reasons the hypothetical economy remains stable.

What Schumpeter treated heuristically as an ideal type, however, the classical and neo-classical writers[1] treated in terms of empirical generalizations which extended to both economic and non-economic spheres. First let us consider those dealing with labour supply and the relation between consumers' spending and saving.

The classical assumption for labour supply is simply that a conventional supply curve, with an upward slope, covers the entire relevant range of variation of real wage rates. For any level of real wages, therefore, a corresponding "quantity of labour" seeks employment. The wage level "clears the market." Hence so-called involuntary unemployment is impossible, except as a matter of the friction involved in adjusting to random disturbances.[2] The classical assumption is, therefore, that the marginal disutility of labour schedule is coincident with its range of prices, i.e., real wages.

In connection with labour supply we might note the difference between Ricardo's and Marshall's respective positions. Ricardo assumed a conventionally fixed standard of living which (through mechanisms which neither he nor any economist adequately understood) regulates the reproductive process. Over a long period, the pressure of numbers forces labourers to accept a wage barely sufficient to support this standard of living. The doctrine of the "iron law" thus emphasizes numbers in defining the quantity of labour; each

[1] Besides Ricardo and James Mill and their predecessors, Keynes included J. S. Mill, Marshall, Edgeworth and Pigou in the "classical school." *General Theory*, p. 3.

[2] Cf. Pigou, A. C., *Theory of Unemployment*, 1933, p. 252: "Such unemployment as exists at any time is due wholly to the fact that changes in demand conditions are continually taking place and that frictional resistances prevent the appropriate wage adjustments from being made instantaneously."

labourer is under pressure to work to his capacity to support the requisite standard for his family. The question of differences in motivation of workers is not problematical.

Marshall assumed the Ricardian position to be true of the "more ignorant and phlegmatic of races" in the past and present. But in cases of greater "enlightenment and strength of character"—where wants had become "adjusted to activities"—the quantity of labour is a function of the effort put forth by the individual worker. Effort in turn is dependent upon the size of return for his expenditure.[1] Hence Marshall felt that in "advanced" countries at any rate, the quantity of labour is a continuous function of real wages independently of numbers as such.

Keynes modified both these versions of the classical doctrine with the concept of the "stickiness of money wages."[2] Essentially he holds that the supply curve of labour services, relative to money as opposed to real wages, does not have a continuous upward slope throughout the relevant range, but flattens at a certain point below which no labour can be hired. If wages fall below this level the effect is with withdrawal of labour services from the market rather than acceptance of employment at the lower wage level which will clear the market.[3]

In one sense the *logical structure* of Keynes' argument is identical to Ricardo's. The latter held that at levels below the established standard of living, *potential* labour is withdrawn simply by not being born. At the point of the minimum standard[4] the supply curve of labour becomes horizontal. Keynes postulated a comparable minimum (for the short run) below which part of the potential labour supply is withheld from the market. In both cases the lower wage limit is a constraint on the perfection of the labour market. The meaning of this imperfection is that a certain rigid element is introduced into the labour market, in the sense that supply ceases to be

[1] *Principles*, Bk. III, Chap. I.

[2] *General Theory*, Chaps. 1, 19.

[3] It is curious that Keynes postulated a "stickiness" in connection with labour supply but not the supply of other factors of production, for which an equally good case might be made. Cf. Tobin, J., "Money Wage Rates and Employment," in *The New Economics*, ed. S. E. Harris, pp. 572–587.

[4] Ricardo emphasized that this standard was not mere physical subsistence, but was "conventional."

dependent upon economic sanctions beyond a certain range.[1]

Our position, argued above, is that the decisions on the basis of which labour is supplied to the economy relative to the supply price are not decisions within the economy in a strict sense, but decisions within the household as a primarily extra-economic sector of society. Labour-supply decisions concern terms on which this factor of production is to be *made available for* economic use; the strictly economic decision concerns the ways in which an already available factor is *put to use*.[2] The fact that the main traditions of economic theory are not in agreement about the nature of labour supply is not, in our opinion, a failing of economic theory as such. It is rather a reflection of the fact that empirical determination of certain economic problems is impossible without resort to extra-economic assumptions. Ricardo, Marshall, and Keynes supplied several possible assumptions; these do not, we feel, exhaust the possibilities.

Essentially what our paradigm promises—and what the history of economic thought has not accomplished—is to locate with some precision the non-economic area within which the problem lies. Of course, if one wishes to make a particular empirical choice between, say, Marshall and Keynes, one should investigate the facts. Empirical studies of labour behaviour relative to real and money wage rates thus far have not conclusively rejected or accepted either the classical or Keynesian schedules, or any alternative. This is not to say that competent empirical investigations cannot throw light on the subject. But all that empirical studies by labour economists can tell us is *that* money wages in a modern industrial-

[1] In terms which we will develop in the following chapter, this point of rigidity marks the point at which the G-component of the contract o employment (that component dealing with the advantageous balance of occupational performance against wages) becomes secondary to one or both of two other components of the contract of employment: (1) the L-component, which deals with the common values linking the household and firm (e.g., the flattening of the labour curve may mean the labourer's relinquishment of valuation of production), and (2) the I-component, dealing with the diffuse symbolic rewards of the occupational status (e.g., the flattening of the labour curve may mean complete withdrawal is associated with a deficit input of diffuse loyalty to the organization. Cf. Chap. III, pp. 116–118.

[2] Cf. pp. 54–55.

capitalistic type of economy tend to be sticky or flexible or something in between. Economists have no mode of analysis, comparable in precision with economic analysis of certain consequences of this fact, on the basis of which they can determine *why* it should be so. The latter question is sociological; we will subject it to a substantive analysis in terms of the theory of social systems in Chapters III and IV.

In the performance-sanction interchange involving consumers' spending for consumers' goods and services, the major decision on the demand side—what proportions of income to spend for goods and services and to save, respectively[1]—is again within the household rather than the economy. How have economists conceptualized this decision?

In Schumpeter's circular flow model, variations in the savings-consumption balance pose no significant problems for analysis of the circular flow. Schumpeter acknowledged that rates of consumption expenditures vary empirically with the extension of credit and that the respective proportions of income spent for immediate consumption and for durable goods—e.g., residential housing—vary. The mechanisms governing these variations, however, involve decisions other than those necessary for the maintenance of the circular flow.

The classical writers were concerned with the fact that not all consumers' income is immediately spent, and that this fact is related to capital accumulation. The classical conception of interest as the reward for "abstinence" is relevant here, as well as Marshall's modification of this view with his concept of "waiting." By and large, however, the classical concern has been with the *fact* that there is a difference between the flow of consumers' income and that of current expenditure; all causes or consequences of variations in this difference are subsumed under the interest rate, which, by determining both rate of saving and rate of investment, immediately draws excess savings into investment.[2]

1 Expenditure for durable goods is, of course, an intermediate case; since consumption of such goods extends over a long period, part of the expenditure is a form of "investment" by the consumer.

2 Cf. Marshall, *op. cit.*, Bk. VI, Chap. II, p. 534. "Interest, being the price paid for the use of capital in any market, tends toward an equilibrium level such that the aggregate demand for capital in that market, at that

At this point Keynes introduced his famous "consumption function,"[1] which is that when the total volume of consumers' income increases, the *proportion* of that income currently spent for consumers' goods and services declines—at what precise rate Keynes did not attempt to say. This function, like the classical representation, has the status of either a postulate or an empirical generalization, depending on the point of view. Keynes was concerned primarily with analysing the consequences of this postulate or empirical generalization for the short-run stability of the economy. His essential point is that, if the assumption about the consumption function is correct for given empirical cases, then it, combined with that of the "stickiness of money wages," can go far toward accounting for a severe short-run decline of the level of productive activity. In terms of our paradigm, Keynes postulates the possibility of significant decreases of rates of input for both of the categories of input (labour supply and consumer demand) operative at this economy-household boundary of the economy.

We have attempted neither to justify nor to refute Keynes' empirical assumptions about this boundary process. We have merely shown that *logically* these assumptions fit at definite points in our paradigm. Whether or not the assumptions are true is, from the economists' point of view, an empirical question. If they are true, the ensuing consequences are the business of economic theory. At the same time, *only* from the economists' point of view are these assumptions purely empirical questions. We are interested in the larger question of a cognate theory of the family system from which assumptions in this area can be derived. If there is such a theory, certain determinations can be made on theoretical grounds which constrain the degrees of freedom left by purely economic analysis. In the following chapters we will investigate a few such constraints in terms of the institutional structuring of markets and in terms of

rate of interest, is equal to the aggregate stock [savings] forthcoming at that rate." This does not deny that the amounts of savings and investment differ at varying levels of income; it says that changes in income will not disturb the equilibration of savings and investment *via* the interest rate. Since investment is infinitely contractable or expansible, full investment is merely a matter of adjustment for any money saved in response to a given interest rate.

[1] *General Theory*, Chaps. 8 and 9.

the family as a consuming system. In the meantime we wish merely to summarize various economic doctrines. The classical writers tended to postulate—and often to justify on broad and vague empirical grounds—a situation minimizing such constraints; they represented a situation in which the rest of society "adapted itself" to economic processes. Schumpeter, for the purposes of the circular flow model, went to the opposite extreme; he postulated nothing but random sources of variation in non-economic data. Keynes, on empirical grounds, selected specific assumptions or generalizations from this wide range of possibilities.

Let us now turn to the economy-polity boundary (G_A–A_A). The first interchange involves the balance of capital funds against various rights to intervene. In connection with the latter the interest rate has significance both as a direct reward but even more as a special symbol. As we have seen above, the classical theory subsumes the determination of saving and supply of capital under the rubric of the price mechanism as expressed in the rate of interest. This doctrine eliminates the independent significance of any extra-economic determinants of (*a*) the balance between consumers' spending and saving, and (*b*) the balance between the holding of liquid assets and their lending. It closes the circle by postulating that both of these balances are simple functions of the same price. Both the relevant supply and demand functions are assumed to have continuous variation and an appropriate slope over the whole range of values. Given these assumptions, a situation in which the market does not clear itself of funds cannot occur. Funds will be lent if there are disposable funds, an adequate rate of interest, and a given level of security. The system is closed on economic grounds alone; there are only frictional disturbances.

Keynes questioned such assumptions. True, so long as a certain level of confidence holds, the supply of funds is a continuous function of their price.[1] But Keynes called attention

[1] This assertion applies only to the speculative demand for money as opposed to the transactions and precautionary demands which are interest-inelastic except for high interest rates. Furthermore, while the demand curve for speculative funds is generally moderately interest-elastic, at low absolute interest rates it tends to flatten even more. Cf. *General Theory*, Chaps. 13, 15.

to the level of confidence itself; it is not always appropriate, he held, to consider it as given. As a matter of fact, when confidence undergoes change, gains from interest payments may be negligible as far as the motivation of the lender is concerned. Even when the interest rate is high, a holder of funds may refuse to lend or insist on withdrawing loans and maintaining his funds in liquid form. The level of confidence is furthermore not a simple function of the interest rate; it is influenced by attitudes which are "economically irrational."

We suggest that our analysis of the A_A–G_A boundary provides a framework for a more specific solution of the problem of attitudes toward liquidity than the rather vague concept of "confidence." More specifically, many of the determinants of the attitudes to liquidity are connected with the status of the "rights to intervene" and the "encouragement to enterprise" sanctions. The level of confidence is in large part the result of the degree of *symbolic* significance which the lender attaches to the various signs—of course the interest rate and its fluctuations are one complex of these signs—relative to the status of his ultimate rights and expectations. Confidence always relates to his rights to intervene, i.e., to withdraw funds if they happen to be jeopardized. Further, the rights to intervene are related, in ways which we have spelled out,[1] to the input of encouragement or discouragement to enterprise by the relevant political authority. This framework, plus more dynamic considerations which we will develop later,[2] should lead to more definite statements about the significant economic problems of "confidence," "uncertainty," and "risk."

The Keynesian modifications of the classical position therefore boil down to the assertion that the empirical state is governed partially by economic laws but is based also on certain non-economic "irrationalities." We have investigated these modifications for the labour supply, the consumption and the liquidity preference functions.[3] The classical formulation reduced as much of the non-economic as possible to

[1] Cf. above, pp. 72–75.

[2] Cf. Chap. IV, pp. 234 ff.

[3] For a comparison of Keynes' marginal efficiency of capital function with the classical formulation, cf. the discussion of investment, Chap. IV, pp. 214–15.

economic conditions; Keynes, on the other hand, introduced certain discontinuities at crucial points to explain a state of affairs, e.g., unemployment, which classical theory could not account for without theoretical embarrassment.

The interchange at the A_A–G_A boundary between productivity and political encouragement of such productivity has occupied a peripheral place in economics in the sense that it has not been incorporated into theory with as much formal elegance as the other interchanges. On the other hand, economists from Adam Smith to the present have been aware of the relation of the polity to the whole problem of productivity or productive capacity. We will choose only a few scattered examples to illustrate this awareness.[1]

Adam Smith himself, who developed the case for free trade to a point of high sophistication, argued that on military and defence grounds, a protective tariff is defensible.[2] This is a clear recognition—indeed, by the father of the school of economists who scorned political entanglements with the economy—that the pursuit of collective system goals or sub-goals requires the relinquishment of short-term gains in wealth. Governmental protection of national defence industries is an input of encouragement of (a certain type of) productive capacity, and development of these industries is an output of productive capacity to the polity. The protection of infant industries—one of the few effective arguments against the classical case for free trade—involves a similar input of encouragement balanced by an output of productivity.

Subsidies are a second instance of direct government sanction to encourage productive capacity. For both protection and subsidization, we include only those encouragements aimed at the achievement of productive capacity for the pursuit of system goals, such as subsidies and protective tariffs in wartime. Encouragements of industry which stem from "purely political" considerations—such as graft, patronage, and submission to

[1] In these examples we will emphasize only the aspect which deals with the encouragement or discouragement of productivity. In some of the examples other political aims might predominate, e.g., the restriction of unfair trade practices may deal more with the integration of certain economic units with the rest of the society.

[2] Smith, Adam, *The Wealth of Nations*, ed. Cannon, E. (4th ed., 1925), Vol. I, pp. 427–429.

pressure groups—are significant primarily at *another* boundary interchange.[1]

In the past few decades the theory of imperfect competition has grown to major theoretical proportions in economics. Discussions of imperfect competition and its implications for output, pricing and efficiency have been closely associated with discussions of public policy *vis-à-vis* trusts, interlocking directorates, etc.; many attempts have been made to formulate governmental policy toward these impingements on efficiency and productivity.[2] Regardless of the correctness or incorrectness of these recommendations, we wish merely to point out that economists concerned with public policy in the area of imperfect competition and unfair practices have tended to assume that government *dis*couragement of imperfect elements represents simultaneously an *en*couragement of productivity in the economy. Hence the whole range of public policy relative to imperfect competition can be interpreted in the light of this boundary interchange.

Problems of monetary and fiscal policy have occupied the attention of economists, particularly since the beginning of the Keynesian revolution. While analysing the economic *effects* of government policies via the multiplier, accelerator and other mechanisms, economists have devoted little attention to the broader interchange between the economy and polity. That is to say, the wider aims of monetary and fiscal policy—whether successfully fulfilled or not—are to stabilize certain elements in the economy in order to keep it productive.

To choose a further example, economists have investigated, particularly since World War II, the problems of *direct control*—import restrictions, rationing, import quotas, etc.[3] Certain of these measures are for purposes of short-term allocation, but some can be interpreted as inputs from the polity encouraging the development of productivity along specific lines; the result-

[1] Most probably this is at the interchange between the polity and the integrative sub-system, though we will not develop the rationale for the assignment to this boundary here.

[2] Cf. Mason, E. S., "Effectiveness of the Federal Antitrust Laws," *American Economic Review*, June, 1949, pp. 712–713.

[3] Cf. Wiles, P. J., "Pre-War and Wartime Controls," and Worswick, G. D. N., "Direct Controls" in Worswick and Ady, P. H., eds., *The British Economy*, 1945–50 (1952).

ing productivity is the corresponding performance on the part of the economy.

Encouragements to productive enterprise are not limited to the so-called "free enterprise" economies. For instance, one of the components in the well-known all-out governmental mobilization of resources, including coercive measures in the interest of the economic development programmes of the Soviet Union and China, is an attempt to further, by one form of direct control, the productivity of the economy for the purposes of pursuing system goals.[1]

As we have said, these various encouragements to productivity are not incorporated into economics at the highest theoretical level, but are important concerns of economic analysists. Toward the end of the chapter, when we investigate formal parallels among the boundary processes, we will indicate certain lines along which formal incorporation of this polity interchange might proceed.

Like a great number of economic theorists, Keynes ignored the special analytical features of the interchanges at the A_I–I_I boundary altogether.[2] This is one reason why it is justified to speak of the Keynesian model as a short-term equilibrium analysis.

The problems of "organization" were neglected in the older classical tradition as well. Logically, such neglect is possible because of a tendency to tie theories of the structure of the economy rigidly to particular assumptions or empirical generalizations about the extra-economic environment. Under such assumptions no independent factor of "organization" is necessary. Classical writers tended to think primarily in terms of the two "active" factors of capital and labour; their preoccupation with long-run processes concerned the supplies of these factors and their relation to rent. For example, the Malthusian principle of population, applied to the iron law of wages by Ricardo, is a typical classical concern. Another is

[1] This final example indicates that the term "encouragement" extends for our purposes beyond its common meaning of "persuasion" or "exhortation" to the realm of coercion and direct management.

[2] Of course, he refers to the "entrepreneur" often; he does not consider him in his unique capacity as shifting and recombining factors of production, however.

Ricardo's view of the tendency of profits to decline and his pessimistic outlook on the prospects of capital accumulation. In one sense Marx broke from the Malthusian and Ricardian laws. But the *area* of his concern was the same; he emphasized the power of capital over labour as the basis of the longer-run developmental trends. Hence all these writers, in so far as they included only the household-economy and economy-polity relations, ignored the factor of "organization."[1]

Marshall introduced an important change. In the first place, he added organization as an independent factor of production to land, labour, and capital. Secondly, he called attention to the firm as a social organization, i.e., to the functions of management as well as the simple supplies of capital and labour. Optimum combinations of factors do not produce themselves automatically. Marshall thus laid the foundation—for the English-speaking world, at least—for explicit attention to the integrative problems of the economy and to the relevant boundary processes.

The pre-eminent theorist in this field, however, is Schumpeter. His circular flow analysis of a stable economy was intended merely to clear the ground for a treatment of economic development centring on the integrative boundary. Under certain conditions there is an input of entrepreneurial service, as shown in Figure 7,[2] which is qualitatively different from labour input in the circular flow. The function of entrepreneurial service is to *change* and hence integrate the combinations of the factors of production stabilized in the circular flow.[3] This stimulates the foundation of new enterprises and the

[1] For an excellent comparative treatment of classical theories of growth along these lines, cf. Löwe, A., "The Classical Theory of Growth," in *Social Research*, September, 1954.

[2] As will be noticed, our treatment of this boundary process is heavily influenced by Schumpeter's theory of development.

[3] It should be clear in exactly what sense we use the term "integrative." A great many interpretations of the Schumpeterian entrepreneur are that he is the great "disrupter" and certainly anything but an "integrator." These interpretations are not contradictory by any means, however. From the standpoint of the circular flow the entrepreneur disrupts established patterns; but from that of a higher system level, he integrates the new combinations into a new equilibrium position. It is from this latter vantage-point that we apply the term "integration" to the entrepreneur's function. (Cf. Chap. V, pp. 264 ff.)

reorganization of old ones. Profit, in Schumpeter's sense, is the monetary sanction which balances the input of entrepreneurial service.

Reorganization cannot occur, however, unless there is some balance between new combinations and their marketing and consumption. In the circular flow, the basic patterns of consumption are stable. The entrepreneur, on the other hand, feeds on changes in demand. At this second interchange, therefore, advertising by entrepreneurial interests as a mechanism for creating demand is relevant. The output of the economy is qualitative change in the patterning of consumption offerings; these are matched by changes in effective demand. This demand is not a matter of aggregate consumers' purchasing power—thus it is not the Keynesian problem—but of the allocation of this purchasing power among qualitatively different channels of expenditure. As we have shown, such allocations tie closely with the integration of society itself.

Schumpeter treats the balances at the adaptive boundary of the economy as subordinate to the entrepreneurial function. Credit creation is a function of the entrepreneur's demand for capital. In the circular flow, interest has no particular significance; it is merely a deduction from entrepreneurial profits which flow to bankers or other holders of liquid resources.

We suggest that Schumpeter is correct regarding the basic processes of changes in the factors of production. We question whether he is correct in his view of the capitalization function. It is clear from the Keynesian and other analyses of the liquidity and capitalization problems that an independent set of processes is involved at this boundary. In this connection it is interesting to note that Keynes and Schumpeter both dichotomized the dynamics of the economy, though in different ways. Both took the economy-household boundary as a sort of starting-point; Keynes combined this boundary with the short-term capitalization boundary (A_A–G_A), whereas Schumpeter combined it with the integrative boundary (A_I–I_I). It is necessary, we feel, to take account of both theories before anything approaching a thorough analysis of economic boundary processes can be developed.

To conclude the discussion of the boundary processes, we might point out some formal dynamic parallels common to all the boundary processes. Each boundary interchange has, as we have indicated, two distinct performance-sanction systems. How are these two interchanges co-ordinated at each boundary?

By introducing particular restrictions, Keynes formulated a particular relation between the two household-economy interchanges. The two household decisions—relative to the supply of labour and consumer demand—are mediated by the decisions to save; they determine the proportion of the wage input to be "returned" to the economy as demand for consumption goods. In this special sense saving relates the wages and spending quanta. On the economic side a corresponding "decision" to produce mediates between what is received via the consumer demand channel and what is offered as wages to the household. Assigning value to these decisions, it is possible to establish various types of equilibria. Keynes emphasized the under-employment of labour equilibrium, typically established by a deficit input of sanctions via the consumer demand channel, resulting in production decisions to offer less sanction for labour, resulting in turn in decisions to withdraw labour from the market.

By introducing similar restricting assumptions at the other boundaries, it is possible to construct certain formally equivalent equilibria, and to isolate the concepts formally parallel to "savings" and "production" decisions at the A_G–L_G boundary.

The polity possesses a body of generalized rights to intervene with respect to the supply of capital funds: the most common form of these rights, but not the only form, is the right to withdraw funds or restrict credit. Furthermore, it is a decision of public policy[1] precisely how far to encourage or discourage productivity via the second A_A–G_A exchange. The concept of "public policy," or at least a large portion of it, is analogous to the concept of "saving" in the sense that it deals with the proportion of generalized rights concerning capitalization that the polity translates into direct encouragements or discouragements of productivity. On the economic side, the economic decisions co-ordinating the "rights-to-intervene" sanction and the "encouragement-of-productivity" sanction are certain

[1] In *one* particular context; *vis-à-vis* the economy of course, not all public policy.

"decisions to capitalize" which are analogous to the producers' decisions to produce (cf. Figure 5).

Let us introduce certain "Keynesian" restrictions on these sets of decisions and thus create an "under-employment of capital equilibrium." A starting-point is the existence of a certain legal *dis*couragement to corporate enterprise expansion and improvement of plant. This discouragement of productivity is analogous to oversaving in the sense that it is a deficit input of sanction. The discouragement leads, in accordance with a given "supply-demand" schedule, to a diminished output of productivity from the economy. But just as lowered production leads to a lowered demand for labour, lowered productivity leads to jeopardy of the rights to intervene on the part of suppliers of capital.[1] With reduced rights to intervene as a deficit sanction, suppliers of capital withdraw capital funds from the market, again in accordance with some supply schedule. The final result is an unemployment of capital funds analogous to the unemployment of labour services. The creation of this model is in a sense artificial; the relevant liquidity preference and governmental policy functions are presumably not the same as the labour supply and consumption functions, respectively. But reasonable dynamic parallels to the A_G–L_G processes appear if the appropriate assumptions are introduced. Furthermore, conceptualizing the process in terms of the double interchange shows that "public policy" is parallel to "saving" in a way which has never been indicated in economic theory.

At the A_I–I_I boundary exchange between entrepreneurial services and new combinations, it is possible to create an "unemployment-of-entrepreneurs" equilibrium by employing the same logical scheme. The sets of "decisions" in Figure 7 which co-ordinate the sanction of "profits" with the sanction of "demand-for-new-product combinations" are those sets of integrative decisions which have to do with the distribution of income.[2] Only if profits are distributed to a certain extent throughout the society will demand for new combinations of

[1] I.e., risks are greater, and the likelihood of losing one's capital is thereby greater.

[2] Distribution enforced by political finance is relevant here, as well as voluntary distribution through charity and philanthropy.

products—in their significance as symbolizing an integrated position in the community—be forthcoming.[1] On the economic side, the set of decisions co-ordinating the input of demand and the "offer" of profits to entrepreneurs is the complex of "decisions to innovate."

Let us again introduce Keynesian restrictions. By virtue of a serious maldistribution of profits over a given period, an under-demand for new combinations develops. The sequence of deficit inputs and outputs is familiar enough by now: decreased new combinations lead to a decrease of opportunities for profit, which lead in turn to under-employment of entrepreneurs.

In this final section, by developing certain under-employment models at other points in the economic process, we have tried to show the power of the boundary process paradigm to elicit parallels among certain extra-economic decisions—"savings," "public policy," and "distribution"—at the different boundaries; and it shows parallels among more strictly economic decisions—"decisions to produce," "decisions to capitalize," and "decisions to innovate." We hope the analysis indicates the general lines along which disparate concepts such as "government," "distribution," "savings," etc., can be incorporated with a higher degree of formal elegance into a more general theory of economic processes.

[1] In terms of the savings analogy, it can be said that unless decisions as to the savings-spending balance are made in a particular way, demand for consumption goods will not be forthcoming.

CHAPTER III

THE INSTITUTIONAL STRUCTURE OF THE ECONOMY

In the last chapter we applied the general paradigm of fourfold differentiation of four functional problems of systems at two levels: (1) to the economy as a system. In this connection we showed that not only the classification of the factors of production and the shares of income, but also the structural differentiation of the economy can be ordered in terms of the paradigm. (2) to the total social system, in which the economy bears specifiable relationships to the other sub-systems of the society. Land, a special case in economic theory, is cognate with the pattern-maintenance function as used in general social system theory. As for the other three boundaries of the economy, the inputs of the other three factors of production and the outputs of the corresponding shares of income result from interchanges with each of three other cognate sub-systems of the society: the interchange of labour and consumers' goods with the household as a part of the pattern-maintenance system, the exchange of control and the creation of capital funds and productivity with the polity, and the interchange of entrepreneurial service and new combinations with the integrative sub-system. At each of these boundaries we located a double interchange involving an intervention of an intermediate symbolic control mechanism, which controls the main substantive inputs and outputs.

We then interpreted a range of problems of traditional economic theory, as developed by the classical writers, Keynes, and Schumpeter, in terms of the boundary interchange paradigm. We isolated certain central problems of economic theory and defined the differences between the various schools of thought. Important sources of these differences are empirical generalizations about the behaviour of workers, consumers, and creditors in their respective markets; from the point of view of economic theory, moreover, such generalizations rest on extra-economic assumptions. These assumptions in turn are dealt with by other special cases of the general theory of social systems, i.e., those cases concerning the other three primary sub-systems of society.

Another set of theoretical problems in economics deals in large part with the *internal* processes of the economy as well as the inter-relations between the economy and other societal sub-systems. These problems are in the area of economic fluctuations, and include detailed mechanisms such as the multiplier and the accelerator and their operation through time lags as they produce cyclical movements. We will deal with this range of problems in the next chapter.

The focus of the analysis in this chapter is the structure of *institutions* which integrate action within the economy itself and at its external boundaries. We will deal primarily with the institutional regulation of the external boundaries, because they are more readily apparent institutionally than the internal regulating structures.

For a long time the concept of institutions has been a vague meeting-ground between the economist and the sociologist. The "institutionalist" movement in American economics a generation ago attempted to formulate the social framework of economic processes, albeit on the whole not very successfully.[1] At the same time institutions have become a central focus of sociological theory; we wish to use the concept in the sociological sense.

Formally defined, institutions are the "ways in which the value patterns of the common culture of a social system are integrated in the concrete action of its units in their interaction with each other through the definition of role expectations and the organization of motivation." Institutions define the broad rather than the detailed conditions of the balancing of performances and sanctions; they define the conditions of maintaining a stable state in terms of meeting the functional prerequisites of the system under more or less typical conditions.

[1] For a sample of institutionalist writings, cf. R. G. Tugwell, ed., *The Trend of Economics*, 1924.

They set limits within which sanctions (economic and other ones) are permitted to operate. When these limits are exceeded, not only are advantages gained or lost, but rights and obligations are violated or infringed. Such violation activates not only rational measures to re-establish such rights and obligations, but also various non-rational psychological mechanisms of the sort involved in the genesis of deviant behaviour. Hence indignation is often directed at the ostensible source of violation; sometimes the indignation is displaced on a scapegoat; anxiety about others' future performance arises, etc. Psychologically these are typical reactions to the violation of role expectations internalized in the personalities of the acting individuals. Such reactions are often involved in what economists sometimes describe as a concern for security.[1]

As the formal definition shows, the value-patterns themselves are the primary reference point for the description and analysis of institutional patterns. But institutions relate these value-patterns to the main types of exigencies which units of the system encounter in actual action processes, in the first instance in social relations with other units. The most fundamental function of institutions is therefore to regulate these social relations. There are two main aspects of this regulation: (1) the maintenance of relative *conformity* with the normative requirements of the value pattern, and (2) the maintenance of relative *consistency* of the system of institutionalized patterns themselves, both in terms of generality of application and in terms of the different "fields" or ranges of application. In both these senses institutions contribute to, indeed constitute, the primary focus of the integration of any social system.

Like other features of social systems, institutions tend to be specialized in relation to the functionally differentiated sub-systems of the society. Therefore there are elements in the institutional complex which are "primarily economic," in the sense that they regulate the processes of the economy more directly than those of other sub-systems.

[1] Cf. *The Social System, op. cit.*, Chap. VII. A general discussion of the nature of institutionalization is in the same reference, Chap. II.

CONTRACT: THE CENTRAL ECONOMIC INSTITUTION

In accord with the established tradition of economics, we consider economic institutions as that set of structural features of a social system which arises from the division of labour and its social consequences. Specialization is intimately related to the economy because in the first instance it is a mechanism which improves the social system's adaptive position. Put a little differently, specialization is a structural change in the direction of efficiency of operation. It is also traditional in economics, and in accord with the general theory of social systems as well, to regard economic production as a process which combines the factors of production into products which have properties not to be found in the original factors.[1]

As the division of labour develops, the process of production brings together the requisite factors from a variety of sources, above all from different locations in the social system, and combines them under the right conditions and in the right proportions (more or less, of course). But what does "location in the social system" mean? Most clearly it means that initial control of the factors lie in non-economic sub-systems. It also means that in these sub-systems the factors are not automatically adapted to the process of economic production. A central feature of the economic process, therefore, involves coming to terms with those who control factors of production and inducing them to utilize or permit utilization of these resources for economic purposes.

The most general term for the process of inducement is *contract*.[2] A contract—the process of reaching a contractual settlement of terms—may be analysed initially into two broad sets of components: first, the process of bargaining for advan-

[1] In much the same way as the chemical process combines elements to produce compounds which have properties different from those of the original elements.

[2] It has long been recognized that contract, in both the legal and sociological senses, is somehow central to the development of a differentiated economy. Classical discussions of contract may be found in the work of Sir Henry Sumner Maine, Herbert Spencer, and Durkheim.

tage, in which each party, with particular goals and interests and the particular advantages or disadvantages of his position, seeks to make the best possible bargain; second, the socially prescribed and sanctioned rules to which such bargaining processes are subject, such as the guarantees of interest of third parties, restrictions on fraud and coercion, and the like.[1] We wish to develop here the second set: the nature and functions of formal and informal rules by which those engaged in contract are regulated in their relations to each other. These rules are largely independent of the particular positions of the contracting parties and of the particular resources or factors in question. They will be related to the form in the discussion of markets later in the chapter.

Contract thus constitutes the institutional framework for the basic economic process of exchange; hence contract is the institutional basis of market structure. First we will analyse the institution of contract itself and relate it to the other main economic institutions; then we will illustrate the economic implications of this analysis by discussing some of the different types of markets and indicating the sociological reasons why they differ.

There is a very close relation between the concepts of contract and organization. Of course, some types of exchange are relatively independent of the existence of organization. In the tradition of utilitarianism these have been treated as prototypical; e.g., the two savages who exchanged one deer for two beavers in Locke's famous example that was taken over by Adam Smith and Ricardo. Even such cases occur, however, in a social system regulated by the institutionalization of contractual relations.

In the general case, however, organizations are built up and maintained through exchange and contract. Exchange is the process by which the organization is set up and by which factors of production are incorporated into the organization over its boundaries. Contract is the institutional framework which regulates such processes and defines the limits within which the input-output processes of the firm may operate in a

[1] Durkheim called these the "non-contractual" elements of contract. Cf. *Division of Labour in Society*, translated from the French by George Simpson, 1949, esp. Book I, Chap. 7.

given society. Naturally, a single individual may constitute a "firm" if he performs all the productive tasks himself, and contracts for tools on the one side and for disposal of his product on the other. But this is a limiting case. The important unit of production is the *organization* of a plurality of individual actors whose co-operative activity constitutes the relevant production process.

The same applies at higher system levels. Hence we may speak of the contractual regulation of relations between the economy and cognate sub-systems of the society. We will refer to these higher-level boundaries in the discussion that follows.[1]

What is contracted for in an exchange relation subject to institutionalization in terms of contract? It is precisely two of the basic object-classification categories discussed in Chapter I, namely, goods and services. Goods are physical objects which have economic value and which can be controlled by actors for economic production or for other uses. Services are performances of individual or collective actors which also have economic value. The former category is the focus of the major complex of economic institutions classed under *property*; the latter is the focus of the institutional complex referred to as *occupation*.

The third category, "cultural" objects,[2] may be treated in at least two different ways. First, certain cultural objects often behave like physical objects if there is a like basis for their control. For instance, technological information may be monopolized by a particular firm; if it is more widely known, patents may protect its use in particular contexts. If, on the other hand, cultural objects are freely accessible, they are "givens" of the economic process. The latter type of objects has primarily non-economic meanings and functions. The second fundamental class of cultural objects relevant to economic processes includes money, credit instruments, certificates of indebtedness, etc., which constitute rights or claims on objects of economic value. This category of objects is obviously of the greatest importance in a differentiated economy. Because money does not respond in a process of interaction, it is identical

[1] Some of the contractual regulations of intra-economic processes will be discussed in Chap. IV.

[2] Cf. Chap. I, pp. 11–12.

to physical objects as possessions, but in many respects it is a special case.

With due regard to the special properties of monetary objects (which we will discuss further later), we may classify the primary complexes of economic institutionalization as three: contract, which deals with the institutionalization of the exchange process itself; property, which refers to the institutionalization of rights in non-social objects, and occupation, which refers to the institutionalization of human services. This classification coincides roughly with that of the factors of production themselves: contract is associated with organization as a factor, property with capital, and occupation with labour.

As for the fourth factor of production—land in the broad sense—one further institutional complex deals with the institutionalization of the givens of the productive process. These givens are not the objects of contractual negotiations with regard to their input into the economy, though their intra-economic allocation involves contractual regulation. As we have noted, the land complex breaks down into physical objects, cultural objects such as the state of the arts, and a component in the services of human beings. Analysis of this complex leads to the field of economic motivation in the wider sense; we will treat this at the end of the chapter.

Let us now distinguish the elements in a typical contractual relation which we may expect to be institutionalized. The crucial fact in a contract is that it links *two* systems of action; it is the social relation by means of which boundary interchanges take place.

To analyse the social relationships which obtain in a contract, we will use the same fourfold functional-problem paradigm, though in a slightly different way. A party to a contractual relationship is acting in a role in the ordinary sociological sense. This role is a sub-system of the social system in which he currently participates. As a system of action, then, the role has a goal orientation (G), is subject to adaptive exigencies (A), integrative exigences (I), and operates in terms of an institutional value system (L). This role system of a contracting party (whom we conveniently designate as ego) articulates with the corresponding role of the other party, alter, and the two become integrated, in ways that we will indicate, into a partially independent social system.

With respect to any boundary interchange, therefore, each participating system pursues a *goal* which is the establishment of a desired or needed relation between the acquisition of input (with due regard to quality and amount) and the corresponding output. In interaction terms, system A's output is its principal performance, whereas system B's input is the corresponding sanction.[1] For instance, a firm produces a line of goods and sells them in the consumers' market for the desired and needed monetary returns. These goal elements constitute the *primary* performances and sanctions in an exchange relationship. The first condition of stability in a contractual relationship is a certain balancing with respect to this reciprocal goal attainment; this is what we mean by the mutually advantageous settlement of terms.

Each contracting party, however, acts in a situation, the character of which imposes certain constraints on him. The most salient aspect of this situation is the structure of the principal collectivity which ego represents as member when he engages in the exchange process. Hence, as salesman ego represents the firm; as purchaser in a consumer's market he most frequently represents the household.

If we refer to the action system which has the settlement of contractual terms as its sub-system goal, then the rest of the system of which the goal is a part constitutes the relevant environment for the pursuit of the goal. Above all, the representative (e.g., salesman or purchaser) must *adapt* his actions to this environment, which tends to set the limiting conditions under which he must operate. Thus the salesman is constrained by the kinds of goods he sells and the terms he must accept, and the purchaser is constrained by the income limits of the household and its taste standards.[2]

The problem of the "interests of third parties" in a con-

[1] The performance-sanction distinction is relative; what is performance for A may be sanction for B, and vice versa.

[2] As we shall see in Chap. IV, the situation to which ego and alter must adapt in a contractual relation has many implications for the behaviour of certain crucial economic functions, such as the marginal propensity to consume and the marginal efficiency of capital. Cf. pp. 221 ff.

tractual relation is relevant at this adaptive focus. For each contracting party the other members of the respective collectivities represented are the most important third parties whose interests must be taken into account in the settlement of terms. The institutionalization of this interest is above all in the limits of contracting agent's powers of "representation." The law of agency is a formal legal statement of certain powers of representation.

The goal interests and the adaptive situations for the respective contracting parties are distinct for each party. But in the interests of stability, ego and alter must constitute parts of a single social system. That is to say, there must be some kind of *integration* and some kind of *common value pattern* which they share.

The basis of integration is apparent in a sort of *secondary* performance-sanction exchange. Relative to the primary exchange (which constitutes the goal orientation of the contracting parties), this integrative interchange involves a higher level of symbolic generalization; it defines the "meaning" of the primary goal objects. The secondary exchange may or may not be concretely distinguishable in any given transaction. To continue with the consumers' market example, proceeds from sales are of course a necessary facility for remaining in business; this aspect of the proceeds is the primary sanction aspect of their acquisition. On another level, however, proceeds from sales are *symbols* of the firm's successful operation, of its approval by a category of customers. In the usual commercial case, even though both the primary and secondary components of input are included in the firm's monetary income, it is possible to estimate the relative salience of each. For instance, in recession periods when consumers' purchasing power is low, in general, relatively poor returns are usually not interpreted as a symbolic disapproval of the firm's market position.

This symbolization of attitude, over and above the attainment of a good bargain, is the primary integrative element in contractual relations. A stable contractual system tends toward some kind of equal balance on this level as well as on the level of the primary settlement of terms. As a matter of fact, apparent imbalances on the primary level are often compensated by an imbalance in the opposite direction on the secondary level. For instance, the fact that "name" firms exact higher prices undoubtedly reflects not only the intrinsic quality of the goods, but also the prestige which customers "buy" in trading with such a firm.

Certain common value patterns among the contracting parties constitute the last element of the contractual complex. Thus, in the contract of employment there is a kind of common valuation of the function of production in the society. From the firm's point of view it is defined in terms of the valuation of efficiency and worker reliability; from the worker's point of view it is defined on the basis of having a "worth-while" job (and not only in terms of wage level).[1] In the case of the consumers' market the corresponding common value pattern is valuation of production in another context—the evaluation of the "worth" or utility of the specific goods in question.

The common value pattern, as the reference point for defining the meaning of the integrative symbols referred to above, has a double significance. In the first place, it sets the background for integrating the exchange system itself by mitigating or eliminating the effects of inherent conflicts of interest. Such conflicts are given meaning in terms of a superordinate system of solidarity which includes *both* contracting parties. In the second place, it tends to integrate any particular contractual commitment with the respective systems which ego and alter represent. For instance, one major reference point for the meaning of a business firm's contractual commitments is precisely the bearing of the commitments on the general financial state of the firm. In the consumer case, both the household budget and the style-of-life patterns provide such reference points. Thus in some sense the secondary interchange must provide equivalence between the two symbolic meaning-foci of the contracting systems.

Figure 8 shows these functional elements in a contractual relationship, stated in terms of the paradigm of action-system analysis. The formulation of the figure is from the point of view of only *one* party to a relationship which of course always involves two parties. We have, that is, confined this formal

[1] For an excellent empirical analysis of the components of "worth-while" employment, cf. Bakke, E. W., *The Unemployed Worker*, 1940, Chap. I.

statement to one side, e.g., the purchaser in a consumers' market transaction. The total relationship would be represented by juxtaposing *two* such paradigms.

The *G*-component includes the elements which are the usual objects of the exchange relation; these are the foci of "self-interest" as it operates through bargaining for advantage. The *I*-component concerns the less obvious and often implicit symbolic overtones of the transaction. On occasion these integrative elements become the object of explicit bargaining as well, but very likely at the expense of certain elements of

FIGURE 8

FACTORS BEARING ON DECISIONS IN CONTRACTUAL RELATIONSHIPS

G	Interest in advantageous terms for exchange of primary output for relevant primary input: goods, services, cultural values.
A	Constraints imposed by ego's representative status in relation to both contracting systems: *other* interests of ego's parent collectivity and its members and that of contracting party (including ego's other roles).
I	Symbolic value of "secondary" performances and sanctions: success, approval, esteem, etc. (Balance of symbolic rewards.)
L	Common value pattern: e.g., valuation of prevalent category of production.

stability. The *A*- and the *L*-components constitute the *conditions* of the exchange; hence from the point of view of a particular contractual relationship they are "given." These involve what Durkheim called the "non-contractual" elements of contract; they are, properly speaking, the *institution* of contract. When they change, the process involves a change of the structure of a relevant contracting system (e.g., the economy or some unit of it), not merely process in the system.[1]

One of the sources of variation of the concrete structuring of contracts is the degree to which each of these components is explicitly stated and formally accepted by both parties. Some of the components, particularly the *I*- and *L*-components, are probably always implicit.

This paradigm of contractual relationships may be applied

[1] We will develop this problem of the structural change of institutions in Chap. V.

to empirical cases on three levels: (1) The illustrative case above is that of the role of *one* of the parties to a given contractual relationship. The goal is to settle terms advantageously from his point of view, and the other components fit accordingly. A typical instance of this case is that in which ego acts in a *representative* role on behalf of a collectivity, e.g., firm or household. (2) The contractual *relation* itself may be treated as a system, with the two parties performing differentiated roles. The goal in this case is to attain agreement, i.e., a mutually satisfactory settlement of terms. This means that the other components have to be redefined appropriately.[1] Again the chances of attaining *G* depend not only on the parties' "interests" as defined in *G* and *A* terms, but also on the emergence of a common value system and an adequate basis of integration. (3) An indefinite plurality of parties on each side of the contractual relation constitutes a system as well; in the economic case, this system is a market. The goal of the *system* is to establish a set of market-wide terms, of which price is the most prominent, though by no means the only component.

In all three cases the *institution* of contract concerns neither the specific terms of exchange nor the specific adaptive exigencies which affect them, but the common values and integrative bases of solidarity (mutual trust) which transcend the parties' immediate conflict of interest.[2]

Now we are in a position to examine closely the "quids" and the "quos" involved in the *quid pro quo* of contractual exchanges. As we have pointed out, they fall into two fundamental classes: (1) rights with respect to non-social objects, or objects of *possession*, and (2) expectations with respect to the performance of social objects. The two great institutional complexes which follow from this distinction are property

[1] It is well known that a two-member system, by itself, is a particularly unstable type. Hence the need for certain stabilizing mechanisms. Cf. Bales, R. F., and Borgatta, E. F., "Size of Group as a Factor in the Interaction Profile," in Hare, A. P.; Borgatta, E. F., and Bales, R. F. (eds.), *Small Groups*, 1955, pp. 396–413.

[2] Since a conflict of interest is inherent in the contractual relation, the institution of contract is parallel to the legal system in which the authority of judge and jury and the rules of procedure and of evidence transcend the conflict of interest between the parties to a litigation.

and occupation. In the last analysis both refer to the structuring of expectations in the process of social interaction. Thus, in ownership or possession, ego's relation to the physical thing is certainly problematical, but so are the expectations of the behaviour of *others* with reference to ego and the thing.[1] In occupation, on the other hand, there are expectations of behaviour on the socially interactive level on the part of the role incumbent himself. Put another way, the differences between possession and occupation lie in the fact that things are not expected to interact in the same way as persons.

In this whole institutional complex the concept of *organization* occupies a central place. To define it formally: an organization is a boundary-maintaining system of action of a plurality of individuals, membership in which is defined by contractual commitments[2] to given kinds and levels of performance (i.e., commitments to contribute to the organization function or goal and to perform agreed services to that end); further, an organization commands contractually committed objects of possession as facilities for its functioning.[3] The organization—or in the economy, the firm—is the unit of the productive system; *its* product, whether goods or services, is the economically significant contribution to the national income. With respect to both possessions and actor services, the fundamental dividing line is between institutionalization of roles or sub-systems *within* the organization and institutionalization of rights and commitments *among* organizations or other cognate collectivities. We will consider the elements of contract which regulate the latter relationships and thus constitute a market.

[1] For instance, the expression "my hat" refers not only to the fact that I "have" and am at liberty to wear a particular hat at will, but also to the fact that others are, under most circumstances, restrained from taking possession of or using my hat without my permission.

[2] When a person or collectivity gives another party a right to expect certain types of behaviour under specified conditions, we say that he (or they) makes a *commitment*. This is a more general use of the term than that in Chaps. I and II, when we referred to land as a set of economic commitments.

[3] In cases where concrete membership in an organization is ascriptive, e.g., by kinship, we may speak of an "implied contract." In the modern type of economy the firm has tended to eliminate all ascriptive bases of membership.

LABOUR, OCCUPATION AND THE CONTRACT OF EMPLOYMENT

An occupational role is the role of an individual within an organization in so far as it commits him to productive functions on behalf of the organization through personal performance and in so far as the commitment is established and/or maintained by an explicit or implied contract with the organization.[1]

The occupational role is thus a type of contractual relationship between an organization and an individual usually acting in a representative role as member of a household or possibly some other collectivity. The primary "quid" is his commitment to continuing performance as a member of the organization in a capacity defined in the contract of employment. The primary but not exclusive "quo" is money income—wages, in the economic sense—paid by the organization for satisfactory performance. The income is a source of facilities for maintenance of his household in the first instance. From the standpoint of the occupational role incumbent, the "quid-quo" relationship constitutes the goal-attainment aspect of the contract-of-employment sub-system of his larger role system. The balancing of *two* expectation-commitment components—the commitment to performance and the expectation of wage-income—is the primary direct function of the contractual settlement.

The typical occupational contract integrates three partially independent systems of action: (1) the organization in which ego is employed; (2) the household of which ego is a member, and (3) the personality of ego. Via this integration the relevant components of these other three systems *themselves* constitute a partially independent social system with its own boundary-maintaining properties. Occupational performance is the primary output to the organization and money income is the primary output to the household. Other components of the contractual interchange, to be taken up later, are the primary output to the personality system.[2] This integration through contract of three otherwise distinct systems is an example of the *interpenetration* of systems of action. By employment in the

[1] As we suggested above, the case of the fully independent professional or artisan is a limiting case; he constitutes a one-man organization.

[2] Cf. below, pp. 179–184.

organization ego does not cease to be a member of the household; nor does he simply part with that element of himself which he "puts into" his occupational performance. It becomes part of the organization as a system of action, but it also remains part of his personality. All three systems are partially reorganized, to a degree, therefore, by the assumption of the occupational commitment.[1]

What are the other components of ego's contractual commitment? In social system terms, the adaptive component consists of the relevant features in the two sub-systems integrated by the contract of employment. On the organization side, ego's contract involves him in a set of adaptive relations to other units; this is the *organizational context* of his role,[2] which includes both the availability of non-social facilities and the co-operation of other role incumbents. These relations either facilitate or hinder his effective role performance. On the household side, ego must be left a margin of freedom from organizational involvement to adapt to certain household exigencies (and secondarily those of other roles). Conversely, household demands must be adjusted to allow fulfilment of occupational obligations. The problem is to strike a balance. The regulation of the amount of time for work is obviously one of the main mechanisms which facilitate this balance. There are other more subtle problems, however; for example, too much "worry" associated with one role may react unfavourably on the other.[3]

[1] Further discussions of the integration between partially independent sub-systems of a system of action are in Parsons, Bales, *et al.*, *Family Socialization and Interaction Process*, esp. Chap. III, pp. 157 ff. The two most essential ideas developed there are those of (1) the interpenetration of systems in the same concrete behaviour process which must be understood as part of two or more action systems and (2) integration of contiguous systems through "cross-ties" which are the patterns of diffuse symbolic meaning and the common values we have discussed here.

[2] This concept was first crystallized in personal discussions with Robert K. Merton.

[3] This implies that the famous economic dichotomy between "work" and "leisure" is psychologically and sociologically misleading if it means merely an indifference curve or indifference map in which leisure is viewed as the simple "alternative" to continuous work. Rather, the alternatives to involvement in the organization include the whole range of commitments in relevant collectivities—commitments which are not fulfilled by choosing "leisure."

In one primary aspect this adaptive component is a special case of the interchange between the economy and polity. As we have pointed out, the adaptive function concerns the capacity to iron out fluctuations over time. Only in limiting cases is employment simply momentary. Implicitly it creates the expectation of continuation of wage income and through this a base for credit. In exchange for this credit creation, the firm acquires certain "rights to intervene"[1] in the operation of the household. These rights, which are exercised primarily through the denial of employment through discharge, constitute a form of power not merely to cut off the household's income momentarily but to some degree to control its longer-run interests.[2]

As we have seen, the integrative balance deals with symbolic meanings associated with the *G* and *A* elements. Such meanings tap more general (i.e., "regressive") levels of motivational structure.[3] On the side of commitment to the organization, the symbolic output consists of diffuse loyalty to the organization as such, over and above the obligation to perform a specific role function effectively. By virtue of this loyalty an individual tends to develop a sense of organizational responsibility and to accept, as the occasion demands, responsibilities beyond any specific contracted function. The integrative input into his personality consists of diffuse prestige associated with his occupational role and status in the organization.

This integrative component is a special case of the exchange between the polity and the integrative sub-system at the societal level. Since we have barely mentioned this interchange in this

[1] Cf. Chap. II, pp. 73–74, for an outline of this concept and the exchange between control of the creation of credit and rights to intervene.

[2] For certain implications of this adaptive interchange for the structure of the labour market, cf. below, pp. 146–149.

[3] This refers to certain characteristics of the motivational structures of personality. We conceive the personality as a system that develops by a process of structural differentiation over time. The more specialized motivational structures are thus derived by differentiation from more general ones which are established at earlier stages of the individual's life history. Hence the more general structures are also the more "regressive." We hold that a contractual relationship therefore "taps" at least two layers in a motivational system. Cf. *Family, Socialization and Interaction Process*, *op. cit.*, Chaps. II and III.

study,[1] the present statement must necessarily be cryptic. In this interchange the firm provides the worker and his household with "contingent support" which is important to him in two contexts: (1) in his occupational role, management gives generalized diffuse support for meeting the various exigencies which may arise in connection with this role; this support is over and above the remuneration for job performance; (2) the firm also adapts to some degree a supportive orientation toward the worker's household, usually in supplying fringe benefits, relative security of employment, etc. In exchange for such support, the worker contributes a type of power which we may call "influence"; the firm gains a reputation in the community as a good employer if workers continually lend their name and good will to it. This "influence" includes a readiness to take a diffuse responsibility for the firm's welfare above and beyond meeting the strictly defined job specifications. Hence a mutually supportive attitude is the essence of this integrative interchange.

Finally, certain value patterns unite the three systems in the contract of employment. For the organization this is primarily the evaluation of effective production (of course at a level appropriate to the firm's position in the economy). For the household it is the acceptance of the responsibility to be a "good provider" for the needs and prestige of the household and its security. These primary evaluations are not incompatible, however, with a secondary commitment in an inverse direction. A "good" organization recognizes an obligation to pay "good" wages and salaries; furthermore, it is proud of its prestige position and the prestige that its personnel derive from this position. Conversely, a "good" family in our society recognizes the obligation of its employed members (especially the husband-father) to be "good at his job" and to consider his job "important" above and beyond the remuneration level.

This interchange involves the same components as the general interchange between pattern-maintenance and integrative sub-systems of the society.[2] The household makes a very significant commitment in entrusting its fundamental security to the labour market and its constituent employing firms. In one respect this commitment reflects its "confidence"

[1] Cf. Chap. II, pp. 67–68.

[2] Cf. Chap. II, pp. 67–68.

in the economy. In exchange the firm provides symbolic rewards which take the form of moral approval of the performance in terms of achievement values. This interchange is the symbolic implementation of the values of economic rationality which we will discuss at the end of this chapter. Figure 9 summarizes the contract of employment.

Within this context a few major axes for the classification of occupational roles may be isolated. An occupational role, if fully differentiated, is a role within an organization which has a relatively specialized function in the society. One mode of classification of such roles concerns the type of organization; the incumbent of the occupational role may be employed by a business firm, a government agency, a university, a hospital, etc. This range of variation concerns the *L*-component of the contract of employment.

A second basis of classification is the type of function assumed *within* the organization. The function may be relatively specialized or "technical," or it may emphasize "diffuse" responsibility for the operation of the firm as an organization. The former accents the *G*-component of the contract of employment, the latter the *I*-component. On the higher levels the diffuse type is what we call an "executive" role. Further, both the *G*- and *I*-components can be broken down into types of content.

Further, the technical role may be assessed according to whether the technical function involved is in line with the function of the organization in the society, e.g., the physician in a hospital, the professor in a university, or the engineer in an automobile plant, on the one hand, or whether the technical function is auxiliary to the organization's primary function, e.g., the physician in a school system, the secretary in a hospital, the lawyer in a manufacturing firm.

Technical roles may be classified finally in terms of their "content"; this refers primarily to types of functions in social systems. Since the differentiation by type of organization has already been noted, the relevant basis in this case is function *within* a given organization. The differentiation of technical roles in these terms is thus based on a classification of types of content of the *A*-component.

Given these several components of occupational roles, any

given concrete role is to be defined in terms of a combination of each of the relevant categories.

One of the characteristics of a contract is that a fluid state of a system of action becomes more definitely structured. For instance, we consider a man's role as an unemployed member

FIGURE 9

LABOUR MARKET

	L_G "Household"		A_G "Firm"
G	L_G Labour services	→ ←	A_G Wages (purchasing power)
A	A_A Rights to intervene (Attitude to authority in organization: acceptance of authority and executive responsibility)	→ ←	G_A Credit creation (credit standing: capital "making advances" to labour)
I	G_G Influence (Reputation as good employer)	→ ←	I_G Contingent support (Responsibility for household welfare: fringe benefits)
L	I_A Confidence (Defined in terms of security of household—entrusted to the economy)	→ ←	L_A Moral approval (Defined in terms of values of economic rationality: production for standard of living)
		Value system of the market as a synthesis of economic rationality and security	

of the labour force to be less structured than his contractual involvement in an organization; that is, the definition of his role is more specific in the latter case. Such structuring, which takes place sociologically in terms of discrete levels which we shall discuss presently, is related to the problem of the "levels of generality" of the cultural systems of meanings which are a central component of social action.[1]

In terms of the contract of employment, the society possesses what may be conceived as a body of resources relatively more fluid than those embodied in occupational roles. Economists

[1] For an extended theoretical treatment of the "levels of generality" problem, cf. Parsons and Bales, *Family, Socialization and Interaction Process*, *op. cit.*, Chap. VII.

and others identify these more fluid resources by the concept of the *labour force*. The labour force, that is to say, is a highly generalized resource available for various specific productive performances in specific organizations. Its generalization is limited, however, by the degree of substitutability of skills and motivational commitments of the members of the labour force. At any rate, however, an abstract unit of the labour force alone is not effective as a factor of production. It must be combined with other types of labour and other factors of production in organizations. The contract of employment marks, therefore, the transition from membership in the economic category of available labour (i.e., labour as a factor of production) to a particular collectivity within the economy. Commitment to a particular organization involves, however, a sacrifice of fluidity, mobility or "generality" of the status of a unit of labour as a factor. Thus we can distinguish two levels of the hierarchy of fluidity-generality in the labour market: membership in the labour force and employment in a particular organization. The transition between these two levels marks the change from the technical status of "unemployed," i.e., not committed to an organization but willing to be so, and "employed," as these terms are used by economists and others.

A similar process of "particularization" occurs at the next level down (in terms of generalization) within the organization. This is the transition from acceptance of employment to assignment to a specific job role. It is possible to be employed by a firm but still be relatively uncommitted to any particular technical specialization and to change jobs without leaving the firm. Hence, a firm's labour force is more fluid and generalized than particular job roles within it. The executive role is more attached to the firm as such, is more "diffuse" than technical roles.

To make labour completely effective, however, human action must be brought to bear in a particular act or series of acts in a particular situation, e.g., operating a particular machine with specific materials. This level, which we may call *task assignment*, is even more particularized than that of the role, which, however specialized, is never confined to a single functional context.

The hierarchy of levels of generalization also proceeds

"upward" from the level of membership in the labour force. Labour does not enter the labour force from a completely undifferentiated state; it incorporates many types and levels of "trained capacity" which are a function both of innate ability factors and of relevant experience. In terms of the life-history of the individual, entry into the labour force is in our society typically from the formal educational system; particularly in the case of women, however, it is possible to move in and out of the labour force at different periods of adult life. The composition of the skills and capacities of a labour force is clearly at least as important a factor in productivity as its sheer "size."

"Training," i.e., the differentiation of the working population in terms of skill and capacity, is the end-product (in the relevant respects) of what sociologists call the "process of socialization." For purposes of analysing the sequence by which "labour power" is created, on the one hand, and utilized in production, on the other, we may distinguish two stages prior to training in skills and capacities: (1) the establishment of what we may call "generalized performance (or achievement) capacity" which in a highly differentiated society is what the normal child possesses on emergence from the oedipal transition, from primary involvement in his family of orientation into the system of formal education; (2) the very first stage of emergence from the status of completely unsocialized organism as neonate, to possessing the first and most general level of "socialized motivation"; in technical socialization terms this is the level of "orality."[1]

[1] The considerations of this paragraph are of little direct interest to economists. All the processes occur primarily within the pattern-maintenance system of the society, i.e., family and education system. The labour force is interstitial between the pattern-maintenance system and the economy, then the last three stages of specification, employment job-specification and final productive action occur primarily within the economy. Naturally the further removed is a process from the boundary of the economy the more remote its economic interest. Nevertheless the origins of labour power within the total society have an important bearing on economic problems, notably those of the motivation to work in an economic context.

We might mention a further set of formal considerations. We have distinguished seven steps in the transition from the most generalized level of socialized motivation to the final concrete utilization of labour in production. Of these the generalized category of labour as a factor of

Thus the institutionalization of the provision of labour for productive service involves not merely one transition—from pattern-maintenance system to economy—but probably six, as follows: (1) from the most general socialized motivation to "generalized performance capacity"; (2) from general performance capacity to "trained capacity"; (3) from trained capacity to membership in the labour force; (4) from membership in the labour force to employment by a specific firm; (5) from employment to specific job or occupational role assignment; and, finally, (6) from specific occupational role to specific "task."

Since the first two transitions are subjects for the theory of socialization, we will not develop them further. But *given* a population and its trained capacities, there must be four relatively independent decisions before labour can be concretely utilized in production, namely; (1) the decision to enter the labour force, i.e., be available for employment if and when suitable and acceptable terms can be arranged; (2) the decision to accept employment by a particular firm, involving the settlement of these terms between firm and household; (3) the decision upon the role to be assumed within the employing organization; and (4) the decision upon the particular tasks to be performed. Two or more of these decisions may be compressed into one, but the conditions relevant to all of them always must be considered. Hence, this transition series is a general paradigm for the analysis of the commitment of human resources to production.

Sensitivity to short-run economic sanctions focuses at the third and fourth transitions in the general series (the first and second in the shorter one). Once employment with a firm has

production, the labour force, is the middle term and is, as we noted, interstitial between two primarily functional sub-systems of the society. We believe that this pattern can be generalized for all the factors of production of the economy, and for cognate factors in carrying out the functions of other sub-systems. In logical structure this paradigm corresponds with that set forth by Parsons and Bales (*Family, Socialization and Interaction Process, op. cit.*, Chap. VII) for the stages in the completion of a decision in group performance and for a phase in the internalization of a norm through socialization. We believe that the seven-step paradigm applies not only to the "factors" but also throughout many types of systems of action. The series of stages for labour and capital as factors are shown in Figure 11.

been accepted, a certain "loyalty" to the firm is expected and even some job changes are likely to be acceptable relatively independent of short-run economic sanctions. The allocation of labour *within* an organization is a function not of a market in the strictest sense (though of course it is influenced by the outside labour market); it is a matter of "administration." Task assignment is even less a function of the market. Proceeding up the hierarchy, we have repeatedly stressed that neither the family nor the educational system function primarily in relation to short-run economic sanctions. Finally, of course, the degree of sensitivity of economic sanctions found in our society cannot be automatically generalized; in many societies there is little or no "employment" in our sense at all and a negligible labour force since household and productive units are fused in a single unit of social organization.

PROPERTY, OWNERSHIP, AND THE CONTRACT OF INVESTMENT

We defined property—the second great complex of institutionalization of contractual relations—as the institutionalization of rights in objects of possession or non-social objects which function as facilities in the process of production and as reward objects to the factors of production.[1] In connection with this institution we will treat "ownership" as parallel to "occupation" in the case of labour.

Ownership in this sense is a contractual relation between a holder of property rights (a "proprietor" in one sense) and an organization, by means of which the proprietor's property is committed to the organization's productive functions. The commitment is established and/or maintained by an explicit or implied contract of investment between the proprietor and the organization.[2] Like occupation, ownership is typically a

[1] I.e., possession often operates as a positive sanction.

[2] To define ownership in this contractual framework is by no means to exhaust the legal and sociological meanings of the term. Our definition is derived from the framework of *interaction*, especially contractual interaction, and hence we treat the organization and its contractual relations as the general case. Much legal, economic and sociological tradition has treated the rights of the individual, *qua* individual, as the general case.

contractual exchange between an individual or collectivity acting in a representative role and an organization engaged in production. The primary "quid" is ego's commitment of rights of possession to the firm. The primary "quo" is some increment of value to ego's property (i.e., to his rights in possession) above and beyond its worth if kept in a liquid state.[1] The parallel between occupation and ownership is essential, but certain differences derive from the fact that possessions belong in the non-social environment of action and are not as such components of the action process. In particular, when a society is highly differentiated, objects of possession are inputs over a different boundary from that at which labour services are incorporated. In Chapter II we argued that labour is interchanged between the goal-attainment sub-system of the economy and the pattern-maintenance sub-system of the society and that capital is interchanged between the adaptive sub-system of the economy and the goal-attainment sub-system (polity) of the society.

In the contract of investment, therefore, the firm's exigencies are similar to those of the firm in the contract of employment, but on the non-economic side the values and exigencies are quite different.[2] In so far as liquid funds accrue to the household as income from labour service through the contract of employment, the decision to save is *not even in the boundary sense* an economic decision. For most purposes it is an intra-latency problem; with respect to the establishment of an appropriate

Hence our position parallels that taken in connection with the independent professional or artisan in the contract of employment. When the proprietor is also the controlling manager of the organization in question, we can speak of the "self-capitalization" of the organization as a limiting case. To put this in a slightly different way, the completely self-sufficient firm with full reserves for financing its own investment is a special case whether it be a corner grocery or a giant industrial firm. In this case the contract of investment is not realized, in the sense that this contract is an institutionally regulated exchange between two distinct collectivities.

[1] We will treat investment so far as it is an intra-economic process, according to the paradigm of the boundary interchange, in the next chapter. Then we will combine the analysis of this process with the analysis of its contractual regulation in an attempt to contribute to an understanding of the *investment function* as this term is utilized by economists.

[2] This is true analytically in spite of the fact that concretely a good deal of investment originates in the property of private households.

level of reserves for the creation of credit, it involves a relationship between the pattern-maintenance system and the polity.[1] The actual creation of purchasing power from this base of reserves, however, is first and foremost a political process in our sense. To encourage productivity by enhancing credit standing or to create purchasing power for units of the economy is to make the political decision that capitalization, i.e., increase of *productivity*, has a certain importance *for the society* relative to other goals. Thus the receipt, manipulation and application of capital funds by the borrower places him—whether he recognizes it or not—in a role of public responsibility. By the same token, the contract of investment, which is the commitment of capital funds to particular firms, is a political decision; the relevant environment which imposes exigencies on the investor is not in a differentiated society the household but the polity or some organizational sub-system with political functions.

Let us now review the paradigm for the contract of investment corresponding to that presented for the contract of employment. The commitment of fluid property resources to the firm is the primary performance of the investor as contracting party and hence is the first *G*-component. The difference between the performance in the investment and the employment cases is that only in a passive sense does the investor have to make a "continuing" commitment, i.e., he must refrain from withdrawing his funds without considering the consequences.[2] This is one aspect of the problem of liquidity.

[1] Cf. Chap. II, pp. 67–68.

[2] The reader should keep in mind the treatment of the A_A–G_A boundary, Chap. II, pp. 56–60 and 72–78 throughout the following analysis. We should point out, however, that the analysis of the contract of investment is *not on the same level* as the major boundary between economy and polity, but one level lower, i.e., between the holders of capital funds and relevant firms within the economy. For a discussion of the difference between these two levels, cf. below, pp. 162–3 and Chap. IV, pp. 210–13. The same difference of levels holds in the case of human services. The two transitions are between trained capacity and membership in the labour force on the one hand, and between membership in the labour force and employment in specific firms on the other.

Capital as a factor of production (i.e., fluid capital funds) is thus interstitial *between* polity and economy in the same sense that the labour force is interstitial between the pattern-maintenance system and the economy. In both cases either one of the transitions between levels of

To demand absolute liquidity is to give the security of the funds priority over their commitment to the productive process (at least so far as the particular organization is concerned).[1]

The primary "quo" which balances the property commitment is the expectation of the maintenance of security of ego's property and the expectation of its possible increase of value through interest and other forms of return. These expectations are means to control the productive capacity of certain parts of the economy. They are thus a case of the "rights to intervene" we have discussed above.[2] The essential sanction of the owner's control over the firm's operations is the right to withdraw his investment. This sanction is, however, only *one* of several possible bases of control; it must be balanced against those of executives, entrepreneurs, etc. Not until all of these are considered is it possible to determine the structure of the market organization.

Hence the adaptive situation of the contract of investment concerns the organizational context of the investor's position, both within the firm and outside as "owner" representing some sector of the polity. The adaptive significance of the firm is its facilitating (or hindering) effects on implementing the increase and/or maintenance of the productive capacity of the firm. The quality of management and its policies are thus of paramount importance to the investor. On the polity side, also, the organizational context of ego's ownership role may facilitate or hinder the investment function. Empirically, there is a wide range of possible organizational contexts. The main unit in which the investor is involved may be a kinship unit, in which case the balance between the family's consumption requirements and the investor's role is the main concern. Such

commitment can be analysed in terms of the paradigm of contractual relations. The concrete content, however, varies according to the level. We have singled out the contracts of employment and investment as crucial for our purposes.

[1] The positive functions of this right to withdraw investment, i.e., the right of manœuvrability, are examined below, Chap. IV, pp. 200–203, 210–13, and 233–41. The implications of this structural peculiarity of the investment market for the behaviour of the investment function is also explored in Chap. IV, pp. 233–41.

[2] Cf. Chap. II, pp. 73–74, and Chap. IV, pp. 200–203, 210–13 and 233–241, for a development of these aspects of investment.

involvement was frequent in the early history of capitalism. Again, the unit may be a private corporate organization which occupies some fiduciary position relative to ultimate ownership interests, e.g., an insurance company, a trade union (the Mine Workers' Welfare Fund), a university or hospital corporation, etc. These forms have become increasingly significant in recent history. Finally, it may be a governmental agency, such as the Tennessee Valley Authority. But whatever the empirical case, the principal adaptive questions are the margin of freedom of the investing agent in his representative role, the standards of security he must meet, his accountability in case of loss, etc.

Analytically this interchange is a special case of the boundary between the polity and the integrative sub-system.[1] The firm's adaptive "contribution" to the investor's interest is "binding decisions" which commit a part of the firm's resources (other than capital) to the specific goal of increasing productivity. In exchange the firm receives a special form of influence or "generalized consent" in that the granting of credit is approved on "policy" grounds as appropriate to this firm of good standing. Thus the main adaptive conditions of the contract of investment consist of the political goal-commitments of the contracting parties. These form the basis of a certain stability of expectations which transcends the specific quid-pro terms of the contract.

Paralleling the case of employment, the integrative component of the contract of investment deals with the investor's level of diffuse commitment to the organization in which he invests, which may be stated as his "confidence" in it. It is thus a second component of what we have called "organizational responsibility." At one extreme, that of nominal responsibility, is the investor who "lets it go" at the *G*-component interests; his interest is overwhelmingly in the security and level of financial return of his assets. At the other extreme is the "capitalist," whose investment role includes a commitment to be partially responsible for fairly detailed control of the affairs of the firm and its profits. In some cases, of course, the respective roles of ownership and executive management are fused in a single concrete role, especially in the case of small businesses.

[1] Cf. Chap. II, pp. 67–8.

The investor's organizational responsibility is balanced on the firm's side by a commitment of diffuse responsibility for using the available capital productively. Concretely this involves the commitment of the whole organization, especially management, to the maintenance and/or improvement of its productivity base.

In analytical terms this interchange is a special case of that between the pattern-maintenance and integrative systems. Like the polity and economy, these two systems exchange *facilities*.[1] From the pattern-maintenance side the primary output is a commitment to pattern conformity or socialized motivation in so far as this contributes to the integration of the society, especially through the disposition to accept universalistic rules of behaviour. From the integrative system the reciprocal output is an "acceptance of belonging," which forms one of the bases for psychological security. Applied to the contract of investment, the appropriate form of pattern conformity is the investor's willingness to treat invested funds, which are necessarily less liquid than cash, as genuine operative resources. In fact, the productivity of the economy is the basis for the value of all financial assets. This valuation cannot be sustained, however, without generalized confidence in the operating units of the economy; without confidence, the result is financial panic. The other side of the integrative exchange, therefore, is the firm's commitment of capital to the productivity base of the firm. Such commitment insures the security of the assets themselves and hence underlies the confidence in the economic unit. This security may be defined, of course, over a wide range from specific expectations of future earnings of particular firms to the overall soundness of the national economy.[2]

Finally, a system of common values links the organization and the proprietor in the contract of investment. On the organization side this involves acceptance of the organization purpose, commitment to the goal of production and interest in productivity as a means to more effective production. On the polity side it means commitment to the responsibilities of

[1] Cf. Chap. II, pp. 67–68.

[2] For an extensive discussion of a similar integrative interchange in the market for liquid funds, cf. below, pp. 165 ff.

ownership, not merely with respect to a particular firm but in terms of the "public responsibilities" of capital and its management. This value system is, moreover, a particularization of the general societal value system and political sub-values. In the American value system—with its strong emphasis on adaptive functions in general—investment tends to be treated as a "good thing" so long as it presumably contributes to productivity.[1]

This system of common values is, in fact, that aspect of the major value system which is relevant to the boundary between the economy and the pattern maintenance system of the society; values at this boundary are appropriate to the integration of the valuation of production and consumption. Hence the *L*-component of the contract of investment is a special case of the A_G–L_G interchange.[2] In this special case, however, the firm values the use of capital—hence productivity—in terms of its relevance to consumption values; whereas the investor evaluates capital in terms of its bearing on productivity itself. Figure 10 summarizes in a way comparable to Figure 9 the contractual structure of investment.

Capital, like labour and the other factors, operates not merely on one level, but proceeds through several levels of generalization. Using the commitment of fluid funds to specific organizational units (i.e., the contract of investment) as our starting-point,[3] let us trace capital through its several stages.

Generalized purchasing power represents the capitalized values of the economic assets of the society. The valuation of these assets, we have stressed, rests essentially on productivity. Above and beyond this *basis* for generalized purchasing power, one of its basic characteristics is its mobility. Purchasing power can shift balances at any point in the economy—between production for consumption and production for capitalization, between various lines of production for consumption, etc. Behind this factor of mobility lies the mechanism of credit

[1] This is not to say, however, that investment is not a source of many dilemmas and ambivalences in our society.

[2] Cf. Chap. II, pp. 53–55, 67–68, and 70–72.

[3] This starting-point is parallel to that of the commitment of labour services to specific organizations through the contract of employment. Cf. pp. 119–20.

creation, which is above all the focus of the *political* contribution to the effectiveness of purchasing power.

Generalized purchasing power cannot, however, be rendered effective unless it is committed to production through several stages of specification. As in the case of labour, it is possible to distinguish three levels of progressively increasing specificity of commitment: (1) the transition, through the contract of investment, between generalized purchasing power to commitment to a particular productive organization (usually

FIGURE 10

MARKET FOR CAPITAL FUNDS

	G_A		A_A
G	G_A Control of creation of credit	←——— ———→	A_A Rights to intervene
A	I_G Generalized acceptance of investing agents (consent)	←——— ———→	G_G Commitments to specific productive capacity (binding decisions)
I	L_A Guaranteed value of generalized facilities	←——— ———→	I_A Guaranteed value of productivity *base* for facilities (security)
L	A_G Valuation of capital as basis of maintaining and enhancing activity	←——— ———→	L_G Valuation of capital as societal facilities
		Value system as balance between production and consumption values.	

a business firm) for purposes of investment; (2) the firm's commitment of these funds to the acquisition of "real assets"—equipment, labour, organization, etc.; (3) the operative allocation of these real assets to specific productive tasks. Only at this last level of specificity does concrete production take place.

In a highly differentiated industrial economy, the first of these stages is the result of the contract of investment; the second and third occur as the result of decisions *within* the productive organization. As always, however, the empirical lines may not coincide with the analytical stages. Through ploughing back its earnings, for instance, the industrial firm may make its own contract of investment with itself, as it were, while the stockholders remain relatively passive.

Capital (generalized purchasing power), like labour power, does not merely spring into existence; it must be "produced" through institutionalized processes. Taking the level of generalized purchasing power as a starting-point again, let us work "up" the ladder of generalization to its origins.

One of the factors in purchasing power is the political element which underlies credit creation; the other major component is productivity in terms of both the current value of real assets and the expected future production from them. Productivity of course is a property of the economy and depends upon the combination of all the factors of production. Aside from its incorporation in the economy, what is the nature of productivity? Its most general component, it seems to us, is what we may call "technological know-how," i.e., empirical knowledge directly applicable to the technical tasks of production. This technological capacity sits at the next stage "above" generalized purchasing power, just as trained capacity of labour sits above membership in the labour force. Of course the total store of technological know-how may not be at the disposal of the economy, i.e., responsive to demands for its "employment" through the expenditure of generalized purchasing power, just as only part of the total supply of trained capacity is in the labour force. Technical know-how is not empirical knowledge as such, but is knowledge differentiated into modes of application and adapted to realistic production situations. It is the capacity, independent of particular resources, to control natural processes in the interests of productivity.

In order to assess the nature of the transition from technological know-how to generalized purchasing power, let us return momentarily to the labour problem. The step from trained capacity to membership in the labour force is as follows: given the trained capacity of the individual, which is the result of the socialization process, *plus* the motivation to enter the labour force and accept employment, then the worker becomes a member of the labour force. Likewise, given technological know-how, which is the result of certain previous processes, *plus* a power factor, then the facilities take the form of generalized purchasing power. This power factor is precisely the political control of funds through credit creation, which renders them acceptable as generalized resources throughout the economy and is the primary factor in their mobility as indicated above.

The next higher level above technological know-how in our series refers to the body of organized empirical knowledge itself, independent of its adaptation to any particular technological use. This codified knowledge is, in a word, the body of *scientific* resources which is potentially available for technological application. Finally, at the highest level of generality is the "given data" or "information" about the world of nature which is as yet unorganized into scientific or protoscientific categories. It is the cognitive "raw material" from which the technological component of productivity evolves, but several stages are necessary before concrete technology results.[1]

The common link between these several stages of generalization is the concept of *facilities.* As these facilities, which, as the "given data" about the natural world, in their most general form, progress toward greater and greater specification in the productive process, they are combined with certain other factors to make them more and more operative concretely.[2] Thus in the transition from "given data" to codified knowledge, there is an addition of cultural organization. In the stage from codified knowledge to technological know-how a certain type of situational information is added. As we have pointed out, the transition from technological know-how to generalized purchasing power involves the introduction of a power element which guarantees the general applicability, mobility, and acceptance of the facilities throughout the society. Generalized purchasing power, then, is interstitial between the economy

[1] In discussing these various "levels" of knowledge we make no claim as to the epistemological status of the several types we have isolated. For our purposes we treat these types of knowledge in terms of their significance as *facilities* ultimately to be applied to the productive process.

[2] The logic of this process of greater and greater specification is similar to the logic of "value added," which is used widely in characterizing the productive process.

and the polity in the same way that the labour force is interstitial between the economy and pattern-maintenance system. As the facilities progress further toward specification through investment, commitment to the factors of production, and assignment to specific tasks, various forms of social organization and concrete factors of production are added to make the facilities fully operative in the productive process. The higher stages of this diminishing series are internal to the pattern-maintenance system of society and hence are unfamiliar to economists; the lowest three levels of specification are, however, essentially a codification of familiar economic analysis.

Just as the scheme of levels of generality of the labour factor gives us some points of reference for analysing the institutional structure of occupational role types, so the scheme which discriminates among levels of capital resources or facilities gives us similar points of reference for analysing the institution of property. We may say that the three lowest levels in the scale concern the foci of property rights in physical objects of possession. There is a well-known classification of such rights which distinguishes rights of use, control and disposal. Use concerns the right to manipulate and to a degree "consume" objects of possession in a set of processes specified by the owner; thus a house may be "rented" to be used for residential purposes on terms agreed upon between tenant and owner. Control, then, means specification of *what* use shall be made of the assets and *by whom*, whereas disposal involves the right to alienate through sale or gift, and conversely to acquire, e.g., through purchase. We may say that the organizational echelons involved in task-performance necessarily have rights of use of equipment and materials. But in a developed organization it is generally a higher echelon which has rights of control, which has the authority for the *allocation* of equipment and materials to tasks and task-performing teams. Finally, it is the organization as a whole which has rights of disposal and acquisition.

Investment in the sense of commitment of monetary funds takes place between the holder of generalized purchasing power and the organization. The property rights held by the investor then are not rights in the "real assets" of the organization as such at all, but are "equity" rights held *against the organization.* The differentiation of these two levels of property rights is of course carried out with the establishment of corporate forms of organization, which distinguishes the operative part of the organization from the association of shareholders which has certain equity rights and rights of control.

Finally, the highest levels of the scale of generalization of facilities bring us into the cultural realm. But here also, in a highly differentiated society, we have classes of property rights. Thus patents constitute rights in the exclusive use of specific bits of technical know-how, and copyright is the form taken by property rights in codified knowledge as such.

Of course, only in a highly differentiated society are all these components of property rights clearly differentiated from each other. One basis of classification of property types is the degree to which this differentiation has taken place. There will also be further institutional variations in the specific ways in which each component is defined and limited and in the extent to which lower-order rights (in our scale) are controlled by higher-order rights.[1]

At several stages in the two hierarchies of generalizability which we have outlined—for human and non-human resources, respectively—a very important empirical asymmetry between these two factors appears. Let us explore a few of the implications of this basic bifurcation for economic analysis.

At the lowest level of generality the asymmetry concerns the difference between the application of labour to the process of production and the application of the "physical" means of production to the same process. The essential difference is that the human factor has to be "motivated" or "rewarded," whereas the physical factors merely have to be "maintained." In the case of the latter, the category of motivation applies only to the human agents which control the physical factors, not the instruments of production themselves. In different terms, human agents are involved in the *interplay* of performances and sanctions, whereas physical instruments are not.

In economic terms the basic distinction we have in mind is that between "goods" and "services" as a resultant of two

[1] Thus in Chap. V we will show that the separation of ownership and control as this has occurred in the American economy has led to a loosening in the subordination of the three lower-level property rights to equity rights.

further distinctions in the general theory of action: (1) between social and non-social objects, and (2) between quality and performance.[1] From a strictly economic viewpoint it can be argued that the distinction between goods and services should be obliterated.[2] All that is required for *economic* analysis on the most abstract level is that some service is contributed to the productive process, whether this service be the heat produced by an oil burner, the services produced by a typewriter, or the advice produced by a lawyer. Presumably all these services can be calculated according to their economic value, even though they emanate from different sorts of objects in different contexts.

Given this strictly economic logic, nevertheless to erase the distinction between human and non-human restricts the analysis of many problem-areas that are fundamental to economics as well as to its linkage with the rest of the general theory of social systems. Another aspect of the importance of the distinction lies in the fact that both capital goods and productivity as the basis of capital as monetary funds are produced partly at least *within* the economy and hence require investment decisions which are primarily economically oriented. Labour services, on the other hand, are not generated within the economy at all but in the household and the educational system, neither of which *can* be primarily an economic system. Of course there is an economic investment *aspect* involved in the commitment of resources to the "production" of labour power, but empirically this process is never guided by economic considerations nearly so directly as is investment in capital goods.

Certain very definite economic consequences follow from the distinction between human and non-human objects. In the first place, because of the *interactive* nature of human social action, only in markets for human services can cases of certain types of extensive and complicated feed-back mechanisms be found. This is illustrated in the case of the differences between the simple accelerator and multiplier concepts, respectively. It is no accident that the accelerator has been treated primarily as a mechanical ratio, involving only depreciation rates and

[1] Cf. Chap. I, pp. 11–12.

[2] This point is closely associated with the thought of Frank H. Knight. Cf. "Capital and Interest," *Encylcopaedia Britannica*, 1954, Vol. 4, p. 800.

capital requirements for expansion and/or contraction. Once the stimulated investment is completed the problem is to calculate depreciation rates, replacement, etc.; these rates do not react to changes in managers' behaviour, for instance. The multiplier, while it is often treated as a simple diminishing series based on the size of the marginal propensity to save, involves a whole complex of human roles and motivations dealing with the maintenance of patterns and management of tensions within the household as a social system. Thus the multiplier effect can be "interrupted" by human responses in a way in which the accelerator principle cannot. Of course, the accelerator principle is dependent upon human responses (human agents must order, purchase and build capital equipment which grows in response to rise in the income level), but because of the "non-human" character of the capital equipment itself, it differs in important characteristics from the multiplier principle.[1]

A much more fundamental series of consequences follows from the human-non-human distinction in the area of market structure. Because of the interaction and mutual response which always attend the incorporation of human services into the economy, we would expect *a priori* the proliferation of much more complicated types of imperfection in those markets which involve human services than in those for physical and/or cultural objects. While this distinction provides only the most general basis for investigating imperfection in markets,[2] it is sufficiently important to be maintained as a broad underlying characteristic of imperfection in various markets. To take an extreme example, because of the fact that slaves are human beings, not physical objects, certain restrictions on the market for slaves must be observed, even though *legally* slaves may be defined as indistinguishable from physical possessions. Even in

[1] For instance, it is theoretically impossible for the accelerator to work as fast on an income downswing as it does on an upswing of income, whereas the multiplier can work equally rapidly in either direction. Cf. Hicks, J. R., *Some Contributions to the Theory of the Trade Cycle*, 1950. We shall investigate the multiplier and accelerator concepts more thoroughly in Chap. IV, pp. 219–220.

[2] Cf. the analysis of the markets for labour, consumers' goods and services, capital funds and "productivity" below, pp. 146–175, for a more complex classification of types and bases of imperfection.

the most extreme cases of the institutionalization of slavery, there has always prevailed a minimum concern for the family life of the slaves, at least minimal concession to the fact that the slave must be motivated, if only by coercion and/or intimidation, etc. Economically this means rigidities such as immobility, non-transferability and indivisibility. Market structure, even in such extreme cases, cannot be independent of the fact that the economic object is human and hence subject to limiting exigencies. In less extreme cases, when the difference between social and non-social is recognized legally, the differences in market structure are even more apparent.

The same basic asymmetry appears at the higher levels of generality. Labour, when committed to a firm, cannot be dissociated from the person of the worker. Hence in all stages of the utilization of labour his total motivational system—from which his willingness and capacity to work have been derived—is in some sense operative in the work process. On the other hand, there is no necessary empirical connection between the specific technological process by which a quantity of purchasing power is generated and those by which it is utilized in production. Hence the utilization of labour at all levels involves specific constraints which the utilization of capital does not.[1]

This completes our analysis of the general framework of the economy's organization in terms of the institution of contract and the regulation of the economy's two most "active" boundaries. We have tried to show that, if the role or market is treated as a system of action, the primary quids and quos of the market interchange are synonymous with the goal-components of these systems. (Of course the statement of the goal-interchange differs according to whether the system of reference is the role of one contracting party, the interactive relation of a contracting pair, or the total market as a system.)

[1] In terms of the theory of action, labour as a factor corresponds to the input of motivation or "motive force" into systems of action, capital to that of "information." In slightly different terms they correspond to the categories of rewards and facilities, respectively. We will use this distinction again in Chap. V. For its most general statements, cf. *Working Papers in the Theory of Action*, *op. cit.*, Chap. V, and *Family, Socialization and Interaction Process*, *op. cit.*, Chap. IV.

The other relevant elements of contract define the adaptive facilities, the integrative patterns and the common value system of the contract relation. Only when all four components are considered can the basis of market equilibrium be understood, even though for some purposes one or more components may be held constant.

In a very tentative way we tried to illustrate that the four components in any contract are special cases of the types of content which are exchanged between the primary functional sub-systems at the societal level, as outlined in Chapter II. Or conversely, all the major interchanges at the societal level are involved in every contractual relation within the society, but in different combinations. The *G*-component of any given contractual system is always governed by the position of this contract *vis-à-vis* the major boundary interchanges. The other components of the contract will vary, however.

This line of analysis, which we could barely begin at this time, is an extension of the proposition that every one of the primary functions of the society is involved in the functioning of every concrete collectivity in society. Thus a firm is primarily economic, but it has political, integrative, and pattern-maintenance functions. Similarly, even though a contract is primarily economic (i.e., the exchange of some economic good, such as consumers' goods, has primacy), all the other types of symbolic interchange are involved in the transaction or set of transactions. This follows from our treatment of the contractual relation as a social system.

Finally, the symbolic content of any boundary interchange stands in a series of different levels of generality; we spelled these series out for labour and capital, which are introduced into the economy through the contracts of employment and investment, respectively. In each case the generalized factor of production, as treated by economic theory, stands as the middle term of a seven-level series. Both labour and capital, as they proceed toward greater specificity, are incorporated more and more fully into the economic process. As labour and capital proceed toward higher levels of generality, however, the processes become further and further removed from economic considerations. In the case of labour the three highest levels of generality are identical with the major stages of socialization as sociologists and psychologists have analysed them. In the case of capital the first stage "upward" is partly political, partly cultural; it is the implementation of technical know-how in the interest of productivity. Higher still stand two "cultural" levels, that of codified empirical knowledge and that of the given data of nature. Figure 11 shows the several stages of diminishing generality for both human and non-human resources, as well as the several transitions between these levels.[1]

FIGURE 11

LEVELS OF GENERALITY OF ECONOMIC RESOURCES AND THEIR IMPLEMENTATION IN PRODUCTION

Levels	*Human Resources*	*Non-human Resources*
7	Primary Socialized Motivation [Intra-latency]	"Given data" (information) [Intra-latency]
6	Generalized Performance Capacity [Intra-latency]	Codified Empirical Knowledge [Intra-latency]
5	Trained Capacity [Interstitial: Latency-Economy]	Technological Know-How [Interstitial: Economy-Polity]
4	Generalized Labour Power (the Labour Force) [Commitment to Economy]	Generalized Purchasing Power [Commitment to Economy]
3	Labour Committed to Firms [Intra-firm]	Capital Funds Committed to Firms [Intra-firm]
2	Labour Assigned to Productive Functions (Roles) [Intra-firm]	Acquisition of Capital Goods [Intra-firm]
1	Utilization in Task Performance	Utilization in Task Performance

FACTOR GENERALIZATION AND ECONOMIC ORGANIZATION

Occupation and property are the institutional foci of labour and capital, respectively, as factors of production. We will consider the institutionalization of land factors toward the end of the chapter. First, however, we will compare and contrast the institutions of occupation and property a little further, then apply some of this and the foregoing analysis to the problem of the structure of markets.

[1] In Chap. V we will attempt to show the bearing of this scheme of levels of generality for the process of structural change in the economy.

Following long economic tradition, we have treated the goal of production as the provision of consumers with *concrete* want-satisfying goods and services. For this function, concrete processes within organizations and concrete exchanges at their boundaries involve the factors of production at the lowest levels of generality and fluidity. What, therefore, is the significance of the higher levels we have distinguished? Are they not merely some kind of superfluous epiphenomena?

In a sufficiently "primitive" economy, economic processes and decisions can operate at the level of concrete physical means of production and the concrete services of individuals. This is possible, however, only in societies in which the economy is undifferentiated from other systems. Among the necessary conditions for such a state are: (1) some organization exists independently of specifically economic functions (this is almost universally a kinship unit in primitive cases); (2) claims to labour services are defined ascriptively by virtue of these organizational (kinship) solidarities; and (3) the unit of organization has rights of residence and possession in land which is the source of physical capital. Modification of these conditions usually means direct acquisition of resources of lower-level segmentary units by economically and politically superior larger units.[1]

Of course, the kinship unit must have at least some rule-of-thumb means of estimating economic and other values of labour and capital resources. But articulation with other units is at a minimum.

When a number of such units becomes involved in economically significant interaction (i.e., when a market situation arises), a more generalized basis of evaluating and comparing economic goods becomes necessary. Lowest order money appears at this point; it functions as a symbolic representation of economic value in consumers' goods and services and—by generalization—in the concrete factors of production. Without such a measure of value and medium of exchange these units could not continue to function as an interdependent economic system. The appearance of money in some form, therefore, is

[1] Cf. Firth, R., *Primitive Polynesian Economy*, 1939, and Fortes, M., *The Web of Kinship among the Tallensi*, 1949, for detailed analyses of these segmentary societies.

closely associated with the break-down of self-sufficient, segmentary units and the appearance of the division of labour.

The division of labour creates the further functional problem of closing the circle of feed-back relations in the system of interdependent units. As long recognized, if unit *A* specializes in the production of goods and services for units *B*, *C*, *D* . . . *N*, then it receives money which is useless unless this money has purchasing power over *other* goods and services. With the division of labour, therefore, a system of exchange develops whereby units can use some of the money returns for their specialized products to acquire other specialized products.

In turn, for the exchange of specialized consumers' goods to be possible, there must be a market for labour and for capital goods as factors of production whereby these particularized factors are evaluated in terms of a more generalized standard. Such a market also implies institutionalized willingness to contract for the use of labour services and capital goods by units other than the original possessors. Finally, these labour and capital goods' markets must have standards commensurable with those in the consumers' goods and services markets; hence the generalization of a common monetary system generalizes to all the existing markets.

At this point the third level of generality emerges. It becomes possible to exchange not only goods and services, but also *generalized power* to command whatever particular factors may be required. This transfer of generalized power takes place whenever units exchange money funds.

By this time, the asymmetry between the two most "disposable" factors of production has appeared.[1] This asymmetry arises, firstly, because labour service is not separable physically from the performing agent, and secondly, because the agent has anchorages outside the economy which cannot be abandoned. Unless, therefore, the household or its functional equivalent is destroyed or absorbed into the economy,[2] there must be certain adjustments between the occupational role and extra-economic roles. Physical goods, on the other hand, do not present obstacles to complete economic control; they

[1] Cf. above, pp. 134–137, for discussion of the asymmetry between physical resources and labour resources.

[2] Either of these situations implies slavery.

can be fully owned and controlled within the organization. Notwithstanding the extra-economic involvement of the agent of labour services, however, generalized purchasing power can come to "stand for" and to a degree "control" both physical goods and labour services.

A final problem—the *extent* of the control of money—rests upon the degree of ramification of the system of interchanges of both consumers' goods and services and the factors of production. Generalized purchasing power is, as we have emphasized, a symbolic mechanism for controlling human behaviour. Of course, it never stands alone; other mechanisms can counteract it. But as the system of social interaction, within which it is an indispensable mechanism of control expands and ramifies, it becomes imperative to define the boundary between the core area within which it operates as a control and the peripheral area where it is of secondary importance.

Because of the phenomenon of *interpenetration*, an economy, where "money talks," cannot be strictly and absolutely segregated from a contiguous sector of the society which excludes monetary considerations entirely. There must be certain "boundary zones" between the economy and other sub-systems of the society in which generalized purchasing power is relatively effective as a means of purchasing, as an ingredient of power, etc. These boundary zones are the foci of some degree of institutionalization whereby distinctions can be made between the commitment of money to the economy as capital funds and its availability for important alternative uses. This is purchasing power institutionalized at its *most* general level, one level higher than fluid capital resources.

The level of generalization of the factors of production is therefore not merely adventitious; it develops in accordance with the differentiation of an economy from other sub-systems and its simultaneous maintenance of integrative ties within itself and with these other sub-systems. Without such mechanisms, the economy could maintain neither its own differentiated level nor its boundary relationships with other sub-systems. One of the major institutional parts of the whole complex of economic institutions, therefore, is the set of expectations with respect to the uses of money, the conditions of its transfer, etc. It is as much an economic institution as the contractual regulation of employment and investment and the exchange of concrete goods and services.

The upper (i.e., more generalized) levels of our seven-level scheme involve considerations less relevant to economic theory. In a sense these higher levels are precisely the obverse of those reviewed in the above paragraphs. In the case of labour, the problem is not the *requirement* of a mobile labour force and the mechanisms of its allocation; rather the question is how motivation can be organized so that people will allow their activity to be controlled in the interest of production goals, especially outside the household context. This can occur only through an elaborate process of socialization; we will develop this subject at the end of the chapter in connection with economic motivation. Suffice it to say at present that adequate motivation for productive performance in a highly differentiated economy can no more be taken for granted than the availability of the complex products of production themselves.

The problem of the genesis of fluid purchasing power for use as capital is parallel. Just as the industrial economy requires greater discipline and a higher degree of socialization of its labour force than less developed economies, so it requires more fluid capital which is disposable over wider ranges of production. A prime condition of this is not only technological development but the underlying scientific extension of empirical knowledge.

THE INSTITUTIONAL STRUCTURE OF MARKETS

Having outlined some of the sociological bases of market transactions, we may now turn to a central problem area of economic theory—the structure of markets. What is meant by the "perfect market," and by the differing degrees and kinds of "imperfection"? What is the relationship between the structure of contractual regulations and the imperfection of the market?

Contract, as we have developed that concept, is at the focus of the notion of the market; every market transaction involves an explicit or implicit contract. In any contractual relationship, and hence in any institutionalized market, we have distinguished four components in the orientation of each of the contracting parties: (1) *G*, the primary immediate goal sought by the contracting partner, ego; this goal is always a balance of his performance contribution against the sanction-contribution expected from alter; (2) *A*, the relevant organizational context on both sides of the relationship, adjusted, of course, to the relevant time span of the relationship; (3) *I*, the diffuse symbolic significances to ego of both *G* and *A* on both sides of the contractual relationship; (4) *L*, the common value patterns which, in their respective ways, ego shares in the interactive context with alter.

It seems to us that certain economic theories of imperfect competition concern on the *G* and partially the *A* components of the market relationship. The other two components are either eliminated completely or assumed explicitly or implicitly to be constant for purposes of economic analysis.

To illustrate this conclusion: the economic analysis of the continuum from pure competition to pure monopoly is a matter of the *G*-focus of the contractual orientation, i.e., the "quid" and "quo" elements. In pure monopoly certain advantages accrue to the firm so that it is able to control the supply and price of "quids"; within the limits of the strength of the buyer's need and his capacity to pay, the firm may exact its own terms in the transaction. In pure competition no one firm has any advantage over any other, so that if one firm attempts to charge higher prices, the buyer turns to an alternative source of supply. Imperfect competition is an intermediate state where advantages leading to a certain degree of control—but not full control—accrue to a limited number of firms. At the base of the theory of imperfect competition, therefore, is an assumption of a certain imbalance of power which results from a differential advantage on one side of the market.[1]

Economists have outlined conditions of supply and demand, optimum productivity and efficiency, cost curves, etc., under varying conditions of imperfection. The major contribution of Mrs. Robinson's work in this field, for instance, is her elabora-

[1] Whether this power or control is used in a "political" sense or whether it is the result of the pursuit of "economically rational" values on either or both sides of the market is an irrelevant issue; the point is that some power imbalance arises between the contracting partners.

tion of the varying conditions of equilibrium for supply and demand schedules other than those of perfect competition.[1]

But what are the conditions of imperfection? What are the *sources* of the power imbalance? In terms of our paradigm, what are the conditions to which either ego or alter (or both) must adapt which lead to relative disadvantage or advantage in the market situation and to the development of features of the market which are not obvious cases of economic rationality? Economists' elaboration of these adaptive conditions has not, in our terms, been carried very far. For instance, Professor Chamberlin defines two empirical conditions—number of sellers and differentiation of product—as the bases of classifying forms of imperfection.[2] These are, in a general way, *adaptive* bases of classification. In the first place, the number of sellers is one aspect of organizational context on the side of the firm, to which both the firm and the household must adapt. Depending upon the number of sellers, the household is placed at a greater or lesser bargaining disadvantage; the supply-demand equilibrium is correspondingly modified to produce an imperfectly competitive market situation. In the second place, the specific adaptive needs of the household require a certain differentiation of product; hence substitutability is limited or altogether out of the question. This places the household at a kind of disadvantage, which is overcome by offering greater sanctions.

These two bases of imperfection in various combinations produce pure competition, oligopoly, monopolistic competition, monopoly, etc., and equilibrium conditions in the usual economic sense can be specified for each. While certain extensions of the classification of the bases of imperfection have been suggested,[3] it is our impression that the theory of imperfect

[1] Robinson, Joan, *Economics of Imperfect Competition*, 1933.

[2] Chamberlin, E. H., *Theory of Monopolistic Competition*, *op. cit.*

[3] Bain, for instance, extended Chamberlin's bases of imperfect competition on the grounds that the classification to be derived from these two is too limiting theoretically. We agree with Bain's criticism. But what categories does he suggest as a sample supplementary list? Whether the goods are durable or non-durable; whether they are producers' goods or consumers' goods; the importance of product variation, and the number of buyers. While the supplementary categories on this list are undoubtedly relevant, the question of the sociological structure of the market situation

competition is not a point of departure for the sociological analysis of markets, for two reasons: (1) its analysis of the adaptive conditions of the market situation is undeveloped, and (2) there has been a nearly complete lack of attention to the *I*- and the *L*-components of the market situation.

We would like to take this brief critique of certain writings in the field and the institutional groundwork earlier in the chapter as the starting-points for outlining some sociological reference-points for the empirical analysis of various types of markets.

In our terms the concept of the perfect market thus implies two assumptions: (1) either sufficient regulation or sufficient competition so that the settlement of terms is not skewed toward the advantage of either side of the market as a whole or toward any unit or units on either side. This assumption includes an equality of power on both sides of the market. (2) symmetry of "type of interest" with respect to the contractual components of the market in question, with the exception of the *G*-component, which is the focus of the power factor. On these grounds, plus the usual economic ones, only a market internal to the economy can approximate the ideal type of market perfection closely. The basic reason for such an assertion is that the second assumption cannot be met when parties to the contract are governed by primacies of different functional sub-systems of the society.

We will deal with four markets which link different sub-systems. At the goal-attainment boundary of the economy we will treat the labour market and the market for consumers' goods; at the adaptive boundary we will discuss the capital funds market and the market for "control of productivity," in that order. These four are most definitely not imperfect in degree, but show different *qualitative types* of imperfection. At the end of the section we will introduce, more or less systematically, a method of classifying such types sociologically.

Let us begin with the labour market, since certain constraints which underlie its imperfections are particularly salient. In order to illustrate the range of constraints we will deal with

is not considered problematical. Cf. Bain, Joe S., "Market Classification in Modern Price Theory," *Quarterly Journal of Economics*, 1941–42, pp. 560–574.

three sub-types of the market for labour: (1) the market for labour services at a low level of technical competence and a low degree of organizational responsibility, (2) the market for executive services, and (3) the market for professional services.

Since the American value system and its institutionalization is skewed in the direction of a strong adaptive emphasis, we would expect a relatively heavy general input of labour services relative to corresponding outputs from the economy. High wages in the United States are, therefore, more a consequence of high productivity than of high bargaining power of labour relative to other factors. In our terms, the labour market is skewed toward the economy in its *G*-component.

The nature of the *A*-component rests upon the fact that labour, unlike capital goods and liquid funds, cannot be separated from the person of the contributor. The labour input at the adaptive boundary is certain "rights to intervene"; in exchange for these the worker gains access to credit on behalf of his household. This adaptive input is probably as important as labour service itself, since it is the basic immediate acceptance of authority and discipline in the work situation.

The more diffuse integrative (*I*) and value (*L*) components of the labour market are, respectively, "contingent support" and "moral approval," on the part of the firm. These form the basis for the worker to return a positive diffuse acceptance of the firm as well as a sufficiently strong valuation of the labour relation to justify confidence in placing the security of the household upon the labour market.

Given these components, the special exigences of the household are particularly crucial in determining the imperfections of the labour market. In modern industrial society the household has been segregated from other social structures and typically has been reduced in numbers to the members of the operative nuclear family. Thus specialized, it has surrendered its economic independence to the labour market. Hence the "breadwinner" has assumed a special responsibility, since the economic security of the household and its position in the community depend largely upon his ability to secure and maintain a good job. An essential characteristic of the labour market, therefore, is that the worker stands, almost by definition, in a low level of organizational responsibility in the firm since he has given up important rights to intervene to the employer; but his organizational responsibility for the security and prestige of his household is paramount.

Economic writers since Adam Smith have emphasized the relative bargaining disadvantage of the individual worker; *viz.* one employer employs many workers; an employer can dispense with the services of a worker more readily than the latter can do without a job; the employer can afford to wait while the worker cannot, etc. Such imbalances in role systems usually give rise to compensatory mechanisms in the social structure. The most significant of these mechanisms in industrial countries is the trade union, which has not failed to appear in the labour market of any industrial society.[1]

The functions of the union, we feel, strongly highlight the importance of the terms of the labour contract *other* than the specific balance between work and wages (G). Unions are conspicuously concerned, in the first place, with the firm's rights to intervene (A), i.e., the extent to which the worker is subject to management's authority and the terms on which disputes in this area are settled. These elements are often the subject both of explicit bargaining and of implicit compromise between management and union. In the I and L contexts the union's significance, however, lies not so much in its efficacy as a bargaining agency as in its reinforcement of attitudes. These attitudes concern the acceptance of the general conditions of employment in the industry, if not the individual firm, and hence the willingness to entrust the household's interests to the labour market.

Some of the union's functions are thus semi-ritual rather than bargaining. They integrate the individual worker and his household into a larger collectivity, membership in which enhances his self-respect and confidence in the justification and success-prospects of his occupational role. In turn, such enhanced self-respect and confidence can stimulate management, under the proper conditions, to give a larger output of contingent support and moral approval of the labour role to the household.

[1] Soviet Russia, where there are unions but no collective bargaining, is a special case because both unions and management are absorbed in a single superordinate organization, the party-state apparatus.

Of couse, as usual economic analysis shows, the union is in part a counter-monopoly to the inevitable monopolistic elements in large-scale industrial organization; indeed it sometimes goes beyond this counterbalancing position. But its equally important non-economic functions adapt the "human element" of the labour force to the exigencies of an occupational role; in particular the union helps the worker to reconcile his inevitable involvements in both firm and household with each other. It performs these functions both by protecting the worker's "interests" through bargaining and by symbolizing his anxieties and other sentiments and reinforcing his self-respect and confidence.

In such cases the mechanisms of social control often break down, resulting, in the labour market, in the exacerbation of the latent conflict of interest between management and labour. It is difficult to believe, however, that so massive a phenomenon as trade unionism in the Western world is significant only on the level of protecting labour's narrow "interest," particularly since its development has coincided with rapid increases in the productivity and real wages of labour. We interpret unionism as a necessary reinforcement of the heavy input of labour service and rights to intervene which are demanded in an industrial economy. Furthermore, this occurs largely through *non-economic* mechanisms of the type involved in rituals, political campaigns and therapy.[1]

The second illustrative occupational complex is the market for executive services. In earlier times the executive role was primarily "capitalistic" in the specific sense that ownership and executive responsibility were fused. Through the "separation of ownership and control,"[2] however, especially in the United

[1] Another phenomenon in the American labour market in the recent past seems to fit into the context of protecting the interests of the household. This phenomenon is the trend of involvement of more than one member of the household in the labour force, particularly through increasing employment of married women (cf. Dewhurst, F., *et al.*, *America's Needs and Resources*, 1955, pp. 91 ff). Although additions to earnings are one basis of this trend, the reduction of risk by not placing all the household eggs in the basket of a single breadwinner's occupational role may have something to do with it.

[2] Berle, A. A., and Means, G. C., *The Modern Corporation and Private Property*, 1932.

States, responsible management functions have passed to occupational roles in the organization rather than "proprietors." The manager's relation to the organization rests at present more on a contract of employment than on a contract of investment.

While the primary interchange in the executive contract of employment is between household and firm, the labour and executive roles differ substantially (above and beyond the latter's ownership status in the firm, if it exists at all). As we have seen, the degree of organizational responsibility must be realistically low for the industrial worker; for the executive, however, his occupational role prescribes a high level of responsibility. If anything, this responsibility is greater than his responsibility to his household. Hence there are likely to be repercussions on the structure of the executive's family; more particularly, the wife tends to assume a disproportionately large share of the household responsibility in even broader spheres than the traditionally feminine ones.[1]

Because of the superiority and power of his position in the firm, the executive on the whole need be concerned less realistically with his household's "security" and with his acceptance by the firm than the labourer. Even though he has a higher standard of living to maintain, he is far less likely to be "laid off" when business is slack, and the resources to carry his family over difficult periods are incomparably greater. The one great hazard is his death or incapacitation. It is probably significant, therefore, that American business executives carry a large volume of life and disability insurance.

Given the executive's extensive control and responsibility, it is not surprising that no "bargaining association" represents this occupational group against the firm either in its "intrinsic" or its "symbolic" functions. It would be wrong, however, to conclude that some functional equivalent of the union is altogether absent. Above and beyond the firm is a "business community" segmented into trade associations, executives' clubs, and so on. These groups perpetuate a business "public opinion," with respect to problems of the suitability of salary

[1] For an interesting journalistic account of the extent of this, cf. Whyte, W. H., Jr., "Corporation and the Wife," *Fortune*, November, 1951, pp. 109–111.

levels, retirement plans, bases of promotion, dismissal, etc.—many of them, problems of the type which concern labour unions. This business community is also responsible for a conspicuous output of ideological matter[1] which expresses business leaders' concern for matters of organizational responsibility with special reference to the "principles" on which the whole economy is organized. This concern we believe derives from the integrative and value aspects of their roles, not primarily from their "economic interests" in the usual sense.

The market for executive services, therefore, involves no more a "purely economic" balancing of advantage than does the contract for labour in the narrower sense. Several mechanisms provide an integrative "compromise" between the firm's more nearly economic interests and values and the household's non-economic interest and values. These mechanisms involve a set of structures organized about the status-security problems of executives. Investigation of these problem areas would contribute to the analysis of stratification in the upper ranges of American society.[2]

The market for professional services points up even further departures from the norm of the perfect market than the two previous cases. From the point of view of the structure of the contract of employment, there are three main types of professional role. The first is the professional role in a business firm.[3] The employment market is similar to the market for executive services, with the important exception that a professional's level of organizational responsibility in the firm is necessarily lower than the executive's.[4] He has, however, an integrative type of responsibility for his professional group besides his firm and his household.[5] By virtue of a commitment to his profession, the engineer, for example, is responsible for the maintenance of technical engineering standards even if this at times is not fully in accord with his business employer's

[1] Cf. Sutton, Harris, Sawyer, Tobin, *et al.*, *The American Business Creed*, 1956.

[2] *Ibid.*

[3] This is becoming an increasingly important case in the United States, especially for engineers and lawyers.

[4] Empirically there are many transitions and combinations, of course.

[5] Cf. Parsons and Bales, *Family, Socialization and Interaction Process*, *op. cit.*, Chap. II, pp. 165 ff.

interest. His freedom to give weight to "professional integrity" is at least an implied element in the contract of employment.

In the second type, the professional person is not employed by a business firm at all, but, as in the case of the physician in private practice, is "employed" piecemeal by a plurality of patients. In this case a conspicuous set of phenomena—the "sliding scale" and others—distort the relevant markets greatly from the perfect market model.

The sliding scale is the provision[1] whereby the physician charges not by "value of service," but according to the capacity of the patient or his household to pay. This is a clear case of price discrimination from the economic point of view. It is usually accompanied by other restrictions on the "pursuit of economic self-interest," such as the prohibition of advertising and open price competition on the part of the physician, of "shopping around" on the part of the patient, etc.[2]

We explain such phenomena by the fact that a certain type of solidary collectivity is established between doctor and patient when the patient is being treated. In this relationship—to which ego either belongs or does not—each member assumes an obligation to contribute according to his ability, financially and otherwise, to maintain the collectivity. The patient has obligations to his household while the physician, like any other worker in the division of labour, has imperatives stemming from his family membership. The sliding scale is the resultant balance. But it is not *primarily* a balance between economic and non-economic interests and values, but between two primarily non-economic ones; the economic considerations which, of course, inevitably enter are subsidiary to *both* interest-value complexes.

Remembering that the patient is the employer and the physician is the "worker," let us apply our technical analytical terms to the market for medical services. First, a taboo is imposed on any explicit bargaining for settlement of terms (G). Closely related is the prohibition of "shopping around" in the sense that the prospective patient seeks the independent advice of several physicians before choosing among them. Such taboos clearly impede short-term economic adjustments between the supply and demand of such services.

[1] Most common in the more specialized branches of medicine.

[2] Cf. Parsons, *The Social System*, Chap. X.

In the *A*-category the professional practitioner gives up only a small quantity of rights to intervene by virtue of his technical competence and corresponding authority; he remains the judge of how his labour power is to be exercised, in striking contrast to the industrial worker.

This heavy deficit in the *A* output category from the household and the rigidity of *G* indicates the likelihood of a balance by heavy outputs in other categories. The solidary collectivity as the crucial feature of the physician-patient relationship means a concentration on the *I*-component of the employment relation. It is an output of "contingent support" to the physician by the patient, without too specific reference to the value of given services. This implies an obligation to be "loyal" to the physician, or to "have confidence" in him, in terms current in the profession itself. This *I*-component more than the others governs the "wage" payment. Instead of paying the physician "what his services are worth" on a marginal productivity basis, the patient pays "what he can afford" as his contribution to the collectivity.

Finally, the values governing the relationship do not give primacy to economic considerations on either side. The service of the professional man is not to be defined primarily as a factor in "production" in the technical economic sense, but as a mechanism of control. Hence the sanction of moral approval is not in the economic sense a reward for the "efficiency" of the physician, but rather for his competence and integrity in the performance of a non-economic function. Economic considerations of course enter as necessary conditions; the physician "has to live" and the fee is the patient's contribution to meeting this exigency.

In less obvious forms, the principle of the sliding scale is fairly widespread in our society.[1] Clergymen, for example, receive their salaries from the voluntary contributions of their parishioners. In a sense the parishioners "purchase" this service. Clearly, however, they contribute according to their ability to pay, not at a rate commensurate with the "marginal utility" of the service.

A third situation in which professional services are marketed is in primarily non-economic organizations, such as the

[1] Cf. note, Chap. IV, p. 226.

university, the hospital, or the government agency. All such organizations in our society are characterized by concealed or indirect versions of the sliding scale. In part this is because the beneficiaries of their services do not pay their costs in fees based upon marginal productivity; the *G*-component is fixed by some kind of administrative decision of reasonableness or fairness to the beneficiaries. Voluntary contributions or taxation make up the balance. When contributions are voluntary, they are expected to be in relation to the income of the contributor—to "what he can afford" not to the specific "value of service." In cases of taxation, the progressive principle has become established firmly in Western countries.

In all these cases the professional man's remuneration is primarily by salary and is mediated through the organization. Hence this *G*-component resembles the market for executive services in a bureaucratized firm rather than individual fee-for-service markets. For example, salary levels are differentiated according to levels of competence and degree of organizational responsibility. It is permissible for candidates for professional jobs to consider the financial advantages of alternative opportunities. The main difference between the market for executive services and that for professional services is the "level" of salaries in the latter is something for which the "authorities" must take responsibility; they often must raise the money to make a fair level remuneration possible. This phenomenon stems in part from the competitive pressure of alternative opportunities in business organizations; but it also stems from the relative importance of the two functions in society. Given the adaptive emphasis in the American value system, it is no accident that the remuneration levels in professional organizations are significantly lower (by a factor of perhaps 3–5) than those of corresponding levels of competence and responsibility in "business."

Another phenomenon in this area which deserves special attention is the institution of tenure. This is the institution by which the contract of employment is protected against termination by replacing ego's services either at a lower salary or by a more efficient performer. It is most widespread in the academic profession, though it is also prominent in the civil service aspect of government. So far as we know it is not recognized *explicitly* in business organizations, though a great deal of informal practice accords with it.

One aspect of the tenure problem is associated with the fact that the product, of, say, a university, cannot be "sold" on a free market at anything approaching a break-even point. It is sufficiently highly valued in non-economic respects, however, for some agency to take the responsibility for its "production." The fact that a university needs subsidy[1] means that those who commit themselves to such a function on a professional basis (involving years of expensive training and sacrifice of alternatives) take a special kind of risk *vis-à-vis* their household responsibilities. Their commitment to the academic profession's values and its internal psychological rewards are some recompense, but seem not to be sufficient. Tenure may thus be interpreted as part of the compensations for assuming such a risk. It is not an "economic" arrangement in a direct sense, but is grounded in non-economic considerations on *both* sides. Naturally it may entail the economic cost of paying an economically sub-standard employee over a long period.

In technical terms the explanation of tenure follows from the relative predominance of the *L*- and *I*-components of the labour contract, especially the former, over the *G*- and *A*-components. It is significant that tenure is found only in organizations with non-economic primacy. We interpret this phenomenon of tenure as a symbol of moral approval which "compensates" the risk involved in commitment to an occupational role which cannot be supported directly from the proceeds of production; it justifies confidence in entrusting the security of the household not primarily to the "market" but to those agencies responsible for economically "non-productive" functions.

Tenure in the university context seems to be most closely related to the common values (*L*) of the contract of employment. Both education and research are primarily pattern-maintenance functions. They cannot be expected immediately to "pay off" in production terms. In the academic profession, furthermore, the standards of successful performance are overwhelmingly universalistic; i.e., they cannot be referred to

[1] Which in turn is associated with some obstacles to full mass acceptance of the product.

any specific solidary collectivity.[1] Tenure is a mechanism of insulating the university personnel from other pressures, particularly economic ones. Thus it may be especially important in a society with a heavy emphasis on economic values.

Government service is the other most conspicuous case of the institutionalization of tenure; its basis differs from that of tenure in the academic case, however. From the standpoint of "making its way in society," government employment is not such a bad risk to the employee as is academic employment. Even more than in the industrial firm, however, government employment requires a heavy input of rights to intervene by the worker. In our society, furthermore, this input is balanced neither by high prestige (as in England, for example) nor by high financial remuneration (as in business). In this context tenure functions to render the position of the civil or military servant motivationally more tolerable in our society.[2]

To conclude this discussion of the labour market, we must make clear what we are *not* saying. By pointing up the *sociological* variability of the structure of the market for labour services, we do not assert that labour supply curves in the usual economic sense cannot be drawn. To say this would be to eliminate *any* economic elements from the market. We do suggest, however, that on theoretical grounds, it is possible to establish the basic characteristics of such curves rather than treat them *post hoc* as "conditions of the market." In short, our purpose is not to establish the facts of the market in the narrow sense, but to provide determinate sociological standards whereby the facts of the market may be established before rather than after the fact.

The market for consumers' *goods*, we have noted, is likely to be less imperfect economically than any of the variants of the labour market. The fundamental reason underlying this proposition is that control of a physical commodity can be

[1] Which is one reason why the university is suspect when integrative pressures are high.

[2] For such reasons, the use of security clearance procedures in ways which threaten tenure in civil service may be particularly disruptive of service morale in this society. Furthermore, businessmen may not be duly sensitive to the importance of this problem, since tenure does not have the same order of significance to them.

transferred completely from its "producer" to its "consumer," subject only to very general "public interest" forms of regulation. But a *service* is inseparable from the performer's person; his other role-involvements inevitably impinge upon the situation in which the service is performed.

Under certain circumstances, therefore, it may be misleading to refer to the consumers' market in terms of goods *and* services without distinguishing between the two. Since the performance of a service for a customer is analytically a part of the labour market,[1] to lump goods and services together in the same market confuses the labour market and consumers' market. Of course, in a highly differentiated society some organization often intervenes between customer and performer of service in order to settle financial terms and other matters. In such cases, however, the employing organization overlaps in function with a trade union; analytically, the employers are still the customers.[2] Hence in our discussion of the consumers' market we will deal with goods only; services are to be treated in terms of the labour market paradigm.

Most economic analysis of the consumers' market has been concerned with the balance of price and output in the settlement of terms (*G*-component). To illustrate the importance of the other components, let us concentrate on a familiar phenomenon in our society, often referred to as the "one-price" system. This institution tends to eliminate bargaining over price in the immediate transaction; the purchaser decides whether or not to buy and in what quantity, *given* the set price. Of course this system is far from universal in our society; discounts of various sorts are often offered. By comparison with other societies, however, it is conspicuous in the United States and most of north-western Europe. The one-price system is combined with a high degree of "consumer sovereignty," i.e., there is relatively little obligation to continue

[1] For the rationale for this assignment, cf. Chap. I, pp. 11–12, where the sociological basis for the distinction between goods and services is developed.

[2] Thus the purveyor of a service is analogous to a professional practitioner, once the step has been taken from purely "private practice" to his employment by an organization for the performance of professional services, e.g., a hospital.

patronage of a particular retail outlet on grounds of "loyalty."[1]

As in the case of the taboos on bargaining and shopping around in the professional relationship, the one-price system rigidifies the *G*-component of the market to some extent. It constrains the free pursuit of economic interest of one or both parties in the immediate transaction; its explanation therefore must be sought in some pressure operating through the other components. What are the sources of such pressure?

First, because of the prominence of adaptive values in American society, the input-output balance presumably is tipped in favour of the economy in a particular sense. The impetus is to maximize *production*; hence the marketing problem is more serious than in a less production-oriented system. Furthermore, a variety of sociological considerations suggest that the problem of such an economy is not to "satisfy" essentially insatiable or expanding wants, but rather to break through the "traditionalistic" barriers to change in established consumption standards. The motivational structures which stabilize consumption standards, like those involved in motivation to labour, involve primarily integrative and value-pattern components and hence are not most directly responsive to short-run economic sanctions.

Before discussing these problems, we might note another important feature of the American market which centres in the adaptive component. An increasingly important share of the consumers' market has come to be dominated by durable goods of a mechanical type, operation of which is in the hands of the householder, e.g., automobiles, automatic heating, refrigeration, washing machines, etc. The household itself has thereby become capitalized to an unprecedented degree.

This affects the perfection of the market for such goods in two main ways: (1) Quality depends so much upon technical considerations that the average consumer is less able to judge quality competently than in the case of more traditional goods (e.g., foodstuffs). He must rely on the reputation of the

[1] In France, attachment to such outlets is very important; where this particularistic tie does not apply, relatively unrestricted *ad hoc* bargaining tends to develop.

manufacturer and the dealer.[1] (2) The *operation* of such equipment in terms of repairs and servicing requires technical competence and equipment which the householder does not command. Hence the consumer assumes a continuing dependence either on the manufacturer or on some servicing organization. Both these imperfections make it more difficult to treat the contract of purchase as an isolated, *ad hoc* transaction. In technical terms, the customer presents a substantially larger output of "control of productivity" to the economy than in the case of traditional consumers' products.

Such factors suggest the importance of solidarity and common-value factors in such transactions. These must have a particular structure, however, in order not to interfere with the "extent of the market." This provision precludes what we think of as the "French" solution of the problem, i.e., the particularistic attachment of the customer to a particular retail outlet. Loyalty to the retailer, furthermore, is readily associated with traditionalized loyalty to the latter's traditional line of goods. This is incompatible with the high level of "consumer sovereignty" which the American consumer undoubtedly enjoys. Producers must, that is, stand or fall according to the acceptability of their products by a very wide consuming public. The mode of integration must allow a large output of "binding decisions" by consumers.

In the United States this problem has been met by developing a nation-wide pattern of volume production at relatively low prices in anticipation of concrete consumer demand. This involves large speculative risks by industry, of course, since producers must invest extensively on the basis of *anticipated* demand. Besides this, however, the high level of consumer sovereignty has been met by a heavy output of "service" to the consumer. This exchange of "good service" for "binding decisions" forms the basis of the solidarity of industry and consuming public. Hence industry has sacrificed its short-term interest in small quantities at high prices in favour of a positive commitment to the development of a high general standard of

[1] In this connection, the brand name or trade mark is a means, even though universalistic, of conveying information to the purchaser and of permitting him to exercise social control by refusing to buy the same brand in the future.

living. Gradually, too, it has been realized that such high standards are the source of purchasing power which underlies high production levels economically. Figure 12 summarizes the structure of the market for consumers' goods.

FIGURE 12

CONSUMERS' MARKET

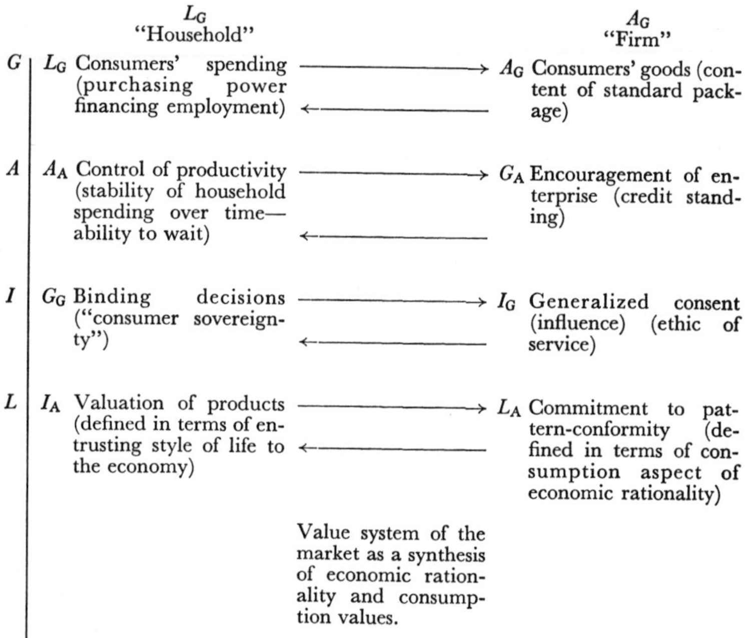

With respect to values (L-component), industry not only accepts the public interest in high consumption levels as a "good thing," but takes over a certain degree of direct responsibility for the content of the style of life. In technical terms this involves an output of a "commitment to pattern-conformity" from the economy to the consuming public.

The one-price system, therefore, is a manifestation of a larger pattern whereby the balance in the consumers' market is shifted away from the primary concern with the G-components and toward a particular type of integrative pattern and common value system. This shift of balance tends to subordinate the significance of *ad hoc* bargaining advantage on *either* side of the market.

Such integration constitutes one reason why certain very general, but particularly Marxian predictions about the "capitalistic" economy have not materialized. Such predictions concern the operation of "economic interests" concerned with the *G*-component of market structures. It is held that producers act, in accordance with their short-run economic interests, to exact the best bargains in the short run. If production is heavily emphasized, therefore, a shortage of purchasing power would develop and lead to overproduction. The patterns we have outlined in the consumers' market and in the labour market illustrate how it is possible to maintain purchasing power in mass markets in a way not incompatible with the continuing expansion of a free-enterprise economy. Such a possibility rests not only on "purely economic" grounds but also on the integrative and common-value components of the market structure.[1]

The above features of the consumers' market are intimately connected with the tendency to dynamic development in the American economy. For the present, however, we wish to illustrate the importance of the market components above and beyond short-term "economic advantage." We will take up the problem of long-run structural change in the economy in Chapter V.

Let us now turn to the market structure of the two markets at the polity-economy boundary (A_A–G_A), the market for the creation of capital funds through credit and the market for productivity, respectively. In both these cases, particularly the latter, we should expect to find imperfections based upon the political nature of capital and the control of productivity.

First, let us summarize the boundary process briefly. One of the interchanges involves the exchange of "encouragement of enterprise" for "control over productivity." To encourage

[1] Current controversies over "fair trade" practices show that the one-price system does not operate without a good deal of strain in the American economy. In particular, the controversies deal with the rights of manufacturers to set retail prices on their products and enforce price maintenance on retailers. Of course, such prices are often undercut by "discount" practices. These practices do not automatically open the door to *ad hoc* bargaining, however, since discounts tend to become established in local markets and provide the basis of a new one-price level. The problem has important legal aspects which are currently under adjudication.

enterprise means to sanction, more or less directly, the continuing contribution of the economic sector in question by means of extending credit standing. Examples of such encouragements are subsidies, tax exemption of ploughed-back profits, protection of industries by tariffs, etc. The control of productivity which the economy surrenders for such encouragements concerns the rights of appropriate political agencies to acquire the productivity as facilities for the pursuit of system goals. In many respects this interchange can scarcely be described as a market, since the role of direct economic sanctions is often unimportant (financial advantages accruing to firms through protective tariffs are fairly indirect). But as we shall see, this limitation upon short-term economic sanctions is at the centre of imperfection in this market. The second interchange involves the exchange of capital funds through credit for certain "rights to intervene," among which the right to withdraw funds is most salient. In this exchange, the relevant economic unit "spends" its credit standing by extending rights to intervene to prospective lenders. Short-term economic sanctions operate in this interchange more conspicuously than in the first, but these are also skewed in ways which we shall discuss presently. Together these two interchanges form a system which links the economy and polity as functionally differentiated sub-systems.

In the market for capital funds (hereafter used to describe the exchange between capital through credit and rights to intervene), the creation of funds is often fused empirically with investment in the narrower sense, i.e., commitment of these funds to a particular organization. Owners of liquid funds, that is to say, may extend control of these funds to productive enterprises. On the other hand, there is considerable commitment *through* intermediaries, e.g., commercial banks, insurance companies, investment trusts, and units of government which operate in the money market.[1] In our discussion of the market for capital funds, we will concentrate on the relationship between the agents of political control and the agents which extend capital funds to productive enterprises at a later stage. Empirically this relationship is often that between the central

[1] Cf. Chap. IV, pp. 217–18, for a brief discussion of the boundary processes which several of these concrete organizations encompass.

bank and member banks. Our remarks apply in many cases however, to the relationship between the agents of political control of funds and productive enterprises themselves. Hence the paradigm of the contract of investment discussed above and summarized in Figure 10, applies at many points in the following analysis.

To illustrate the similarities of the two levels of commitment discussed in the last paragraph, let us refer back to the labour case. The transition between trained capacity and membership in the labour force is usually the result of a household decision; while that between the labour force and labour committed to firms is a joint decision of household and firm. But merely because these two transitions indicate a successively deeper commitment to the economy, the worker as a personality and as member of a household does not relinquish control of his labour power entirely. In this sense the contract of employment is a transaction *between* a household and a unit of the economy. The same holds for the contract of investment. Even if some intermediary, such as a bank or insurance company, is the investing agent, such an agency has an important role in the polity and is not purely a business firm.

Now we may review the functional paradigm for the contract to lend liquid funds. The goal of the transaction is, of course, governed by the A_A–G_A context of the market; hence it is the settlement of mutually advantageous conditions on which the lender will create credit and the borrower will surrender rights to intervene. For the borrower, advantageous terms include the amount available, the conditions of repayment, and the premium payable for the time elapsing before repayment (interest); on the lending side there is similar interest in the security of the loan, its liquidity (i.e., the restrictions on its return on demand) and the premium. Of course, these terms often vary interdependently. In an ordinary checking account, the depositor enjoys a high level of liquidity in that he may withdraw his whole deposit on demand. Before deposit insurance he assumed a certain risk of losing the funds altogether, which the interest rate reflected in part. Now the depositor receives no interest; indeed he pays a service charge (partly negative interest). The goal of the contract to lend liquid funds, therefore, is a special case of the overall A_A–G_A interchange.

In connection with the *adaptive* component, the exchange involves the exigencies springing from the nature of the collectivities which the lending agent and the borrowing agent represent. On the lending side there is the necessity for a certain generalized acceptance of the borrowers (as future investors) as economically rational agents. At this point, in our opinion, the values of economic rationality are most thoroughly institutionalized in a market context. The criteria for extending credit follow the dictates of the economically rational use of this credit to a much greater extent than do the criteria for offering labour services or for the sale of consumers' goods. Examples of these criteria are that the borrowers should maintain certain universalistic characteristics of honesty and fairness in allocating the funds among productive enterprises, that they make reasonable attempts to gather information as to the economic standing of such enterprises, etc. In return for the lender's acceptance of the borrowers as economically rational agents, the latter must "carry through" their side of the adaptive component by making definite commitments to specific productive enterprises in order to guarantee the standing of the rights to intervene which they have extended to the lenders. Presumably these commitments are made in accordance with the expectation of the lenders, i.e., in accord with the more or less explicit standards of economic rationality.

This adaptive interchange is a special case of one of the exchanges between the polity and the integrative sub-system at the societal level.[1] What the lender (political agent) extends to the borrower is a certain order of "consent" when he accepts him as an economically rational agent; in exchange for this consent, the borrower undertakes to make certain "binding decisions" to justify the receipt of such consent. In this sense the adaptive interchange in the contract for liquid funds is a system of political control; it is adaptive in the sense that it provides a certain reservoir of guarantees that the goal-interchange of the contract may be carried out more or less effectively.[2]

[1] Cf. Chap. II, pp. 67–68.

[2] The formal logic is perhaps a little cryptic here since we have not been able to develop the underlying analysis in full. The *adaptive* component of the exchange between "consent" and "binding decisions" is appropriate

The difference between the *G*- and the *A*-components of the contract is illustrated in the difference between the concepts of "credit" and "consent." In the capital market these vary at least to some degree independently. In conditions of easy credit (i.e., general availability of advantageous terms) loans may still be refused because of the low level of consent (i.e., the low level of acceptance of the borrower as an economically rational agent). Conversely, even though credit conditions may be rigid, certain borrowers who have a reputation for careful and rational action may be singled out as good prospects. This difference illustrates the semi-independent operation of the goal and adaptive components in this market structure.

The primary *I*-component on the lending side is to provide a guaranteed value of the generalized facilities which are being offered. This is the focus of the problem of the maintenance of the state of confidence in "legal tender" and the problem of the guarantee of certain stability of the funds' value against too rapid inflation or deflation. In return for such guarantees, the borrower supplies certain guarantees for the continuing value of the *base* for generalized facilities, i.e., the state of productive capacity itself. These guarantees constitute the basis for liquidity; if they are not provided adequately, lenders prefer their funds in liquid form rather than based upon an inadequate base of productivity.

At the level of the society as a whole,[1] this *I*-component is a special case of relationship between the integrative and pattern-maintenance systems. The significance of the "guaranteed value of generalized facilities" is a sort of confidence which the latency system gives to the economy; in return for this confidence in the value of money and credit instruments, the economy provides a level of security in so far as it guarantees the state of the productivity of the economy, which ultimately underlies the whole credit complex.

to the market itself considered as social system. At a different system-level, however, namely that of the society as system, the same interchange constitutes the functional relationship between the polity and integrative system. This dual significance of the same interchange illustrates two fundamental propositions: (1) all the functional exigencies are apparent in every social system, and (2) the same concrete series of performances and sanctions may be broken down into different symbolic components.

[1] Cf. Chap. II, pp. 67–68.

The principal common value (*L*-component) lies in the evaluation of capital as facilities for the maintenance or increase of productivity. On the lending side this value is spelled out more in political terms, i.e., from the point of view of the creation of the facilities for power. On the borrowing side it is more in terms of the creation of the facilities for production in the usual economic sense. Together these values strike a balance between the weights to be given to the values of productivity and production for consumption purposes, respectively. In this sense the interchange involved in this *L*-component is a special case of the overall societal interchange between the economy and the pattern-maintenance system (A_G–L_G).

What are the kinds of imperfection which can be derived from this set of components of the capital market, and how are these imperfections structured empirically? In so far as the *G*-component is a special case of an exercise of power by means of the imposition of situational controls over the access to facilities,[1] there is a tendency for the structure of collectivities in the market for such facilities to be highly centralized. This expectation is based upon the proposition that in the interest of the stability of the society as a whole, there must be a relative monopoly on certain of the facilities of power in order to check very deep tendencies to outbreak of violence and consequent disorganization. Since *generalized* facilities have to undergo a series of transitions toward greater specificity to be converted into *effective* facilities for power,[2] the degree of centralization is not so extreme as in the case of the control over certain more specific facilities of power. Yet some centralization should be apparent. We consider the structure of banking systems in highly differentiated societies to reflect in part the exigencies imparted by this *G*-component. In most cases a more or less central bank regulates the distribution of credit throughout the system. As a matter of fact, in all the economic markets (except for certain "natural" monopolies involving special products, special locations, etc.) the Central

[1] Cf. Chap. II, pp. 56–57.

[2] This is another possible "line" of diminishing levels of generality, i.e., from generalized facilities for power to effective facilities of power. Cf. above, pp. 119–39.

Bank conforms most closely to the theoretical norm of a perfect monopoly with single seller.

The *G*-component is not the only factor underlying the centralization of the banking system. A second basis is found in the *I*-component, especially in the liquidity problem associated with this component. In order to understand this basis, let us turn momentarily to the consumers' goods market. One of the characteristics of monopoly, as generally defined, is a certain rigidity of economic response: price does not change in response to changes in output, firms are not driven out of business by decreased demand, etc. This rigidity stems precisely from the centralization of control of the market by one or a few firms. In the market for liquid funds, the obverse is true. Even though there is centralization, the market is geared for economic responsiveness to economic and other signs which may be apparent from time to time. In fact, the market is so institutionalized that it is, if anything, *over*-responsive. Panics may result from small changes in the interest rate, the failure of a single bank, a political event, etc.; in short, one of the institutionalized characteristics of the capital funds market is a certain tendency to over-reaction and consequent disorganization.[1] This tendency is present in spite of the extreme centralization of the banking system. Indeed this tendency provides the second basis for the centralization of the system. Because of this extreme flexibility and the resultant tendencies to panic in the capital market, certain mechanisms of control must emerge as correctives to these tendencies. The central banking system, with its ability to control the movement of liquid funds *throughout* the system, is able to soften and control movements toward disorganization in the capital market. Indeed, it has been a long and painful historical lesson of most central banks that the provision of mechanisms of control over mass reaction in the market for liquid funds is one of its fundamental functions.

Thus we are faced with an apparent paradox of imperfection. On the one hand the banking system is characterized as much as any other market by the presence of a single seller; yet this condition, usually associated with rigidity of economic response in one respect, is combined with, if anything, too much flexibility

[1] For a discussion of the institutionalization of uncertainty and risk, cf. Chap. IV, pp. 233–41.

of economic response in other respects. We think this paradox springs only from the fact that the traditional view of imperfection has been too narrow; it is exceedingly important to recognize that there are *types* of imperfection, not merely degrees, and that combinations of the characteristics of imperfection are more extensive than has heretofore been generally appreciated. We shall discuss this problem presently.

These components lie, therefore, at the foundation of the centralization of the banking structure. They, plus the *L*-component which deals with the balance of production and consumption in society, also lie at the foundation of the "public interest" or "fiduciary" characteristics of financial organizations. The commercial bank, for instance, is definitely conceived as a "trustee of the people's money." In this connection government backing of its security has been readily accepted, whereas similar guarantees of other types of business firms have been vigorously and successfully resisted. Other institutions which collect capital for investment, such as the insurance company, also have a pronounced fiduciary character. Finally, the Central Bank, whether nationalized or not, is expected always to behave responsibly and "in the public interest." One of the keynotes of the fiduciary relationship is a greater concern for the security of funds than for a private firm's use of its own funds. Indeed, this concern seems to parallel the concern for the element of security in the worker's job status in the labour market. It goes without saying that, because of the public character of financial institutions, a great range of restraints are imposed upon action carried out only according to the standards of economic rationality.

Yet at this point arises a second apparent paradox in the market for capital funds. Given the centralization of the banking system and the restraints upon banks' actions because of their heavy involvement in the polity, the market is none the less characterized by a strict application of standards of economic rationality, especially in the *A*-component, in which the condition for extending credit is a generalized acceptance of the borrower as an economically rational agent. Such demands of course are partially rooted in the banks' own need for solvency. But beyond this is the fact that investment (the next step "downward" in the particularization of capital resources) is in a special sense an "intra-economic" process,[1] and hence not subject to such stringent exigencies as the household imposes, for instance, at the A_G–L_G boundary interchange. This institutionalization of the dictates of economic rationality at the economy-polity boundary, plus the complete mobility and divisibility of money, shows that, while certain of the characteristics of the market for liquid funds are governed by the strictest sort of non-economic considerations, the elements of a "perfect market" are also present in their purest form. The presence of such paradoxes argues for a thorough reconsideration of the theory of imperfect competition.

The cluster of financial institutions—banks, insurance companies, etc.—at the economy-polity boundary is an example of the development of a "buffer" ring of interstitial organizations to mediate between the business firm in the economy and the primarily non-economic units of the society. The labour union is another such example. Both unions and fiduciary organizations are "in business" in the sense that they have a *relative* economic primacy in their orientations.[2] But this economic primacy is clearly skewed in the direction of the non-economic values and interests on the other side of the relevant boundary of the economy.

The second market at the A_A–G_A boundary, the "market" for productivity, is considerably more skewed in the direction of political exigencies, hence considerably more imperfect, than the market for capital funds. Before spelling out the kinds of imperfection in this market, let us apply the paradigm for contractual structure.

As in the case of the capital funds market, the *goal* of the market for productivity is governed by the overall A_A–G_A exchange. Hence it deals with striking an appropriate balance between the encouragement of enterprise by the relevant political agency, and the supply of productive capacity which is, under the appropriate circumstances, at the disposal of the polity for the pursuit of system goals. The terms of a "good exchange" from the political side deal with the potential

[1] For an exact conceptualization of the status of "intra-economic," cf. Chap. IV, pp. 210–13.

[2] The union, e.g., has greater economic primacy than a professional association.

importance of the economic sector for the pursuit of economic goals, the "costliness" of the encouragement, etc. On the economic side, the primary interest is in the receipt of sufficient credit standing to render the projected enterprise or type of enterprises profitable from an economic standpoint.[1]

Above and beyond this goal-transaction, the *adaptive* component of the market for productivity involves an element of political control. This political control, while adaptive, is a special case of the relationship between the polity and the integrative system at the societal level.[2] The polity lends a form of "support" to the economy in the form of an endorsement of the importance of the enterprise in the economy. This is the political control element, for instance, in the protection of infant industries or tariff protection. Further, the extension of government contracts to certain forms of enterprise (e.g., research) which otherwise would not be carried out is an obvious form of support. In return for this support, the contribution of the economy is to surrender "influence" to the polity, specifically in the form of rights to utilize the relevant aspects of the resultant productive capacity under the appropriate conditions for system-goal attainment. This interchange is adaptive in the sense that it supplies a base of control within which the goal-transactions proceed.

To integrate the two parties to the contract for productivity (the two parties are characteristically governmental and business organizations) there is a certain interchange which is a special case of the exchange between the pattern-maintenance system and the integrative system at the societal level. The polity provides a kind of motivation to pattern-conformity with the system-goals in question; this motivation is often implemented by various forms of inducement and control, such as appeals to the collective spirit of the enterprise in question or, in more extreme cases, outright control through regulation or nationalization. In return for this motivation, the economy accepts the societal system goals. Of course the success

[1] Of course, the element of "bargaining" is completely removed in some cases, especially in modern totalitarian societies, where the supply of productive capacity is often subject to political coercion rather than other forms of political encouragement.

[2] Cf. Chap. II, pp. 67–68, and above, p. 128.

of the motivation and the degree of the acceptance of system goals may vary widely empirically; at this point we are concerned only with the performance-sanction system which provides the integrative bridge in the market for productivity.

Finally, the common value (L-component) deals with the valuation of productivity. On the polity side the perspective is the facilities base for system-goal attainment; for the economy there is a valuation of the independent economic significance of productivity. Hence the common value-system, which is a special case of the A_G–L_G interchange at the societal level, is not unlike that appropriate to the market for capital funds. The chief difference lies in the levels of application; the value system of the market for capital funds applies to the allocation of *generalized* facilities, whereas that of the market for productivity applies to the allocation of facilities which have been more deeply incorporated into the productive capacity of the economy. Figure 13 summarizes the contractual relation in the "market" for productivity schematically.

FIGURE 13

"MARKET" FOR CONTROL OF PRODUCTIVITY

	G_A		A_A
G	G_A Encouragement of enterprise (granting of credit standing)	←——— ———→	A_A Productive capacity
A	I_G Endorsement of importance in economy (support)	←——— ———→	G_G Rights to utilize productive capacity under appropriate conditions (influence)
I	L_A Motivation to pattern-conformity (appeals, socialization, nationalism, etc.)	←——— ———→	I_A Acceptance of societal system-goals by economy
L	A_G Valuation of independent economic significance of productivity	←——— ———→	L_G Valuation of productivity as facilities base for system-goal attainment
		Value system as balance between valuation of facilities for economic production and valuation of facilities for social system-goals.	

On the basis of almost every one of these components in the market for productivity, the tendency is for the structure of the market to be skewed markedly further from the criteria of perfection than in the case of the capital market. In the first place, the goal-exchange deals with much more specific facilities than capital funds; that is, men and machines are much more immediately applicable than generalized purchasing power. This is an application of the proposition that facilities must be made specific through several stages of decreasing generality before they can be made effective as facilities in production, power, pattern-maintenance, etc.[1] The functional case for centralized control of productive capacity (which is of course almost always latent) therefore approaches more closely the functional case for the monopolization of the force and violence by the state. Hence the agencies which encourage enterprise (in our sense) and control productivity are almost always agencies of the Government, which are both more centralized and more non-economic than the banking system.

A second source of imperfection of the market for productivity is found in the *A*-component, particularly in the predominance of political goals as criteria for the endorsement of the importance of any particular economic sector. The basis for the protection of many infant industries (e.g., synthetics), for certain tariff protection (e.g., the "defence" rationale for the protection against Swiss watches) and for certain government support through contracts (e.g., intercontinental ballistics) is *not at all* economic; indeed to establish economic units in connection with system-goals often means a less efficient allocation of productivity from the standpoint of the economy. Defence, welfare, and other political considerations consistently outweigh the standards of economic rationality. That the degree of imperfection is greater than that of the capital funds market is illustrated by the following example. In the decision to protect a certain infant industry for purposes of defence, only if the economic costs are absolutely prohibitive is the economic basis taken as the primary determining factor in the support of this by tariffs. But once the tariff is enacted, and a certain degree of credit standing has hence been conferred upon the industry, the advance of capital funds to this industry depends upon a

[1] Cf. above, pp. 129–34.

great many more considerations than the importance of the industry for the defence of the nation. Most of these considerations, furthermore, deal with the economic standards by which the funds are to be applied.

The sources of variation or imperfection in the *I*- and *L*-components of this market also imply a degree of remove from short-term economic considerations. Imperfections in the *I*-component deal with the degree of commitment of the relevant economic units to the goals of the political system. Manifestations of a low degree of such commitment would be instances of deliberate corruption of government funds, generalized lack of co-operation in the supply of system-goal facilities, etc. The existence of such imperfection provides a second basis for the centralization of control over productive capacity: such imperfections must be readily controllable. Variations in the *L*-component deal, finally, with the level of valuation of productivity as an appropriate power base. This variation, like that of the *I*-component, is virtually independent of short-term economic considerations.

By now we have analysed the variation in market structures sufficiently to indicate that most economic treatments of the characteristics and bases of imperfection do not take an important range of variation into account *theoretically*. Our general point is that market structures differ in sociological type, not merely along some dimension of competitiveness. To summarize, therefore, let us sketch a few of the lines along which a *systematic* classification scheme of types of imperfection might be constructed.

In the first place, we would break down markets according to the overall boundary processes of the economy. The broadest focus for market structure, therefore, is the economy-latency, the economy-polity, the economy-integrative, and the fourth "closed" boundary of the economy which deals with land factors.[1] Furthermore, each of these boundaries is sub-divided

[1] In this chapter we have analysed only the economy-latency (A_G–L_G) and the economy-polity (A_A–G_A) boundaries in detail. For a brief, less systematic statement of the integrative boundary, cf. Chap. II, pp. 77–78, and Chap. V, pp. 264 ff. For a discussion of the "land" boundary, cf. Chap. II, pp. 69–70. Finally, for a classification and discussion of the major *intra*-economic boundaries, cf. Chap. IV, pp. 205–19.

into two markets, e.g., the economy-latency into the labour market and the consumers' goods market and the economy-polity into the market for capital funds and the market for productivity. Finally, each of the resulting markets is characterized by a contractual structure which is schematically summarized in Figure 14; every market, considered as social

FIGURE 14

THE COMPONENTS OF A MARKET SYSTEM

Unit with Economic Primacy		*Unit with Non-economic Primacy*
± Goal-attainment	⟶ ⟵	Goal-attainment ±
± Adaptation	⟶ ⟵	Adaptation ±
± Integration	⟶ ⟵	Integration ±
± Common values	⟶ ⟵	Common values ±

system, has aspects of goal-attainment, adaptation, integration, and common values which govern the market transactions. Furthermore, each of these aspects may be *skewed* toward the economy or toward the extra-economic system (i.e., the adaptive exigencies of the household may or may not be weighted more heavily than the adaptive exigencies of the economy in the market for labour services). This possibility of skewing is illustrated by the ± signs on each side of each of the four components.

For the characterization of any given market, therefore, the following information is necessary: (1) its significance in terms of overall boundary interchange; (2) its role in the double-interchange of the relevant boundary; (3) the goal-attainment, adaptive, integrative, and value components of the market, considered as social system; (4) the relative weights and/or rank order of these components in the structure of the market. For instance, in the labour market, the *G*-component is weighted relatively heavily, though the others are certainly important; in the market for medical services, the *I*-component is predominant; in the market for academic services, the L-component is the focus of the contract; (5) the degree to which each of the components is skewed in the direction of the economy or the non-economic unit. For instance, the A-component of the market for productivity is skewed markedly in the direction of the attainment of political goals; the A-component in the market for capital funds is skewed more in the direction of economic considerations.

The application of such categories to market structures provides a basis not only for the classification of the types of imperfection within any given economy but, also, because it is grounded in functional categories which cut across cultural lines, for the classification of market structures in different societies at the same time and in the same society over time. It is of course far beyond the scope of this study to extend our analysis into the complex study of comparative market structures, but we feel that these starting-points for systematic development of a sociology of markets might be turned profitably to the investigation of this important field.

THE INSTITUTIONALIZATION OF ECONOMIC VALUES AND THE MOTIVATION OF ECONOMIC ACTIVITY

The institutionalization of the economic value-pattern system itself *governs* processes of a more fluid character (such as the market transactions we have been considering) in any given social system. In our technical terms, the institutionalization of value patterns is most central to the latency or pattern-maintenance aspect of the economy.

What is the economy's value system? We suggest that the primary content is that of *economic rationality*. From the point of view of economic theory, economic rationality is a postulate; so far as it is empirically acceptable economic theory presumably possesses greater validity, other things equal. But from the point of view of the economy as a social system, economic rationality is not a postulate, but a primary empirical feature of the system itself.

In order to interpret this proposition, we must distinguish at least two levels to which the concept of "institutionalized value-system" is applied. The first level describes the values of the total society. These values never can be defined in terms of economic rationality. Rather the societal value system defines the *relative importance* of economic functions (and hence of economic rationality) in the hierarchy of functions on behalf of the society. In Western society economic values occupy a high position in the hierarchy. In the American case they are probably higher in the hierarchy than elsewhere; indeed, there is good reason to believe that economic functions are ranked highest.

The concept of economic rationality applies to a second level, i.e., to the values of the economy as a societal *sub-system*. Rationality refers to a mode of organization relative to a standard of effective attainment of a system's paramount goal. In the case of the economy this paramount goal is *production* in the technical economic sense. Economic rationality in the value-system sense is thus the valuation of the goals of production and appropriate controls over behaviour in the interest of such goals. The meaning of "rationality" is therefore limited to the orientation of action toward maximal conformity with a norm.[1]

Economic rationality on the *social system* level thus refers primarily to the economy, not the society, as a system. Distinct from both of these system-references, however, is the reference to the personality of the individual actor as a system. This is the proper reference of the concept of economic rationality as a *psychological* concept.

The most important similarity between personality systems and social systems is that they *interpenetrate* if they both possess common *content* of value patterns. But there are two fundamental differences as well: (1) Since the contents of personality value patterns are derived by the internalization of social role-objects in socialization processes, their hierarchy differs from that of the values of the social system. This is because the individual is socialized in specialized agencies (e.g., the family

[1] Of course "rationality" often refers not only to the norm itself in the hierarchical structure of value-systems but also to the extent to which this norm is successfully implemented empirically. A description of the level of economic rationality of an actual behaviour system may refer to either or both of these considerations.

and the educational system) and in a determinate time sequence, not in and through the whole social structure all at once. (2) The specific goals and the adaptive and integrative exigencies of personalities differ from *any* social system. The value content is, in its implementation, *directed* toward different problems. Because of this second factor especially, the relationship between social systems and personalities has an element of looseness. In a complex society the same personality has roles in a variety of social sub-systems and each sub-system functions through the participation of a variety of personalities. The value systems of the individuals are internalized under varying conditions and with varying degrees of success. Hence the internalization of values leaves a range of performance-sanction flexibility for the mutual adjustment of personalities to each other. This flexibility is considerable even in the absence of neurotic distortions in the relations between value pattern and action.

Hence it is exceedingly dangerous to reason too directly from the personality system to the social system and vice versa. True, value patterns held in common between personalities and social systems stabilize social motivation and underlie the orderly functions of social systems. But no personality acts *only* in terms of the value system he shares with the members of the collectivities in which he participates. Each has different organic components in his motivation, a different life history, a different combination of participations and a different concrete situation.

In these terms the concept of economic rationality may designate either a property of a social system or a property of a personality system; but these two references must not be confused. In either case, however, the concept refers to the mode of *organization* of the system relative to its values. It refers first to the level of valuation of economic production, and second to the degree to which the system is effectively organized to implement this component of its value system.

On the social system level, though economic rationality has a universal core which is independent of cultural variability,[1]

[1] This is to say that *all* human societies are economically rational to some important degree. There is no "prelogical mentality" to which the concept is irrelevant.

in certain more specific respects it varies greatly. The first dimension of variability is the degree of differentiation between the economy and the other societal sub-systems; only at an "advanced" level of economic development does this reach a high degree. The second dimension is the strength of economic values in a society relative to other value systems.

If the level of differentiation is relatively high and economic rationality relatively strong (as is true in the United States today), we would, as we have already noted, expect greater emphasis on production than on consumption at the economy's *G*-boundary. That is to say, household members would tend to stress their roles as producers in the economy more than their roles as consumers. The high valuation of occupational roles and of occupational success is an index of this stress in our society. Furthermore, we would expect that occupational remuneration would be more a symbol of achievement (*I*-component in the contract of employment) than a means to purchase consumers' goods (*G*-component) at this boundary. This is also true in the United States, relative to other societies.

At the *A*-boundary of the economy, we would expect a high valuation of productivity and hence heavy commitment of general purchasing power to economic production.

Finally, at the *I*-boundary, there would be high valuation of entrepreneurial activity to reorganize both economy and society to increase long-term productivity. We will discuss this boundary briefly in Chapter V.

The value system of any social system controls system processes via the *motivation* of individuals. In general, the value system operates through two channels: (1) the *internalization* of the value system (and its appropriate sub-systems) in the personalities of individual members of the system; (2) the *sanctions* administered by other system members which, in a changing situation, tend to stabilize the internalized orientations and adapt specific behaviour to the changing exigencies. The two are of course interdependent in that the same individual both expresses his internalized values in action and sanctions the actions of others. There is, however, as we have noted, room for considerable flexibility of action in response to situational variations, a flexibility which is regulated by sanctions.

The differentiation of these two channels in the economic

case is in part a function of the degree to which human services within the economy are performed in occupational roles. As we have seen, the occupational role is institutionalized through the contract of employment and includes expectations of performance of function in the context of organization. In so far as the occupational role is highly differentiated, the distinction between these two primary components of an institutionalized value system should be apparent. We will deal here only with the organizational, not the household, aspect of the role.

In speaking of occupational roles and motivation in them, we make the transition from the social system to the personality reference. Here we may assert the following. (1) In so far as the values of economic rationality, in their production aspect, are internalized, the role incumbent will be positively motivated to the effective performance of his function, which is interpreted as a *contribution* to the functioning of the organization. A major part of this motivation is independent of the specific level of reward sanctions. This component is the motivational component of the land complex; it is what Marshall meant by "activities." (2) In part, occupational performance is a direct function of short-term reward sanctions. In our occupational system money income is particularly important, both as a means of meeting household responsibilities *and* as a symbol of recognition or esteem. Of course, *relative* pay levels are very significant in this respect.

As we have argued, each of these components may be further sub-divided into two. The first sub-component involves evaluation of the production goals of the economy (G) and its value pattern realization (L). The second sub-component involves in the first place the G-component of the contract of employment, or money wages as direct compensations for specific labour services; this is usually taken for granted in economic discussions. But an I-component is also involved in the second sub-component of the contract, which we have defined as diffuse sentiments of "responsibility" for the organization. These sentiments are sensitive to *attitudes and their symbolization* rather than to the money value of remuneration as a means to something else. Attitudinal rewards are valued "for their own sake," not for what they can buy.

The I-component of the orientation to employment bridges

the three other components: the *G*- and the *A*-components of the contract of employment *and* the internalized system of values. It bridges, in other words, the control of motivation to production as a land factor, which is relatively independent of current economic sanctions on the one hand, and sensitivity to these current sanctions as defined in the *G*- and *A*-components on the other.

The paradigm for the contract of employment[1] is thus the main framework for the transition between the sociological and the psychological analysis of individual motivation in the occupational role. It defines the value components which he holds in common with the employing organization and the three bases (other than this component of his internalized value system) of "interest" in productive work through which adjustments to the situation tend to be made.

The analysis of the levels of generality of labour as a factor in production, and of its genesis in the socialization process,[2] links this analytical framework for motivation in the occupational role with the analysis of the personality as a system. In the course of personality development the motivational organization which goes into the occupational role differentiates from other sub-systems of the personality which are appropriate to other roles. An adequate theory of occupational motivation must include reference to the relationships among these various sub-systems of motivational organization.

The problem of motivation in a highly differentiated economy is of primary importance in the occupational role, since through it the input of human services into the economy is effected. With certain modifications the motivation underlying occupational roles may be extended to the input of the other factors, since both capital investment and entrepreneurial service both have become assimilated to the occupational pattern empirically. Such roles differ from "labour" roles even at managerial levels, but the differences are based upon the markets for different types of services which we have discussed. The role of the banker, for instance, "skews" from simple economic rationality in a more complicated way than does the labour role. Like the labourer, the banker is the agent of the

[1] Cf., pp. 114–123.
[2] Cf., pp. 121–123.

input of a primary factor of production into the economy; he is also anchored in a household. But his involvement in the polity is of a different order. His occupational role and his decisions will be influenced by a variety of fiduciary considerations.

Even in cases where investment is not within the context of an occupational role, e.g., when individual household members offer funds to firms in a security flotation, the *analytical* components we have outlined still define the context in which the *decision* to invest may be analysed. More generally, the outline of the analysis of motivation in occupational roles is a special case of a general sociological theory of motivation in institutionalized roles. With appropriate adjustments this kind of analysis can be extended to any type of institutionalized role in a society. Above all, the relationship between the motivation of economic activity in a social context and the psychological character of the personality is not completely unique; its institutionalization is not basically different from the institutionalization of other types of roles.

The occupational role differs from others above all in its particular type of institutionally generalized goal, i.e., "success," and in its definition of the values behind the goal and of appropriate situations in which to seek such goals. Apart from qualifications such as these, this account of motivation can be generalized to behaviour in all social roles. Moreover, the process of learning and socialization by means of which such motivational structures develop are, as we have indicated, fairly well understood in broad outline.[1]

Economists should refer to this order of developments in the relation between psychology and sociology when they turn to problems of motivation in a more technical sense. It is possible to take into account the appropriate elements traditionally defined as those of "self-interest" in our analysis; but it is also possible to analyse other problems beyond the scope of

[1] On the general character of motivation in social roles, see Parsons, *The Social System*, especially Chaps. II, VI, and VII. On its application to the economic case, see Parsons, "The Motivation of Economic Activities," *Essays in Sociological Theory*, revised edition, Chap. III. On the process of socialization, cf. Parsons, Bales, *et al.*, *Family, Socialization and Interaction Process*, especially Chaps. II and IV.

traditional utilitarian analysis, such as the difference between motivation in economic and non-economic contexts. For example, it is possible to determine why behaviour in an ordinary intraeconomic market should be defined as legitimately "self-interested" in the usual economic sense and why behaviour in the market for professional services is not.[1]

Contrary to much often implicit economic opinion, an adequate theory of institutional motivation does not rest—in a narrow psychological sense—on a "theory of human nature" which is as yet unavailable.[2] The theory we are developing is, of course, in great degree a product of developments in modern psychology (mostly *since* the time that the accepted economic thinking on these matters crystallized). It is also, however, a product of the development of sociological knowledge. The relation between psychology and sociology lies primarily in the fact that the basic structures of institutionalized motivation are *learned* in the course of social experience. However much they depend on the genetic capabilities of the organism, they are not direct manifestations of hereditary constitution. Furthermore, the essential environment of this learning process is the *structure of social relationships* in which the child develops. Internalization of culture patterns in social situations is the motivational counterpart in the personality structure of the institutionalization of the *same* patterns in the social system. In turn, this institutionalization defines the situation for analysing behaviour processes in any given social system, of which an economy is one subtype.

Above all, in the field of economic behaviour, as well as in other fields, motivation must be treated as complex. It seems to us that the central fallacy in much of economic thought is to postulate some single motivational entity as an explanation of all economic behaviour. Usually this entity is some version of the "profit motive" regarded as an inborn propensity of human nature. But when complex phenomena are subsumed under the operation of one variable, the variable degenerates

[1] It is important to distinguish the *institutional* component of this difference (a social system problem) from the *motivational* component (a personality problem). As we have noted, they need not coincide exactly.

[2] For a discussion of this "bias" in connection with the economic treatment of "propensities," cf. Chap. IV, pp. 227 ff.

into a name for the class of phenomena in question. This is true of the concepts of the "profit motive," the "instinct of acquisition," and the "rational pursuit of self-interest," and others.[1]

Any adequate theory of institutionalized motivation, including that in the context of economic institutions, must include, beside the factor of strength or intensity, *at least four* independently variable components: the relevant internalized value systems of the actors, facilities available in the situations in which they act, the immediate reward sanctions expected for their actions, and the more diffuse symbolic reward meanings of success and lack of it in attaining the goals of their actions.

According to such a theory, economic rationality in its empirical sense is a function of: (1) the degree to which the relevant action is oriented to a central function in a differentiated economy as such, (2) the degree to which it is in accordance with an appropriate institutionalized and internalized value system of the economy, and (3) the degree to which the action is *integrated* within itself as a system relative to the values of economic rationality.

This completes our extensive review of economic institutions. Because of the general nature of this book, we could not expect to provide circumstantial and detailed discussion of a great many empirical problems which the economist finds relevant, above all those involved in comparative variations in the structure of economies. But in order to demonstrate that adequate treatment of the fields on the borderline of economics depends not only on empirical information but also on *theoretical* analysis of the non-economic factors, we felt it necessary to carry sociological analysis beyond the programmatic level and show its possible usefulness to economists.

If the economist is concerned—as indeed he must be—with the relevant inputs and outputs through the boundary processes of the economy, then he *inevitably* encounters problems of the institutional regulation of these processes. Just as inevitably, solution of these problems involves institutionalized non-economic factors. Finally, it is possible to analyse such factors *in direct theoretical articulation* with the logical structure of economic

[1] In connection with consumption and investment motivations, cf. Chap. IV, pp. 261 ff.

theory. This articulation does not merely "extend" economic theory, nor does it simply make it more concrete or empirical in the sense of providing more data; it points up *direct articulations with other branches of the theory of social systems.*

All of these points except the last are almost commonplaces in the tradition of economic thought. Hence we rest our case on the success of our preliminary demonstration of the possibility of logical articulation.

The gist of our case is this: the division of labour and exchange are central background concepts of all modern economics. Exchange processes in a system of division of labour involve relations of contract, which deal with the "quids" and the "quos" on which economic theory has concentrated (the factors and products of production). But because contracts are social relationships they involve "non-contractual elements of contract." These elements articulate precisely with traditional economic theory and promise more specific solutions to many empirical economic problems than are available at present. Furthermore, if we treat contract on the proper sociological level, it is possible to derive from it the fundamentals of the phenomena of organization, occupational role structure, and property, which, along with contract, are the major institutional components of the structure of the economy. Finally, only through the analysis of institutional structure and its relation to the processes of the economy can economic theory be incorporated into the general theory of social motivation, and hence be relieved of the necessity of resting on *ad hoc* hypotheses about "human nature" which are psychologically and sociologically dubious, if not downright untenable.

CHAPTER IV

ECONOMIC PROCESSES WITHIN THE SOCIAL SYSTEM

A thread of continuity which runs through the preceding chapters is the representation of the economy *as a social system.* By means of this representation we have shown that central economic concepts possess the logical characteristics of categories common to all social systems and that the economy as a system faces functional problems common to all social systems (Chapter I); that the economy, like all social systems, has a determinate set of boundaries and boundary interchanges which can be specified and related to categories of economic analysis (Chapter II); and that economic activities proceed within a determinate institutional framework, a framework which is not randomly "given," but is interwoven closely with the classes of economic activities and the content categories of the boundary interchanges themselves (Chapter III).

While the view of the economy as a single social system elucidates the exchanges between the economy and other societal systems, this overview does not have sufficient analytic specificity to interpret some of the problems subsumed under the term "economic processes." To be sure, the functional differentiation of the economy, its boundary interchanges, and its institutional regulation involve at many points dynamic considerations, e.g., the performance-sanction interchange, the interaction among various actors in the economic process, etc. These considerations do not, however, extend to more technical problems of economic dynamics. In this chapter and the next, therefore, we shall deal primarily with problems of process in the economy. First we will treat mechanisms involved in economic fluctuations *within a given institutional framework*—especially the multiplier, the accelerator and time lag. In the final chapter we will explore in a tentative way the problem of the change of institutions themselves, i.e., the problem of economic development.

This chapter has three sections. First we shall analyse critically three models of economic fluctuations selected from the literature on trade cycles—those of Samuelson, Kalecki, and Hicks; each of these models differs from the others in certain respects but all three face common dilemmas. Our selection of the three is not meant to exhaust, or even represent, the types of trade cycle models available in economics. Indeed, we could have chosen much more "sociological" models.[1] Our intention is merely to illustrate that even highly formalized models which apparently are independent of sociological considerations are subject to supplementation and correction on the grounds of sociological theory. We will summarize each model; next we will examine the dilemmas common to them; then we will turn to some of the resolutions of the dilemmas that economists have suggested. In the second section we will lay an extensive theoretical foundation for a further discussion of the dilemmas outlined. This foundation will consist in a further functional breakdown of the economy, an outline of the boundary-processes *within* the economy, and an analysis of some of the regulative mechanisms of these internal boundary relationships. In the third section we will return to the discussion of fluctuations *per se*; more particularly, we will bring the considerations of the second section to bear on some of the dilemmas which economic theory has been unable to resolve.

SOME MODELS OF THE TRADE CYCLE

Samuelson's[2] elaboration of the Hansen formula for analysing changes in the national income is one of the most concise statements of a mathematical trade cycle model. Samuelson notes three components which operate in any addition to income: (1) government deficit spending, g; (2) private consumption expenditure, operating by the multiplier principle.

[1] E.g., Schumpeter, J. A., *Business Cycles*, 1937.

[2] Samuelson, Paul A., "Interactions between the Multiplier Analysis and the Principle of Acceleration," *Review of Economic Statistics*, 1939, pp. 75–78.

This is governed by α, the marginal propensity to consume, which refers to the proportion of national income from the previous period spent on consumption in the current period; (3) induced private investment operating by the accelerator principle. This is governed by β, the relation of induced private investment to the increase in consumption between the previous and current periods. It is possible to calculate one year's income in the following way: if at time t the national income Y_t can be written as the sum of government expenditure g_t, consumption expenditure C_t and induced private investment I_t, and if the following relations hold:

$$C_t = \alpha Y_{t-1}$$
$$I_t = \beta(C_t - C_{t-1}) = \alpha\beta Y_{t-1} - \alpha\beta Y_{t-2}$$
$$g_t = 1$$

then:

$$Y_t = 1 + \alpha Y_{t-1} + \alpha\beta Y_{t-1} - \alpha\beta Y_{t-2}$$
$$Y_t = 1 + \alpha(1+\beta) Y_{t-1} - \alpha\beta Y_{t-2}$$

If Y from the past two periods is known and if the time lag between previous Y and current C is assumed to be one year,[1] then by substituting various values for α and β, the following year-by-year series emerge from calculation on the basis of the formula above: if g is assumed to be constant at 1 throughout, and if a value of ·5 is assigned to α and unity to β, then calculations produce a peak in the third year, a trough in the seventh, a peak in the eleventh, etc. Other values of α and β produce the following: (1) relatively sudden rise and gradual easing back to the original Y but never below it; this is not an oscillatory cycle, strictly speaking; (2) damped oscillatory movements; (3) explosive oscillations around an average Y; (4) explosive upward movement, approaching a compound rate of growth.

Kalecki's theory[2] also depends upon model sequences involving a multiplier and accelerator, but he extends his analysis further than Samuelson. The mechanism of the multiplier, for instance, is subject to two time lags instead of

[1] The assumption of one year has no particular significance. It is necessary to postulate some unit to represent one "consumers' plan revision period."

[2] Kalecki, M., *Essays in the Theory of Economic Fluctuations*, 1939, esp. Chap. 6.

one; in addition, Kalecki assigns values to the lags on the basis of empirical data. The first time lag is between current income of capitalists[1] and previous investment, which determines current income. This is expressed by the equation:

$$Y_t = f(I_{t-\lambda})$$

which gives the functional relation between national income Y at time t and investment at time $t - \lambda$, both expressed in stable values. The assigned value of four months to λ is based on the plotted empirical lag between investment and income in the United States before World War II.[2] The second lag depends upon delays in the construction industry between investment orders for fixed capital goods and delivery. Kalecki calculates this lag at half the construction period, or $\theta/2$, to be between 3 and 6 months, again on the basis of statistics. The total lag between investment decisions and current income, therefore, is λ (4 months) plus $\theta/2$ (3–6 months) or 7–10 months.

For the acceleration principle, Kalecki accepts a function ϕ similar to Samuelson's B:

$$D_t = \phi_e \, (Y_t)$$

or, investment decisions D at time t are the function ϕ of the income of the same period. By assigning different values to the two functions—f, the dependence of income upon previous investment, and ϕ, the dependence of investment upon income—cycles of various magnitudes can be calculated.

Kalecki introduces, however, a second determinant of investment decisions—the level of capital goods—which refines the concept of the accelerator and explains the "turning points" in the cycle's peak and trough. As fixed capital goods accumulate, a decline in the marginal expectations of profit from investment forces a decline in investments; conversely, as capital goods are depleted, marginal expectations of profit rise, and investment decisions rise. The two determinants of investment—the level of Y and the stock of fixed capital—interact with the multiplier to produce the following cycle in outline. From some initial position at which investment covers

[1] Income of rentiers and workers is not significant in Kalecki's model, since they are assumed not to save.

[2] Kalecki, *op. cit.*, pp. 71–73.

only depreciation, a rise in investment sets off an income rise in the future. This in turn stimulates further investment, which produces a further rise in income, and so on. At some point, however, the expansion of capital equipment accompanying increased investment lowers investment decisions and thus dampens the self-stimulation of the interaction between D and Y. This dampening pressure increases and at some point income ceases to grow while investment still adds to the stock of equipment. The final increment lowers investment below the previous period, and income begins to fall. This in turn sets off a self-stimulated downward movement, aggravated by the large stock of capital equipment. On the downward path of Y and D, investment falls below the level of replacement and income ceases to fall. The upturn occurs when shrinkage of capital equipment continues to fall in the face of a stationary income, and investment decisions are stimulated by this decrease of fixed capital.

Hicks,[1] whose model includes the multiplier and accelerator as ingredients, introduces even more refinements. His analysis of the multiplier begins with the savings = investment ($S = I$) formula and with the Keynesian expression that if investment increases by a certain amount, then income has to increase to make S equal to the increment of investment. The point of interest to Hicks (and to us), however, is not *that* savings must equal investment, but *the way* in which the two come to be equal. To determine this, Hicks utilizes the Kahn multiplier "convergent series," which depends upon a certain time lag between the earning and spending of incomes. This means that consumption lags behind, but converges upon increased investment at varying rates according to the length of the time lag assigned. Hicks illustrates the lag with a length of three months[2] but acknowledges that this can be varied freely to one month or to any other period. Hicks further refines the multiplier model for a changing economy, but this is not essential for our purposes.

The accelerator is refined by the introduction of a time lag and by the distinction between fixed capital and working capital. These two refinements produce an upward accelerator

[1] Hicks, J. R., *A Contribution to the Theory of the Trade Cycle*, 1950.
[2] *Ibid.*, p. 20.

of three phases: (1) net disinvestment, or the running down of working stocks to meet the increased demand. In this phase new fixed capital investment is not possible because of a time lag; (2) investment to build up the raided stocks and to install new fixed capital; (3) oscillations running into the future which occur because of the alternate building up and tearing down of the hump of investment in the second phase. The downward accelerator is by and large classifiable into the same phases, except that the second phase must necessarily be spread out over time, since disinvestment is limited by the rate of depreciation.

In constructing the cycle, Hicks begins by temporarily ignoring these refinements. One needs only an appropriate value for s, the marginal propensity to save, and v, the investment coefficient (the ratio of induced investment to the change in output which called it forth).[1] Variation of s values, holding v at unity, produces four cyclical magnitudes, namely, the regular convergence, damped fluctuations, steady fluctuations, and explosive fluctuations.

Hicks then introduces the refinements one by one. Briefly, postponement of the induced investment hump to the accelerator's second phase dampens the cycle and causes sub-oscillations; distribution of this hump over several phases dampens and delays the cycle; further extension of the consumption lag dampens the cycle in general; and the tail in phase three, if it gets into step with the minor oscillations of the postponed hump in phase two, can exaggerate them. Finally the cycle can be made logically compatible with an economy with a constant rate g of autonomous investment, or growth. All these refinements are then incorporated into a model of the cycle. The upswing may be immediate or lagged, cyclic or smooth in its movement from the initial equilibrium. The downturn is explained primarily on the basis of reaching the maximum full employment of resources. The downswing is longer temporally and is governed primarily by the multiplier, since the process of disinvestment on the downward accelerator is extended over time. And finally, the upturn is encouraged by autonomous investment, which continues throughout the cycle at a continuous rate.

[1] Note the similarities of s and v to Samuelson's α and β, respectively.

Formally, each of the three models has a determinate number of variables which do not change in meaning and which bear a consistent relationship to each other throughout; furthermore, the laws governing the interaction among the variables are either fixed or variable within strict logical limits. From the standpoint of formal excellence, therefore, none of the models offers any basis for contrast among them, or for preference of one model over the other. Points of contrast emerge only when one introduces a "breath of realism"[1] into models, i.e., applies them to the empirical operation of the economy. The points of contrast are the number and length of time lags; the values assigned to the coefficients, functions and propensities; and the overall determinacy or indeterminacy of the cycle's path.

How many time lags? Any empirical reference presupposes at least one time lag simply because processes take time. This principle underlies Keynes' distinction between the "logical theory of the multiplier," and "period analysis." The logical theory, "which holds good continuously without time lag,"[2] is subject to no error and is timeless in the sense that it moves from one static position to another. No actual income movements are so simple. The full effect of a change in investment, according to Keynes, occurs only after a lag, primarily in consumption expenditure, but also in the spread of increased investment in related industries. Given the general presupposition of at least one lag, it is apparent that a great number of institutional foci for lags appear in the actual ebbs and flows of economic process. Without attempting any classification of lags as yet,[3] we shall merely note that the three models differ in the number and kind of lags incorporated. Samuelson posits a single delay between income of the previous period and consumption of the current period. Kalecki combines construction delays for capital goods and an expenditures lag into a single lag between investment decisions of the previous period and income of the current one. Hicks accepts the mul-

[1] Hicks, *op. cit.*, p. 82.

[2] *General Theory*, p. 122.

[3] Our analysis of the boundary interchanges and their institutional structure (in Chaps. II and III as well as below, pp. 205 ff) provide the bases, however, for a relatively exhaustive classification of lags. Cf. also pp. 241–45.

tiplier lag, which he divides into wage and non-wage; for the latter, he includes both the period between the effective earning of income and its acquisition and the period between acquisition and expenditure. He also introduces the so-called "output lag" involving a delay between increased output and induced investment to meet it. Such are the differences among the economists we have selected for analysis. Later we will attempt to show that the number of appropriate time lags is by no means an arbitrary matter, and that sociological analysis furnishes a conceptual framework indicating why certain time lags are important within a given social system.

How long are the relevant time lags? In an early exposition of the time-lag notion, D. H. Robertson[1] incorporated the concept of the "day" consumption-expenditures lag, apparently with no serious claim that this period is a literal representation of consumer behaviour. Samuelson extended this period to one year, also with no apparent defence of this period on grounds of consumer behaviour. Kalecki fixed the lag between investment decisions and income change at 7–10 months; and this was supported by empirical reference, at least to the limited data from which he derived the time span. Hicks traces the logical consequences—in terms of the magnitude, speed, and other effects of income and investment changes—of different assigned values. For instance, the difference between a three-month and one-month lag in consumption means a changed period of adjustment in the multiplicative rise of income.

In one sense the methods of assignment of length to time lags are the source of genuine differences in the models of the trade cycle. In another sense the "alternative" solutions are not competitors in the same methodological race. That is to say, to specify a single arbitrary length (Robertson or Samuelson) or to exhaust several possible arbitrary lengths (Hicks) is one set of operations, namely, to illustrate the economic effects of a minimum number of hypotheses. To assign *empirical* value to the length (Kalecki) is another set of operations, to be performed when applying the model from case to case. Some economists create logical models; others apply these models by filling in empirical data. But as we shall show later, this distinction between a theoretical model of the trade cycle on

[1] Robertson, D. H., *Banking Policy and The Price Level*, 1932, pp. 59 ff.

the one hand and the "facts" on the other, as two sets of operations, raises a serious analytic dilemma which limits the scope of economic theory as such.

What value is to be assigned to relevant functions, propensities or coefficients? All three of the representative trade cycle theorists agree that the fluctuations depend upon (besides the lags) the value of the coefficients which determine the magnitude of the accelerator and multiplier. Samuelson and Hicks vary such values numerically and thus derive several different cycles of varying magnitude. Since Kalecki did not calculate any definite hypothetical empirical path, no definite numerical values for the relevant coefficients were necessary. The coefficients are such, however, as to require *some* value, even in the Kalecki model. The important point is that although some value is required, in *all* cases there is no stable criterion in economic theory for assigning value.

Is the path of the cycle determinate or indeterminate? To summarize the problems which appear in determining the time lag and multiplier-accelerator coefficients, we turn to the problem of the determinacy or indeterminacy of the cycle itself, which rests upon the decisions taken on these issues. If the model is assigned fixed values—either at the earlier stage of arbitrariness or at the later stage of introducing a single statistic—it has no *general* reference to empirical economic processes. If such fixity is relaxed by changing the values of variables numerically, then the model can account for various *possible* empirical cases. But merely to change the values numerically gives the economist no criteria other than the logical limitations of the number scheme he uses, for preferring any one of the resulting cycles. This is the central dilemma of economic analysis. On the one hand is the legitimate and desired aim to preserve the scientific integrity of the model; but on the other, any application to economic processes seems to necessitate a degeneration of the model to a lower level of scientific generality. Furthermore, this dilemma will not be solved, in the nature of the case, by appeal to more and more refined economic theory *as such.* With economic theory it is possible to formalize the relationships among the various coefficients, functions and/or propensities and predict the movement of economic series on the basis of changes of such relationships; but it is not possible to choose the original values of the coefficients or to determine the conditions of their variation on economic grounds alone. So long as the economist remains within the confines of economic theory alone, therefore, this dilemma will continue to reappear. It is our contention that sociological theory, by providing an analytical framework within which important economic coefficients can be assigned values on the basis of their relevant sociological contexts, can offer substantive contribution to the resolution of this dilemma.

Before proceeding to the nature of this contribution, let us note a few signs of incipient controversy among economists concerning the adequacy of trade cycle models. Though no sophisticated economist claims that a general model is a realistic representation of the empirical world, there are implicit claims and counterclaims of spatio-temporal applicability of certain types of models. To limit our illustration of such claims to the above authors: Samuelson includes the accelerator on the grounds that the phenomenon of oscillation cannot be explained on the basis of the multiplier alone;[1] Kalecki attacks the Harrod model on the grounds that it truncates the length of the observed cycle;[2] and Hicks repeatedly justifies the introduction of the multiplier and accelerator refinements on the grounds of "breath of realism," "likely to correspond to actual experience,"[3] and "direct power to explain what happens."[4] Certainly it is possible to choose between cycles on the basis of gross errors of exclusion or inclusion of economic mechanisms and their refinements. But as we have shown, such claims are justified only up to that point where economic principles themselves offer no further discriminative power. At that point it is necessary to turn to other conceptual schemes.

A second source of incipient conflict is the overall negation by some economists of the possibilities of a *general* theory of economic fluctuations. Joan Robinson has expressed one side of this controversy under the heading of "Fossils": " . . . we must abandon the artificial device of imagining [a private enterprise economy] to confront each change of fortune with a history of smooth development behind it. . . . Each section

[1] Samuelson, *op. cit.*, p. 75.
[2] Kalecki, *op. cit.*, p. 66.
[3] Hicks, *op. cit.*, p. 89.
[4] *Ibid.*, p. 94.

of the economy has all sorts of vicissitudes even when the whole is developing fairly steadily."[1] Mrs. Robinson is especially concerned with the influence of past variability on expectations of entrepreneurs.

This claim, reminiscent of the "historical relativist" controversy which has plagued every social science at one time or another, is instructive in one sense. The analysis of trade cycles (or other economic phenomena) must rest, that is, on the results of analysis on several system levels, depending upon the order of the problem to be solved.[2] Among the levels required for the analysis of economic fluctuations are certainly subsystems of the economy and their fluctuations, the personal history of entrepreneurs *vis-à-vis* past economic fluctuations, as well as the contemporary functioning economy. But if the claim is meant either to deny the possibility of systematically ordering economic categories because of variations in expectations upon which they depend, or to deny the possibility of systematically ordering the changed expectations themselves according to a coherent theory of social systems, then on the grounds we have spelled out in this volume, we must reject this claim as an unjustified over-reaction to the variability at the boundaries of economics which cannot be ordered by means of conventional economic concepts.

A third "response" to this major dilemma is the familiar endogeneity-exogeneity dichotomy, which is a formally incorporated realization that what is usually assumed for analytical reasons to be constant often varies in empirical fact. Let us take a final example from Hicks. In outlining the cycle, he assumes that the rate g of autonomous investment of growth is constant, i.e., free from exogenous influences. Later[3] he investigates "some of the possibilities which arise when we allow for fluctuations in autonomous investment" in terms of the consequences for the path of the cycle. It is not necessary to go into the details of these possibilities; suffice it to say that Hicks has pointed out a number of possible empirical complications, and that appeal to "exogenous" factors illustrates the importance of the analysis of many system levels in connection

[1] Robinson, J., "The Generalization of the General Theory," in *The Rate of Interest*, 1953, pp. 124–125.

[2] Cf. Chap. II, pp. 60–61.

[3] Hicks, *op. cit.*, Chap. IX.

with empirical phenomena. But, as such, the dichotomy treats endogenous factors as originating within the economic system and exogenous as originating vaguely outside the system but not explicitly as the result of processes in *other specific systems*. Hence within the framework of the bare endogeneity-exogeneity dichotomy there are neither criteria by which to choose among the possibilities of various empirical phenomena nor criteria by which to determine the nature and operation of specific extra-economic sub-systems.

The social sciences other than economics have the task of providing grounds for assigning values to non-economic elements. In Chapters II and III we have shown that elements of the non-economic world possess determinate order. We now wish to push this analysis further. First we will dissect the economy itself according to the principles of the theory of action; next we will turn to the regulation and control of internal economic processes; and finally, with models of the trade cycle before us, we will attempt to demonstrate that such an analysis contributes to the determinacy of a theory of economic fluctuations without sacrificing its generality.

THE INTERNAL STRUCTURE OF THE ECONOMY

The principle by which the economy (or any other social system) can be dissected analytically is one of the fundamental principles of the theory of action: what may be treated as a unit for purposes of one level of analysis may be treated as a system for purposes of another.[1] To illustrate, when the system level is the society as a whole, the economy is a unit functionally differentiated along the adaptive dimension. At the next lower level of analysis the economy becomes a system with four units representing solutions to *its* system problems. We now propose to shift the point of reference once again toward the microscopic, and analyse each of the four units of the economy as systems in themselves. In particular we will treat production, finance and capitalization, entrepreneurship, and economic commitments as sub-systems maintaining boundaries relative to each other.[2]

[1] Parsons, Bales and Shils, *Working Papers in the Theory of Action*, Chap. V.
[2] Cf. Fig. 2, Chap. II, p. 44.

This dissection is, of course, theoretically important in itself; our main aim, however, is to provide the groundwork for the analysis of economic process in this chapter and economic growth in the next.

Let us first recapitulate some principles of functional differentiation which apply at all levels. The most general principle is that any system tends toward differentiation of structure in accordance with four functional problems: goal attainment, adaptation, integration, and latent tension management and pattern maintenance. The meaning of these problems is constant from system to system: the goal-attainment function realizes the primary orientation of the system in question; the adaptive function meets certain situational exigencies, either by adjusting in the face of inflexible reality demands or actively transforming the environmental features in question; the integrative function regulates the inter-relationships between the already-differentiated adaptive, goal-attainment and latency subsectors, mitigates the level of distinct differentiation of each that obtains, and in general promotes harmonious interaction; finally, the latency function furnishes, maintains and renews the motivational and cultural patterns integral to the interaction of the system as a whole. We repeat: the meaning of these four system problems does not change from system to system. At the same time the *content* of the differentiated sub-structures fulfilling these functions does differ from system to system. For instance, the economy differs in content from the finance and capitalization sub-system, even though each is adaptive at its respective system level. Characterization of any functional differentiation, therefore, involves a *general meaning* of the relevant functional problem and a *particular meaning* at the system level in question.

A second general principle is that the statement of functions is not equivalent to the description of any one concrete empirical structure.[1] Rather it refers to a determinate range of structural variation, the empirical referent of which may differ from time to time and from place to place. Thus, later in the chapter[2] we will demonstrate that while certain individuals and collectivities—individual lenders, stockholding bodies,

[1] Cf. Chap. I, pp. 14–16 and Chap. II, pp. 60–61.

[2] Cf. below, pp. 217–18.

investment banks, commercial banks, etc.—differ in the concrete, they all perform, at least in part, the same function relative to the adaptive boundary processes.

These two distinctions—between functional problems in general and functional problems within a given system on the one hand, and between particular functional problems and concrete empirical institutions on the other—should be kept clearly in mind as the analysis proceeds. We will spell out, for each of the four economic sub-systems, (*a*) the general functional problems which all sub-systems face, (*b*) the range of variation of structurally differentiated role types which contribute to the solution of these functional problems in each specific sub-system, and (*c*) instances of concrete roles and institutions which are relevant to the solution in question.

For economy of expression, the following notation system will be used throughout: as above, A=adaptive; G=goal attainment; I=integrative, and L=latent tension management and pattern maintenance. Further, when these symbols are combined in sequence, e.g., A_{G_i}, the combination refers to progressive levels of differentiation toward the microscopic. In the case of A_{G_i}, therefore, A represents the adaptive system at the most macroscopic level, i.e., the economy; the G represents the goal-attainment sub-system of the economy, i.e., the production functions; and the i, at the next level down, represents the integrative sub-sector of the production sub-system, or "production co-ordination" (see Figure 15). Likewise, A_{G_a} (in the same figure) represents "procurement of facilities" within the production sub-system within the economic system.

The production sub-system of the economy (A_G) is concretely the aggregate of production units in an economy. The sub-system is, however, not identical with any particular firm or aggregate of firms. For clarity of understanding, a certain analogy with firm organization will be followed throughout, since the firm is a typical productive unit in a differentiated economy.[1]

[1] We do not view all production, however, as "physical production," as the selection of an industrial firm as a model for exposition might imply. "Production" includes anything of economic significance, not merely physical goods. We have selected the firm for illustrative purposes because it is sufficiently differentiated to provide ready examples of discrete roles

Figure 15 represents the fourfold functional dissection of the production sub-system of the economy. (1) Let us begin with the latency cell A_{G_l}—technical production or the flow of the production line—the general functions to maintain and renew the processes integral to the operation and interaction of the production sub-system as a whole. Concretely, these functions are fulfilled by the flow of materials and labour through the aggregate of production organizations. Some of the relevant technical roles are machine tender, foreman, plant engineer,

FIGURE 15

A_G

PRODUCTION SUB-SYSTEM

Procurement of facilities *a*	*g* Production, distribution and sales
l Technical production (flow of production line)	*i* Production co-ordination

plant inspector, etc. The A_{G_l} sub-sector is, therefore, a sort of reservoir of scheduled obligations which underlie the realization of production goals. (2) By way of contrast, A_{G_g}—production, marketing and sales—involves the manipulation of the production goals themselves, which is usually accomplished by means of "policy decisions." These decisions change the quality, quantity and organization of the A_{G_l} elements in the short run. Relevant roles include top management in all instances, but in more differentiated organizations responsibility falls upon such role incumbents as sales executives, production managers, etc. (3) A_{G_a}—procurement of facilities—is another necessary condition for the realization of production goals in that it is the mode of adaptation to certain situational exigencies. The most common of these exigencies is the need for

which can be assigned to system-problem solutions. In organizations which are not so highly differentiated the same system problems are met, but often by roles which are fused, i.e., multifunctional.

generalized facilities, in the form of liquid assets, to implement a change in the production process or to meet crises such as debt or mortgage foreclosure. The term "financing" is often used to cover these adaptive functions. (4) A_{G_i}—production co-ordination—regulates the production-marketing-sales decisions, the kind and level of financing, the organization of the plant, human relations, and relates these to each other to ensure smooth operation of the production sub-system as a whole. This function operates to establish lines of communication in the organization and to assure successful functioning through the channels; hence it is appropriate to include many of the "trouble-shooting" activities of the executive. In concrete cases these co-ordinating roles often fuse with the financing, production-marketing-sales, and some technical roles; in larger organizations, however, co-ordinating positions tend to be segregated by function in the staff as distinguished from line organization.

FIGURE 16

A_A

INVESTMENT-CAPITALIZATION SUB-SYSTEM

Guarantee of liquidity *a*	*g* Production of productive capacity
l Credit and investment mechanisms (flow of credit and capital)	*i* Guarantee of enterprise

Figure 16 shows the differentiation of the investment-capitalization sub-system. It will be recalled[1] that the goal of the economy as a whole is the production of wealth or utility for the society or its sub-systems. Fulfilment of this goal maximizes adaptation for the social system. Just as production of wealth represents facilities for the pursuit of societal goals and sub-goals, on the next level down—the level of the economy as a system—production of producers' wealth maximizes

[1] Chap. I, pp. 20–23.

facilities for the pursuit of the economy's production goals. This view of capital and the production of productive capacity is fully in accordance with the logic of these concepts as employed in economics.

The investment-capitalization sub-system is therefore that set of roles relevant to the control of the creation of capitalized resources. It is important to underline the word *control.* Investment-capitalization means neither the physical processes of production of, e.g., cement or steel for capital goods, nor the processes of speculation and trading on the stock market. Rather the investment-capitalization function refers to those performance-sanction relationships by means of which these processes and others are controlled. The logic of this assumption of course applies on the production (A_G) level; that is, production is the differentiated role system responsible for the control of concrete production processes.

The investment-capitalization sub-system faces the same functional problems as any system, though their solutions differ in structure from other systems. Thus (1) the investment-credit mechanisms (A_{A_l}) underlie the capital exchange and investment. Concretely these include the institutionalized commitment to the credit system, certain types of accounting, certain conventions in the exchange of securities, and so on. These are the givens of the process of the creation of producers' wealth, just as technical production (A_{G_l}) represents the givens of the production sub-system. (2) The goal of the capitalization-investment sub-system is the control of the creation of producers' wealth itself. We will consider this goal in more detail when we analyse the economy's internal boundary relationships. (3) Given this goal, the creation of productive capacity is not merely random accumulation of capital, just as production of goods and services by A_G is not a simple accumulation of products; the A_A sub-system has a "situation" to which it must adapt. This situation is primarily the current production needs of the economy as defined in A_G. Hence there must be a selective accumulation or allocation of productive capacity in accordance with certain production needs. This allocation is realized primarily by the mechanism of short-term investment, which represents the adaptive interchange between the investment-capitalization sub-system and the production sub-system. We will explore the interchange in detail when we consider the boundary relationship itself and its contractual regulation. In the meantime we will note certain mechanisms by means of which the adaptive function of the investment-capitalization sub-system is maximized. The most salient mechanism is a certain *guarantee of the liquidity of securities* (A_{A_a}) which permits continuous adaptation to the production needs of the society by re-allocating funds to various firms, dropping commitments to particular firms and taking them up again, turning to new investment opportunities, etc. In a highly differentiated capitalization system such liquidity is healthy, for it sensitizes investors to production needs and opportunities and allows for quick adaptation to changes in these. The institutional focus for the adaptive sub-sector of the capitalization-investment sub-system is, of course, the stock exchange. (4) On several grounds, however, adaptation alone is not sufficient to meet the various exigencies facing the creation of productive capacity. Somehow or other there must be a balance between short-term investment and the long-term investment to cover the changing needs of the economy. Furthermore, as Keynes[1] and others have pointed out, excessive attention to the short-term prospects often involves sheer speculation, or interest in short-term appreciation of securities as opposed to the expectation of future yield of income. To account for attention to long-term needs and for correctives to excessive speculation, we turn to the integrative sub-sector, A_{A_i}.[2] These mechanisms of stabilization and correction take the form, if we may appropriate Keynes' term,[3] of *guarantees of enterprise*. Enterprise is defined as "the activity of forecasting the prospective yield of assets over their whole life" as opposed to speculative trading. Investment must strike some balance between enterprise (integration) and short-term gains (adaptation).[4] Concrete examples of integrative restric-

[1] *General Theory, op. cit.*, Chap. 12.

[2] This opposition between the adaptive and integrative dimensions is consistent with the general theory of social interaction. Cf. *Working Papers*, Chap. III.

[3] *General Theory*, p. 158.

[4] Cf. Keynes: "Speculators may do no harm as bubbles on a steady stream of enterprise. But the position is serious when enterprise becomes the bubble of a whirlpool of speculation." *General Theory*, p. 159.

tions are a government transfer tax on all transactions, the requirement of a cash percentage for the purchase of securities, etc. These integrative mechanisms and others guarantee a certain interest in the longer-term state of productivity in the economy as reflected in long-term returns.

The phenomenon of entrepreneurship is seldom isolated institutionally; that is to say, those who perform the entrepreneurial functions are the same individuals who perform various functions in other sub-sectors, e.g., production, co-ordination, procurement of facilities, etc. It is still possible, however, to treat the entrepreneurial function by differentiation of function according to system problems. Accordingly, in Figure 17, (1) A_{I_g} provides the institutionalized mobility,

FIGURE 17
A_I
ENTREPRENEURIAL SUB-SYSTEM

Financing of innovation *a*	New combinations of factors of production *g*
l Mobility, flexibility and substitutability of factors of production (flow of resources)	*i* Opportunity for innovation

flexibility and substitutability of the factors of production which are the latent prerequisites for changing combinations. Instances are the institutionalized motivation of workers to change residence for occupational reasons, acceptance of limited technological unemployment, etc. In short, this sub-sector includes those particular elements of economic rationality which are the value requisites for the pursuit of long-term economic adjustments. (2) A_{I_g} represents the actual process of innovation, or the offer of new combinations of factors of production, which is the goal of the entrepreneurial function. (3) A_{I_a}—financing of innovations—shows that the innovating entrepreneur faces certain environmental restrictions, such as differential availability of resources, the state of the arts, etc. These are the situational exigencies to which the entrepreneur must adapt. (4) The integrative sub-sector (A_{I_i}) is the complex of entrepreneurial decisions based upon the opportunities and incentives for innovation. These decisions are integrative in that they control the introduction of new combinations, limit the demand for inventions, resources, etc., limit the demand for risk capital, and change the market demand for re-allocating the uses of the factors of production.

The analysis of the economic commitments sub-system, shown in Figure 18, involves the classification—in system-problem terms—of the motivational commitments underlying

FIGURE 18

A_L

ECONOMIC COMMITMENTS

Commitment to long-term productivity *a*	*g* Commitment to productivity
l Economic values (economic rationality)	*i* Commitment to planned allocation of resources

the whole economic process. These are the "rent" factors for the economy. (1) A_{L_l} is the most general statement of positive valuation of economic activity as a form of activity, which underlies the commitments of A_{L_g}, A_{L_a}, and A_{L_i}. (2) The goal (A_{L_g}) of the underlying motivational and value structure of the economic system is a willingness to release resources, skills, etc., for capital use. This commitment to productivity is a particular instance of the more generalized commitment to the industrial economy as a salient sub-system of the system. (3) A_{L_a}, or the commitment to long-term productivity, differs from A_{L_g} in that the former is adaptive relative to certain special exigencies such as changes in long-term demand, in market structure, in pools of resources, etc. (4) The integrative function (A_{L_i}) is the commitment to supply the motivation and skills necessary for planning,[1] which regulates commitments merely to capitalize and commitments to change the form of the factors of production.

THE INTERNAL BOUNDARY RELATIONS OF THE ECONOMY

These four sub-systems—production, finance and capitalization, entrepreneurship and economic commitments—interlock by boundary processes governed by the same principles as the boundary processes linking the economy and the other societal sub-systems.

The total number of boundaries for any social system is four, three "open" and one "closed."[2] For instance, three of the sub-systems of the economy maintain open boundaries relative to cognate sub-systems of society. The latency sub-system of economic commitments, however, borders the societal value system and the institutionalized control of situational exigencies through it, in such a way that the commitments of the factors of production are not contingent upon short-term economic sanctions. Similarly *within* the economy, each of the four economic sub-systems has three boundaries relative to other economic sub-systems and one closed boundary. The relevant closed boundary is the latency boundary in all cases: credit mechanisms, technical production, flow of resources, and economic values. In each case the underlying motivational and cultural conditions appropriate to this sub-system are made available. For the boundary at A_{I_l}, for instance, the input (from the value system) is positive valuation of "enterprise" as a type of activity, as opposed to traditionalistic valuation of economic routine.[3]

[1] The word "planning" is not to be confused with governmental planning. As employed here, the term refers to some commitment to co-ordinate economic activities, independently of the source of this commitment. Hence this commitment can be focused in several possible institutional forms: large firms, government, individual entrepreneurs, etc.

[2] Cf. Chap. II, pp. 66–70.

[3] Even though each of these L sub-systems—A_{A_l}, A_{G_l}, A_{I_l}, and A_{L_l}—are the focus of the "closed" boundary in each case, i.e., articulate with the value system, this does not mean that they do not have boundaries *within*

At the three "open" boundaries, each sub-system interchanges with another primarily at one boundary only. For example, the economy's goal-attainment sub-system is contiguous to the latent tension-management and pattern-maintenance societal system, but *not* to the polity. The same logic holds for the boundaries *within* the economy as well. Each sub-system links with each at one boundary, yielding six boundary interchanges:[1]

$$A_{G_g}\text{–}A_{I_g} \qquad A_{A_g}\text{–}A_{L_g}$$
$$A_{G_a}\text{–}A_{A_a} \qquad A_{I_a}\text{–}A_{L_a}$$
$$A_{G_i}\text{–}A_{L_i} \qquad A_{I_i}\text{–}A_{A_i}$$

In Chapter III we attempted to show that every boundary interchange or market structure is characterized, if we consider it to constitute a social system in itself, by an exchange involving all the major components of a social system, i.e., goal-attainment, adaptation, integration and maintenance of common values. Now, for certain purposes in analysis of the market, only the goal-attainment aspect of the interchange (settlement of terms) may be singled out; indeed, a great deal of strictly economic analysis of market behaviour rests upon the supply and demand schedules which are constructed with reference to prices and quantities exchanged. For purposes of our analysis in this chapter, we will discuss only a single goal-exchange in the internal markets of the economy. We feel, however, that with appropriate endeavour the "non-economic" elements of control of the internal boundaries can be developed to levels of discrimination comparable to those of the external boundaries.

The internal boundary processes are *not* identical with concrete organizations or individuals in any given case. What is represented in a boundary interchange is the balancing of *decisions* in the contexts of different *roles*. Whether these decisions and roles are coterminous with any concrete individual or collectivity is largely a function of the level of the division of

the system in question. For instance, we would expect the A_{A_i} to have boundary relationships "at the next level down" with A_{A_a}, A_{A_g} and A_{A_i}. Cf. Chap. II, pp. 51–70, esp. pp. 66–70.

[1] The total is a mathematical exhaustion of possibilities in accordance with the paradigm presented in the footnote, Chap. II, p. 68.

labour in society.[1] Sometimes the two sets of decisions involve only one individual actor; e.g., the roles of executive and entrepreneur often are held by a single individual. Sometimes the two roles are found within the same organization. The fact that the balancing of performance and sanction may be a special case of role conflict or role fusion does not prohibit, however, regarding the balancing of roles or even components of roles as a definite boundary interchange. This is an important caution of the general theory of social systems: to isolate analytical or functional relationships is not necessarily to relate concrete actors or collectivities in any other capacity than certain aspects of their roles.

It is possible to characterize each interchange in conventional market terms; in each case the market is for the supplied performance. It is also possible to construct a hypothetical supply and demand schedule for each of the six internal boundary interchanges.[2] The performance units appear on the conventional "quantity" axis and the sanction units on the conventional "price" axis.

Figure 19 summarizes all the boundary relationships within the economy; it also locates the external boundaries relative to the internal allocation. The reader should refer continually to this schematic representation as we discuss the internal boundaries one by one, for it is the groundwork for our substantive sociological commentary on economic dynamics in the remainder of the volume.

$A_{G_g} - A_{I_g}$ is the interchange between the "production, distribution, and sales" sub-sector of the production sub-system and the "new combinations of the factors of production" sub-sector of the entrepreneurship sub-system. The entrepreneur provides new combinations; in return he receives profit. From the standpoint of *content* this interchange is similar to the interchange between the economy and the integrative sub-system $(A_I - I_I)$[3]. The crucial difference, however, is one

[1] Cf. Chap. I, pp. 14–16.

[2] For purposes of illustration, we will carry out this operation for the A_{G_g}–A_{I_g} interchange by constructing a possible supply-demand schedule. For the other boundary processes, even though the logic of supply and demand applies throughout the analysis, limitations of space make it impossible to carry out the whole analysis.

[3] Cf. Chap. II, pp. 66–70.

FIGURE 19

THE INTERNAL AND EXTERNAL BOUNDARY INTERCHANGES OF THE ECONOMY

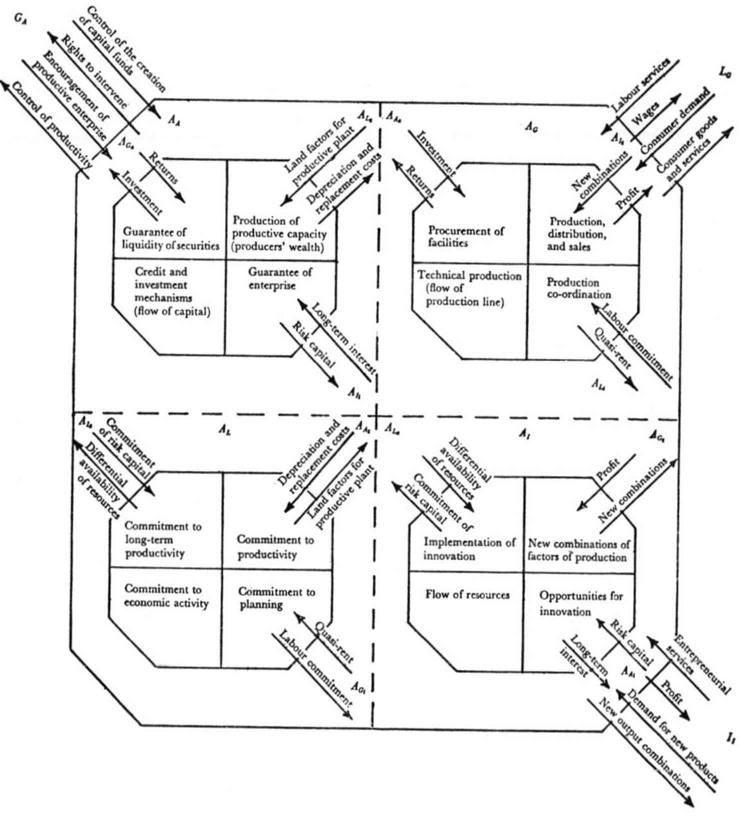

of system reference. That is, in $A_I - I_I$ the system reference is the interpenetration of economy and society; from the present point of reference, the interchange involves two sub-systems *within* the economy. It is not necessary that there be two discreet empirical transactions for us to draw this distinction; at finer levels of differentiation the same factors from the standpoint of content often represent different exchanges at different system levels.[1] On a hypothetical supply-demand schedule in the resulting market for new combinations, profits represent the price and new combinations the quantity. As a first approximation, the supply curve presumably slopes upward and to the right, since greater profits in the production sub-system bring forth a comparably greater quantity of new combinations. The demand curve for new combinations is presumably perfectly elastic if potential profit is above zero, since any profit more than zero represents a lowering of the cost-revenue ratio. At the point where profits equal zero or less, however, the demand for new combinations drops to and remains at zero.[2]

In recent times, as the technological base for production has multiplied in complexity, the market for new combinations has been institutionalized extensively as a "cost" of firms. The gigantic research and development funds of the large manufacturing firms in the United States are perhaps the most striking examples. Certain types of markets for new combinations (e.g., atomic development) were for some time institutionalized exclusively within the governmental framework. Finally, some research for new combinations is pursued in universities, both under government contract and as private scientific research.[3]

1 Other levels of possible differentiation along these lines are organization, sub-organization, role type, sub-role, etc. Exchanges among these levels have different analytical significance.

2 This is a case in which both sides of the "market" are often found in the same concrete role. The balancing of the executive role component and the entrepreneur role component (the two relevant roles in this exchange) may be a problem of role conflict or role compatibility. The fact that the occupant of the roles may be the same individual, however, bears no consequence for our analysis.

3 One of the more interesting of the many forms of "imperfection" in this market is the fact that universities seldom receive contract money from business firms for research programmes, even in cases where specific lines of research and development have not been stipulated.

$A_{G_i} - A_{L_i}$ shows the relationship between the "co-ordination of production" sub-sector of the production sub-system and the "commitment to planned allocation of resources" sub-sector of the economic commitments sub-system. The interchange involves one of the elements classified as a land factor, namely, commitment to labour.[1] The sanction by which these commitments are recruited for the production sub-system is more or less equivalent to the economic term "quasi-rent."[2] This term seems satisfactory, since it indicates the "land" basis for these primarily motivational and cultural factors.

$A_{A_a} - A_{G_a}$. The flow of investment funds balanced by returns is the primary relationship between the capitalization sub-system and the production sub-system, as shown in Figure 19. The performance on the part of investors in the A_{A_a} sub-system is to supply investment funds originating at the $A_A - G_A$ interchange; the sanctions are primarily dividend or interest payments on securities. We will discuss this familiar interchange further when we analyse the contractual regulations and other mechanisms of control of this market. We must clarify, however, the sense in which we treat investment as an *intra*-economic market.

As shown in Chapter III, the term "labour" applies to several levels of generality of commitment of human services to economic use; in particular we distinguished generalized performance capacity, trained capacity, membership in the labour force, commitment to a particular organization (employment), and commitment to a specific job and finally task within the organization. All of these categories are "labour," but they differ in the degree of commitment to strictly economic use and control. Labour becomes analytically

[1] This use of "commitment" as referring specifically to the land elements of motivational commitments should not be confused with the narrower use of the same term in connection with the *G*-component of the contract of occupation. Together the "land commitment" and the "commitment contingent on economic reward" constitute the two elements of the total commitment to accept employment.

[2] The term "quasi-rent" has been used more for managerial recruitment because of the higher visibility of the "fixed cost" element of managerial talents and commitment. We would extend the concept to cover those elements of all commitments to labour which are not contingent on short-term economic sanctions.

"intra-economic" at the transition between trained performance capacity and membership in the labour force.[1]

The labour services are at the disposal of the economy once membership in the labour force has been accepted; however, ego is *still* a member of the household, and the economic use of his services must be adapted to the exigencies imposed by the structure of this collectivity.[2] "Intra-economic" does not mean that the incumbent of the role has no other involvements. The same holds in principle at the transition from the labour force to specific employment; membership in the household still obtains.

The case of liquid resources is analogous but different in important respects. "Capital" applies at several parallel levels of generality of commitment. Not to mention the prior stages, generalized purchasing power becomes capital funds which are put at the disposal of the economy for economic uses at the $A_A - G_A$ boundary; in this analytical sense any use to which these funds are put after this transaction is "intra-economic." Hence the process of investment $(A_{A_a} - A_{G_a})$ and the concrete acquisition of capital goods $(A_{L_g} - A_{A_g})$ are intra-economic. Capital at all these levels still has "political" significance, however. As the regulation of the contract of investment shows,[3] the owner and manipulator of capital funds is continuously involved in a position of public responsibility in the polity; the use of these funds is subject to adaptive and value conditions stemming from the investor's membership in political[4] organizations.

We treat "investment" in a technical sense as the transfer of capital funds from the capitalization-investment sub-system to the production sub-system $(A_{A_a} - A_{G_a})$ or to particular units of it.[5] Given this limited meaning, investment stands at a

[1] Cf. Chap. III, pp. 119–123.

[2] Cf. the discussion of the contract of employment, pp. 114–123, and the market for labour, pp. 146–156, in Chap. III for an account of the exigencies imposed by membership in this collectivity and some of the institutional patternings relative to these exigencies.

[3] Chap. III, pp. 123–139.

[4] In the wider sense of the term.

[5] Capital, in the economic literature, has referred to all of these levels of generality of liquid resources; and investment has referred to at least the lower three of the transitions between these levels.

central point in the whole economic process. On the one hand, certain "political" decisions earmarking the funds for economic uses and not other system goals are made at the $A_A - G_A$ boundary preliminary to commitment to firms. From the political side, therefore, the investment allocates these funds among industries. On the other hand, via the $A_G - L_G$ boundary, the decisions as to which industries are important to the consuming public are made or anticipated before investment is undertaken. The problem, once the demand for production is apparent or anticipated, activates an intra-economic mechanism to gain facilities to carry out this production. In the sense that the investment-returns exchange adjusts these $A_A - G_A$ and $A_G - L_G$ decisions (which are by no means automatically adjusted to each other), it stands between two major external boundary processes. Figure 20 illustrates this central position schematically. Investment is thus the intra-economic allocation of *already-earmarked monetary facilities to already-demanded production.*[1]

The importance of these considerations—relating investment decisions to the two external boundaries, showing investment decisions to be internal to the economy in a sense that the other boundaries are not, and demonstrating the connection of investment functions with an adaptive cross-tie which relates

[1] At this point we might mention a few parallels between the "system vs. unit" distinction and the "levels of generality" paradigm utilized in Chap. III (cf. esp. Figure 11, p. 139). The A_A–G_A interchange between control of creation of capital funds and control of productivity treats the economy as a system interchanging with the polity as system, with the adaptive sub-systems of each considered as units for purposes of this boundary interchange. At the level of the A_{A_a}–A_{G_a} exchange between investment funds and returns, however, what are treated as *units* for the former exchange are treated as *themselves systems*, exchanging with each other. This relativity of treatment as system and/or unit is a general characteristic of the theory of action (cf. *Working Papers*, Chap. V). Paralleling the system-reference change between the A_A–G_A and A_{A_a}–A_{G_a} exchanges are two transitions between levels of generality: (1) from "generalized purchasing power" to "capital funds for economic use" (parallel to A_A–G_A), and (2) from "capital funds for economic use" to "investment funds committed to particular firms" (parallel to A_{A_a}–A_{G_a}). The "system-unit" distinction emphasizes the particular systems involved in a given boundary exchange; the "levels of generality" paradigm emphasizes the status of the exchangeable in the interchange.

the political decisions to relinquish facilities to consumption decisions—will become apparent when we discuss the role of investment in the business cycle.

$A_{A_g} - A_{L_g}$. This boundary relates the capitalization-investment sub-system goal to institutionalized land factors in the economy in the familiar capital goods market.[1] It involves the final acquisition of these capital goods and services with the funds which proceed in decreasing generality via the $A_A - G_A$ and $A_{A_a} - A_{G_a}$ boundaries.[2] The major performance is the supply of land factors, the most obvious instance of which is

Figure 20

INVESTMENT AS AN INTRA-ECONOMIC PROCESS

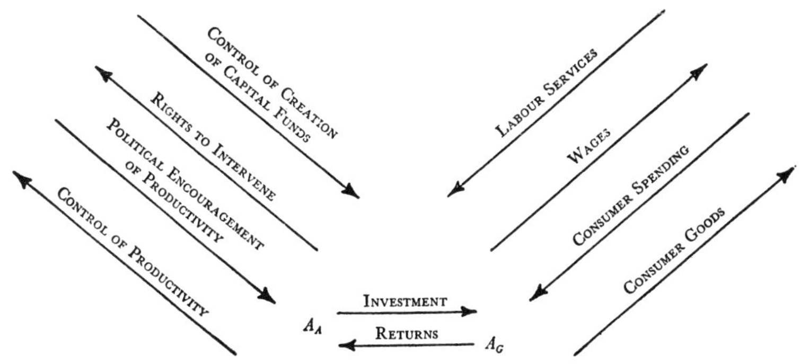

physical plant, to the capitalization-investment sub-system. The reward is payment of rent factors, e.g., depreciation and replacement cost on capital goods.

$A_{A_g} - A_{L_g}$ and $A_{A_a} - A_{G_a}$ demonstrate in what sense the investment-capitalization sub-system acts as an active intermediary in the transfer of land to the consumer and the transfer of

[1] Because there is in the literature a certain bias in the direction of discussing capital plant and the incorporation of land factors into it in terms of "physical" factors, we again emphasize the importance of cultural and motivational factors which go into the capitalization-investment sub-system.

[2] Not all funds acquired via A_{A_a}–A_{G_a} are committed to land factors. Certain of these go to meet current costs, e.g., in labour payments. Cf. Chap. III, pp. 134–37 for a discussion of the asymmetry of these two uses.

certain shares of income to rentiers. Let us return to Schumpeter's acceptance of Böhm-Bawerk's dictum that ultimately the only factors of production are land and labour.[1] The investor, as an intermediary in the manipulation of land by labour to produce concrete goods, adds the value of capital investment as a factor of production in the $A_{G_a} - A_{A_a}$ exchange. This exchange constitutes only half of the addition of capital productivity, however. The $A_{A_g} - A_{L_g}$ interchange consummates, as it were, the addition of capital by exchanging land factors for the costs of depreciation and replacement of capital plant. In the terms utilized in Chapter III,[2] the $A_{G_a} - A_{A_a}$ interchange is the locus of a step down from a higher level of generality of capital resources and the $A_{L_g} - A_{A_g}$ interchange is the locus of a further step in the direction of the decreasing generality of these resources within the firm. So in two senses the A_A sub-system is an intermediary between A_G and A_L: (1) it acts as a repository of generalized facilities which gives greater flexibility to the purchase of land factors (by means of the offer of investment funds), and (2) it renders these land factors more productive in the long run, even though capitalization means a short-term deferment of production.[3]

The whole investment complex has been at the focus of economic analysis from the beginnings of the science. Is it possible to interpret the classicist and Keynesian ways of treating of the investment market in accordance with our boundary process conceptual scheme?[4]

The classical treatment of the investment function parallels the classical conceptualization of the other boundary processes. The businessman cannot borrow and pay interest without the use of concrete capital goods. His alternatives, therefore, are to carry out "real" investment or close down. Investment in plant is the "real" basis of the security of the capital owner's assets, because expectations of returns are based on produc-

[1] I.e., A_L and A_G are the only relevant sub-systems.

[2] Cf. Chap. II, p. 85.

[3] These two contributions of the A_A sub-system constitute a definition, at the economy level, of the concept "adaptation" as we use it more generally.

[4] Our treatment is parallel to our discussion of consumption, labour, and liquidity toward the end of Chap. II.

tivity, not mere promises of the borrower to pay. The classical view is that, apart from frictional disturbances, the market for securities is continuously cleared. The determination of the decisions to invest is primarily in economic terms, i.e., the degree of adequacy of return motivates the holder of securities to decide whether or not to continue holding them. The investor's role in the polity is not problematical.

Keynes introduced an empirical modification of the classical doctrine. The investment function is normally a function of economic factors in the usual sense; the cost of capital goods on the supply side and the expectation of future yield on the demand side determine the marginal efficiency of capital schedule which intersects with the interest rate and determines the level of investment. In connection with the expectation of future yield, however, Keynes emphasized the word *expectation*. Expectations may be oriented to realistic prospects of economic productivity; there is also a speculative element in the investment process by virtue of which the purchaser is oriented to the prospects of short-term appreciation of the market price. Keynes thus incorporated this discontinuity more fully into his theory than did the classicists.

Keynes treated the factors responsible for major fluctuations of the marginal efficiency of capital as "psychological"; this represents an advance over some classical formulations which played down such factors. But as we hope to show below, this label commonly signifies that these factors are conceived as linear, hence reducible to the strength or weakness of *one* variable. We also hope to show that behaviour leading to fluctuations of the investment function is not merely "psychologically" determined, but is determined by the involvement of the investor in a particular market situation and in a particular extra-economic social system of action (i.e., the polity).[1]

$A_{L_a} - A_{I_a}$. The entrepreneur must adapt to the degree of commitment to the land factors (*pools* of physical resources, technological information, commitments to research, etc.) by means of which new combinations are realized. This involves an interchange (shown in Figure 19) between the "implementation of innovation" sub-sector of the entrepreneurship sub-system and the "commitment to long-term productivity"

[1] Cf. Chap. II, pp. 56–64.

sub-sector of the economic commitments sub-system. The input from A_{L_a} is the differential supply of physical resources, information, inventions, etc.; the reward is risk capital funds. The resulting market is for *changing* factors of production.

$A_{L_a} - A_{I_a}$ is the first of two steps in the addition of new combinations. The second is the transfer of the new combinations to the production sub-system ($A_{I_g} - A_{G_g}$). Thus the entrepreneur is in a sense analogous to the investor, an active intermediary between the two factors of land and labour, though his addition of value is through integrative channels and hence qualitatively different from the contribution of the investor.

$A_{A_i} - A_{I_i}$. Finally, we must inquire into the relations between the two "intermediaries"—the entrepreneur and the investor—in the flow from land to production. The boundary shown is between the "opportunity for innovation" sub-sector of the entrepreneurship sub-system and the "guarantees of enterprise" sub-system of the investment-capitalization sub-system. This is the familiar market for venture capital in which the input from the A_A system is long-term risk capital funds and the return is the long-term interest rate or long-term returns. This link between mere investment and development or change of the economy represents, more than any other, the locus of enterprise. Just as $A_{A_a} - A_{G_a}$ sensitizes investors to current production needs of the economy, the boundary between investor and entrepreneur sensitizes investors to the long-term developmental possibilities and supplies the entrepreneur with the funds to co-ordinate the incorporation of these sources of change.[1]

To summarize the allocation of the factors of production within the economy: A flow of land factors converges on the production sub-system, with the investor and entrepreneur "joining" the flow, adding the factors of capital and organization, respectively.[2] Rewards for the factors of production flow in the reverse direction and correspond point by point with the

[1] Cf. Chap. V, pp. 266–67, for a discussion of its relation to institutional change.

[2] This delineation of the respective roles of the "capitalist" and the "entrepreneur" in the narrower sense shows that they occupy the positions in the economy which are in greatest command of short-term and long-term changes in productivity, respectively. We will discuss the significance of their roles in Chap. V in connection with economic development.

flow of factors themselves. A certain proportion of these monetary rewards are "drained off" at each stage as shares of income for the various agents in the addition of value. The model of the economy, including both external and internal boundaries, as shown in Figure 19, represents an exhaustive analysis of the major processes of acquisition of the factors of production and their allocation and combination within the economy.[1]

Before turning to the interpretation and supplementation of economic dynamics, we will illustrate the relationship between the paradigm and the *concrete* structure of the economy. It is inappropriate to *identify* the concrete organizations and roles of individuals in the economy with the actors in the performance-sanction relationships involved in the boundary relations. It is possible, however, to identify the boundary processes in which several collectivities or individuals are primarily involved. The following empirical examples are limited to capitalization in the broader sense.

(1) An undifferentiated case in which four boundary processes are combined is the *self-sufficient farmer* in the transaction of purchasing a tractor. In one role he creates his own credit (A_A–G_A) for the pursuit of economic production; at the same time he invests these funds in his own enterprise (A_{A_a}–A_{G_a}). More remotely, he adds to the productivity of the economy in return for continuing active or passive encouragement to productivity by the political sub-system (A_A–G_A). Finally, the purchasing transaction involves acquisition of the concrete tractor (A_{A_g}–A_{L_g}).

(2) The *commercial bank* as a concrete organization is a mediating structure at several boundaries. In the sense that it is the repository for liquid funds surrendered to it by private holders, it is involved in a boundary between the latency sub-system (household) and the polity.[2] In its capacities as holder of these funds, creator of credit, and distributor of loans to investors, it fulfils both political and economic functions;

[1] This characterization of economic processes in terms of two reverse flows corresponds formally to the more general characterization of the directions of flow which predominate in processes of performance and learning, respectively, in any system. Cf. *Working Papers*, pp. 222–227.

[2] Cf. Chap. II, pp. 61–62.

the crucial boundary relationship in this case is A_A–G_A. If it lends funds to enterprises itself, it is involved in the A_{A_a}–A_{G_a} boundary. The flow of funds in this latter interchange is usually in the form of short-term loans for working capital.[1]

(3) The *investment bank* has, like the commercial bank, the problem of securing liquid funds from savers. On the other hand, it commits these funds to firms for investment purposes ($A_{A_g} - A_{G_a}$). Finally, as a source of venture capital, the investment bank ties in with the entrepreneurial function ($A_{A_i} - A_{I_i}$).

(4) The *individual* or *collectivity* in purchasing a security squeezes two of the investment bank's functions into one, i.e., simultaneously creating credit liquidity ($A_A - G_A$) and placing the resulting liquid funds at the disposal of an investing firm through the medium of the investment contract ($A_{A_a} - A_{G_a}$ or $A_{A_i} - A_{I_i}$).

(5) Neither the investment bank nor the individual investor acquires the machinery, social organization, cultural artifact, etc. Thus, the actor who decides to invest seldom is involved in the $A_{A_g} - A_{L_g}$ boundary; usually the business enterprise is the recipient of the capital goods.

The above empirical examples distinguish between the analytical dissection of interchanges between differentiated decision clusters on the one hand, and the organizational patterning by means of which these interchanges are institutionalized on the other.[2] Our major concern in this volume is the functional, not the concrete organizational patterning of the economy.

[1] Since fixed capital and working capital are more or less arbitrarily chosen points along a continuum, it seems reasonable to include the facilities for both in the A_{A_a}–A_{G_a} boundary interchange. The distinguishing characteristic between the facilities which go for the category of "working capital" as opposed to "fixed capital" is, as a usual matter, the different sort of rewards which accompany the transmission of facilities for fixed capital. The latter usually are sanctioned by returns on securities, whereas loans for the temporary acquisition of working capital are serviced through the interest rate mechanism.

[2] By no means are the categories of fuctional differentiation of any system which we use the sole *determinants* of the concrete organizational structure of the economy. As a matter of fact, we have not addressed ourselves to the problem of the determinants of segmentation and similar structural processes. For a brief discussion, however, cf. Chap. II, pp. 43–46.

RESTATEMENT OF THE TRADE CYCLE

It will be recalled that in the study of short-term fluctuations there are two areas of indeterminacy of trade cycle theory: (1) by what principles do we assign values to the multiplier function and the accelerator function? (2) by what principles do we specify the number and length of time lags?

We will attack the first question as follows: first we will restate the trade cycle model in terms of the internal and external boundary processes: next we will outline some institutional regulations of the relevant internal boundaries; then we will suggest some outside limits for the investment and consumption functions—limits inferred from the structures of property, contract, and occupation; finally we will turn to the problem of the specific determination of the relevant co-efficients above and beyond these outside limits. To end the chapter we will briefly consider some sociological contributions to the time-lag problem.

Which of the boundaries in Figure 19 are involved in a trade cycle roughly equivalent in scope to the models considered earlier? By definition, the effect of the entrepreneurial function (or changes in combinations of factors), is held constant in short-term fluctuations. Hence we may eliminate the following boundary relationships[1]: (1) $A_I - I_I$, between the entrepreneurial sub-system of the economy and the integrative system of the society; (2) $A_{G_g} - A_{I_g}$, between the production sub-system and the entrepreneurial sub-system within the economy; (3) $A_{I_a} - A_{L_a}$, between the entrepreneurial sub-system and the economic commitments sub-system within the economy; (4) $A_{L_i} - A_{G_i}$, the supply of labour commitments to the production sub-system within the economy; (5) $A_{I_i} - A_{A_i}$, between the entrepreneurial sub-system and the finance-capitalization sub-system within the economy. We will return to these relationships, however, in the next chapter when we deal with structural differentiation and economic development.

Of the remaining boundaries, which ones are involved in a trade cycle? In the simple case when the production sub-system does not borrow or float securities in order to invest,

[1] The elimination is strictly analytical; the continuous empirical presence of the entrepreneurial function is obvious.

then only the following two boundaries are relevant: (1) $A_G - L_G$, which involves the balance between wages and labour supply and between consumption spending and consumption goods, respectively, between the economy and the household; (2) $A_{A_g} - A_{L_g}$, which deals with the acquisition of concrete investment goods by the investment sub-system.[1] These two interchanges are the locus for the simple multiplier and accelerator. The multiplier traces the immediate and feedback consequences of a change in investment for the goods-spending flow over the $A_G - L_G$ boundary. The accelerator principle traces the consequences of changes over the $A_{A_g} - A_{L_g}$ boundary in response to changes in rate of flow of the $A_G - L_G$ interchange.

For our discussion we will expand the narrower notion of the accelerator to the wider concept of the investment function. The usual view of the accelerator tends to reduce it to an intra-firm engineering problem,[2] which assumes either that the production sub-system saves enough to finance any required investment[3] or that no irregularities develop between firm and investor on the one hand and between investor and supplier of funds on the other. In a highly differentiated economy, these assumptions seem unrealistic, even for constructing a restricted model of the business cycle. The *investment function* therefore includes the roles involved in $A_{A_a} - A_{G_a}$ (the relation between investor and firm), and secondarily in $A_A - G_A$ (the relation between investor and creator of capital through credit).

These four markets—$A_G - L_G$, $A_A - G_A$, $A_{A_a} - A_{G_a}$, and $A_{A_g} - A_{L_g}$—two external and two internal, mark the points where differentiated roles are co-ordinated in the course of a trade cycle. It is possible to restate a typical trade cycle model in terms of the magnitude of the interchanges across these boundaries at various points during cycle. An upswing is marked by a gradual increase in the rate of all interchanges (in accordance with the operation of the multiplier and accelerator) over *all*

[1] These two boundaries apply only to the limiting case of the self-sufficient firm with complete reserves. As we show immediately below, two further boundaries are involved in investment.

[2] Cf. Samuelson's elementary outline of the accelerator principle in *Economics*, 1951, pp. 389–392.

[3] Kalecki, for instance, assumes this, *op. cit.*, pp. 121–122.

the boundaries. The rate of $A_{A_a} - A_{G_a}$ and $A_A - G_A$ depends largely upon the degree of differentiation of these markets and the degree of self-sufficiency of reserves of the production sub-system. During the downswing and trough, there is a great decrease in rates of interchange over the $A_G - L_G$ boundary and a virtual cessation over those three boundaries dealing with investment and its financing. The principles governing the downturn and upturn are not different from those cited in the first section of this chapter, except that they are rephrased as performance-sanction balances. This descriptive model of the trade cycle in terms of the general theory of social interaction is identical to the strictly economic model.

The restatement by itself, however, adds little to the economic statement; the fundamental areas of indeterminacy remain. Does the general theory provide any principles governing the values of the consumption function (multiplier) and the investment function (accelerator)?

THE CONSUMPTION FUNCTION

In the analysis of markets three elements are normally introduced: (1) the supply side, (2) the structure of the market, and (3) the demand side. In our terms this involves analysis of at least three different system-references. For the market for consumer goods, we have already discussed the first two to some extent. First, though we did not deal with the technical production-function problem as such, we located it in the production sub-system of the economy (A_G). This sub-system is a social system in the usual sense, with its own *A–G–I–L* functional problems and modes of "solution" to these problems.[1] Second, in the analysis of the structure of the consumers' goods market, we treated the relationship between economy and latency systems (only approximated by the relationship between firm and household) as a *social system in itself*, with its own appropriately defined system problems. At this level we suggested a classification of types of market imperfections based on the relative predominance of the various system-problem solutions.[2] To complete the picture of this market, we must

[1] Cf. above, pp. 198–200.

[2] Cf. Chap. III, pp. 143–75.

once again shift our system-reference; in this case we will treat the *household as a social system*[1] and examine the implications of its system-problem solutions for the shape and behaviour of the consumption function, or demand side of the market for consumer goods.[2]

What are the functional problem areas of the family as consuming unit which require the expenditure of income? In the first place, the institutionalization of the family system (say, in accordance with the American value system) implies a certain minimum of possessions in order for the family to meet the cultural definition (as opposed to a mere legal definition) of a family. This list of goods of course varies in accordance with value changes. But it certainly includes a minimum level of nutrition necessary for "cultural survival," which implies far more than mere biological survival; shelter of a certain quality; some minimum symbolic differentiation of intra-familial sex and generation roles; and in recent years the list might include such specific items as some sort of automobile, radio, television, etc. This list—described under the term "standard package"—is relatively *in*variant in the face of moderate income changes. Its acquisition is the culturally defined *goal* of the family as consuming unit.[3]

In addition to this goal a level of spending is required by the consumption unit primarily for the purposes of tension management within the family. In this respect certain aspects of entertainment, leisure and vacations are important. The primary function of such spending is, for the consumption unit, *latent pattern-maintenance and tension management*; i.e., those

[1] To treat the household as synonymous with a part of the latent pattern-maintenance and tension-management system is, strictly speaking, in error, because a single collectivity or class of collectivities do not comprise a functional sub-system (cf. Chap. I, pp. 14–16). We select the household for illustrative purposes because of its latency primacy and because of its empirical salience in the market for consumer goods.

[2] We are deeply indebted to Mr. Howard Roseborough for his work in formulating the consumption needs of the household according to the four system problem paradigm. Most of the analysis of the consumption needs of the family is owed to his suggestions.

[3] We have borrowed the term "standard package" from a forthcoming article by Riesman, D., and Roseborough, H., "Careers and Consumer Behaviour," in Clark, Lincoln H., (ed.), *Consumer Behaviour*, Vol II.

exigencies of personality-tension and small-group management to which the family must adapt in order to function effectively.[1]

Thirdly, class and prestige symbolization are a major area of role involvement for the consumption unit. In so far as the specific items in a family standard of living are culturally defined as symbols of class prestige, differential spending on class symbols obtains from class to class. This component of family spending is primarily *integrative* in that it is the focus of the symbolic location of family units relative to each other in the society.

Above and beyond these three sets of role expectations which define and even require a positive level of spending, a cluster of expectations positively sanctions a level of saving, or liquid funds set aside for *adaptation* to situational contingencies in the future. For the majority of spending units such saving is defined residually[2] as an amount to be set aside only after meeting other role commitments. In other cases, particularly among the community "leaders" defined as most responsible for the goal-attainment aspect of the social system, the norms for saving are defined positively in terms of "public responsibility," "public spirit," "community leadership," etc.[3]

Among these role involvements which lie behind spending patterns, many deal with the deeper levels of personality adjustment and the maintenance of community status. These two types of involvement severely restrict the manœuvrability of the family; in economic terms, they involve relatively "fixed costs." The head of the household cannot afford, for instance, to tie funds in some educational institution for only two weeks with the expectation that his children will receive a proper education and then, deciding that the service is not satisfactory, withdraw his funds and switch payment to some

[1] These, of course, are not the only pattern-maintaining and tension-managing exigencies facing the family unit, but they are the ones most closely associated with the expenditure of income. An obvious example of pattern-maintenance and tension-management not so intimately tied with income expenditures is the early socialization of the child.

[2] A number of such specific contingencies, such as expenses for medical care and education of children, are included in this category, however.

[3] The basic independence of savings and investment and the limited political significance of savings should be kept in mind, however. Cf. Chap. II, pp. 61–62.

other educational institution. In short, the involvements of the family unit preclude anything approaching speculation. Spending patterns must fluctuate within fairly narrow limits. The obvious implication for the consumption function is that it is very stable, both on the individual family level and in the aggregate.

The definition of the family's situation and its involvements in the consumption market sets fairly narrow outside limits, as it were, on the fluctuation of the consumption function. But can we not, by appeal to the above sociological considerations, suggest more specific determinants of the consumption function at any given time?

The "standard package" expenditure differs within limits from class level to class level[1]; its most important characteristic is its relative stability at any given level. The modes of tension management—e.g., leisure, entertainment, methods of socialization—and differential class symbolism certainly differ from class to class of consumers, as does the level of "enforced" saving arising from differential involvement in the "public responsibility" aspects of the supply and management of liquid resources.[2]

We may construct, from these institutionalized differences in spending patterns, a hypothetical consumption function. It is not our purpose to develop a complete theory of consumption here, but to suggest the translation of a few sociological insights into theoretical economic terms.

Figure 21 shows a hypothetical consumption function

[1] Differential class definitions of the "standard package" are certainly visible in the United States, but undoubtedly to a lesser extent than in Europe.

[2] These statements depend upon the propositions that prestige position and income, tension-management patterns and income, and involvement in community goals and income are all highly correlated. The propositions seem to be reasonable. For evidence on the first two correlations, cf. Warner, W. Lloyd and Lunt, P. S., *The Social Life of a Modern Community*, 1945, Hollingshead, A. B., *Elmtown's Youth*, 1949, as well as many other community studies of social stratification. For the correlation between high income and high involvement in community or society goals, cf. National Resources Committee, "The Structure of Controls," in Bendix, R. and Lipset, S. M. (eds.), *Class, Status and Power: A Reader in Social Stratification*, 1953, on the local community level, cf. Hunter, F., *Community Power Structure*, 1953.

which pulls together the consumption implications of the several familial role-involvements: common values, status symbolization, leisure, and community responsibility for goal attainment. Line *CV* represents the level of consumption in keeping with the common cultural values of the family system; its slight upward slope indicates the modified class differentials

FIGURE 21

CONSUMPTION FUNCTION

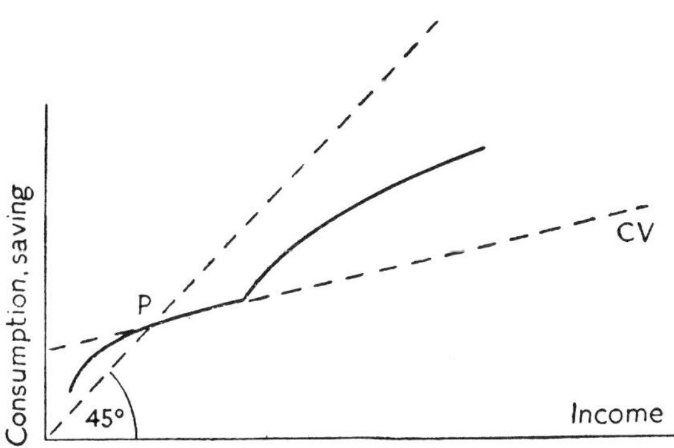

in the definition of these values.[1] Below point *p*, therefore, even though a family earns less than is required to live up to the common value definition, within limits it will continue to overspend and dissave until it becomes such a credit risk that it is unable to dissave further, or until financial pressures become so great that the value definition itself is modified or abandoned, and the curve slopes downward again. Outside assistance such as relief may prevent this final downward sloping, however.

Reading in the other direction from point *p*, the principles of saving differ. As income rises above the level necessary to

[1] The continuous slope of *CV* in Figure 21 indicates the "interlarding" of class levels in the American stratification system. In more definitely stratified societies, e.g., in Europe, *CV* would be represented roughly as follows:

implement the common value base, the consumption function proceeds roughly parallel to the 45° line. Such a slope indicates that pressures to symbolize a rising class position increase with a rising income, so a negligibly greater proportion of income is saved even as income rises. Toward the peak of the income level, the involvement in disproportionately high contributions to societal goal attainment invokes a disproportionately high level of saving to depress the upward slope.[1]

The logic of this simple model derived from a differentiated structure of role involvements of the consuming unit bears important consequences for the analysis of economic fluctuations. More is involved than a simple relation between the consumption unit and the proportion expended; built into the model is the *structure* of the different expectations which govern expenditures at different levels of society. When incorporating this sociologically derived model into a multiplier or into a trade cycle model, the theorist must specify more than aggregate shifts in income level. It is necessary to trace income changes to particular segments of society and to note the structured expectation systems of the consuming units in question, since different role expectation patterns govern the spending and saving habits of the various segments of the curve. Adequate formulation of the "propensity to consume" requires more than a statement that the *MPC* is some relation between *aggregate* income changes and proportion saved. Many economists have noted that changes in distribution of income involve change in the propensity to consume.[2] But such statements involving the expectations governing the various levels of the distribution and the consequent effects of various types of aggregate increases in income have not been incorporated formally into trade cycle models.

Furthermore, a sociological derivation of the consumption function points in the direction of a satisfactory solution of the

[1] In this connection, if taxes are considered as in part a functionally equivalent alternative to saving, then a progressive tax structure is a legal exemplification of the principle that the wealthier "community leaders" contribute disproportionately to the financing of collective goals. It is a case of an indirectly applied "sliding scale." We have discussed this in the medical and other cases, cf. Chap. III, pp. 152–56.

[2] Cf. Kalecki, M., "Three Ways to Full Employment," in *Economics of Full Employment*, Oxford University Institute of Statistics, 1946.

analytic dilemma mentioned above. The dilemma, it will be recalled, is between a model's analytical adequacy and generality *and* its determinate empirical reference. Economists regard the consumption function in the first instance as a series of possibilities; when it comes to applying the model empirically at a later stage of analysis, it is presumably simply a fact to be determined empirically. As we have shown, the dilemma is not resolved by the dichotomy between "theory" and "facts." The derivation of a consumption function from a body of sociological theory, on the other hand, provides a *theoretically determinate* element of the trade cycle model (theoretically determinate from the standpoint of sociological theory) and hence eliminates the necessity for postulating an indefinite series of arithmetical variations of value; furthermore, it provides a *determinate* (not merely *possible*) theoretical basis for predicting the paths of cycles, and is thus not merely a "given" from which economic consequences will follow. In short, a sociologically derived function further specifies the possibilities of types and magnitudes of cycles. It does not reduce the generality of the economic models, but it augments their determinacy.

To derive a consumption function from the characteristics of a *system of action* differs methodologically from current views of the process of saving in economics. The common economic conceptualization of consumption or saving is in terms of a "propensity." Keynes viewed the propensity to consume as a "fundamental psychological law, upon which we are entitled to depend with great confidence both *a priori* from our knowledge of human nature and from the detailed facts of experience."[1] It is difficult to establish the logical properties of a "propensity" (or a "psychological" concept in general, as Keynes used it) from this definition and its subsequent use. But it seems to us that a propensity, as used by Keynes and other economists, is a "psychological" entity which is subject to expression with *more* or *less* intensity as income changes. Any derivative function is high in value if the propensity is strong, low if the propensity is weak. In short, a propensity squeezes the variability of certain aspects of the non-economic world into a single linear dimension which can be assigned values. It is easy, by

[1] *General Theory*, p. 96.

one further step, to assume that these values are the *result* of *one* law: the greater or less strength of the psychological entity as related to level of income.

To generalize the argument, let us look at the problem from the other side of the boundary. Suppose, as sociologists, we are analysing the family. In dealing with this sociological system of action, it is necessary to incorporate statements about the current earnings of the breadwinner which are relevant to various intra-familial problems (tension management, style of life, etc.). Such statements of course involve us in borderline economic considerations. Could we not account for current wage levels by postulating a "fundamental economic law" which manifests itself in a definite "propensity to produce a wage rate," to be expressed with greater or less intensity? Certainly this is not the best account of the wage level in the economy; even more certainly the level of wages is not determined by the operation of a single law, but is a resultant of the operation of a *system* of interacting variables in the economy. The "propensity" logic is clearly methodologically inadequate.

Any function, therefore, particularly one as complex as the consumption function, is unlikely to be the product of the operation of a single psychological law. This is not to say that the function is not sometimes linear; no doubt it *sometimes* is. The important point is that, linear or not, it is generated in a system or systems of *action*. To reduce it to the operation of a propensity and to call this propensity a "fundamental law" is to freeze the boundaries of economic analysis by means of an *ad hoc* proposition in such a way as to suggest that any further investigation would not or even could not be fruitful.

The postulation of a definite propensity falls somewhere "between" two other operations we have noted: (1) varying the value of a function according to a scheme of arithmetical values, and (2) filling in the "facts" from case to case. To assume a propensity is to assert that there *are* grounds for selecting among several possible arithmetical values and that there *is* a way for predicting the facts from case to case. But this restoration of the theoretical determinacy to the non-economic factors, in so far as it rests on the operation of one law, is in our opinion of very limited value. It is not satisfactory to have a multi-variable system of action on one side of the boundary and a simple law on the other, unless we are dealing with some very special case.

Let us, in this connection, first examine Keynes' famous "psychological" postulate concerning the marginal propensity to consume, whereby "when [any modern community's] real income is increased [the community] will not increase its consumption by an equal *absolute* amount, so that a greater absolute amount must be saved."[1] Graphically the Keynesian representation for the aggregate[2] is shown in Figure 22. The 45° line refers to the shape of the function if total income at all income levels were spent on consumption.

FIGURE 22

KEYNESIAN CONSUMPTION FUNCTION

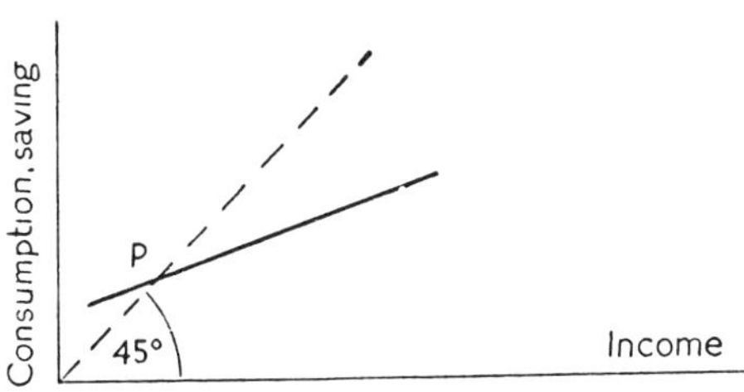

What does this function imply about the social structure? In the first place, the only two terms in the consumption function relation—the consumers and their incomes—are linked by the principle that consumption rises as income rises, though not so rapidly.[3] If this principle is all that is given, what are the *reasons* why the principle should hold? Or in sociological terminology, what are the institutionalized modes of orientation (structured role expectations) that determine this relation between consumption-savings and income?

[1] Keynes, *op. cit.*, p. 97.

[2] There are presumably no complications involved in the simple addition of individual functions to obtain the aggregate.

[3] Keynes lists a good many reasons, both subjective and objective, why persons save and the conditions under which one might expect a change in the saving level. But for purposes of the general theory he assumes the subjective factors as given and proceeds under the assumption that there will be no major changes in the objective factors. Hence for working purposes, the single principle stated above is the governing principle of the savings-consumption ratio. *Ibid.*, Chaps. 8 and 9.

The inferences about structured role expectations[1] which one may draw from the Keynesian principle *per se* are two only: (1) household states involving expenditure of wealth change at a uniform rate as income rises; or (2) household states may change at different rates for different individuals as income rises, but these cancel out to produce a uniform rate. Clearly both inferences defy what is known about the structure of role expectations as institutionalized in the social system and internalized in individual actors. Integrative and other exigencies preclude the possibility that role expectations may be reduced, even in their consumption manifestation, either to a straight linear relation dependent on changes in the rate of income or to random variation around this relation.

Duesenberry's[2] theory of consumption is an outstanding example of a theory which often is considered as an alternative to Keynes,[3] but from the standpoint of our analysis it possesses certain similar characteristics. Duesenberry holds that the Keynesian formulation of the consumption-savings ratio involves two incorrect assumptions: (*a*) that every individual's consumption behaviour is independent of every other individual, and (*b*) that consumption relations are reversible in time. In order to account for the influence of consumers' behaviour on each other, Duesenberry develops a utility index which incorporates the weight applied to the consumer by the expenditure of other individuals. By dividing the traditional utility index by a "demonstration effect," he concludes that in equilibrium, consumption is proportional to income and the savings ratio therefore is independent of the absolute income level. To incorporate the second assumption, Duesenberry develops a formula based on the hypothesis that saving depends

[1] The only hint at structured role expectations which Keynes gives is a sort of "inertia principle," which is related to our conception of "latent pattern maintenance." That is to say, when Keynes holds that "men are disposed, as a rule and on the average, to increase their consumption as their income increases, but not by as much as the increase in their income" (*General Theory*, p. 96), we may infer that there are certain tendencies to maintain spending patterns even though there has been an accumulation of facilities which enables the spender to pursue different patterns.

[2] Duesenberry, J., *Income, Saving and the Theory of Consumer Behaviour*, 1949.

[3] In the sense that the shape and determinants of the Duesenberry consumption function differ from those of the Keynesian formulation.

upon past as well as current income. When income is at the highest level ever attained, savings are higher than at a similar level reached in a decline from a higher level. The psychological principle behind this formula is that when income falls there is a lagged effect whereby previous consumption needs will continue for some period until spending again becomes commensurate with income level.[1]

It is interesting to note that Duesenberry's logic parallels that of reference group theory,[2] even though he does not base his results on reference group theory as it has developed in the last decade. In the case of the demonstration effect, the consumer feels deprived relative to people with the same or other incomes; hence spending patterns will follow from this reference. In the case of the effect of past income on current spending, the consumer feels deprived relative to past consumption level (or perhaps even relative to the consumption level of others in the past who had the same income as his own), and spending is partially determined by reference to this standard.

To the sociologist the Duesenberry hypothesis represents an advance from the Keynesian postulate, for it locates the consumer in the context of at least a generalized conformity to habits of others' or one's own past standards. Hence, Duesenberry moves a little closer to the incorporation of a structured role expectation system within the community.

It remains to be seen how far the "demonstration effect" or reference group theory holds up empirically in the field of consumption. But on the basis of the demonstration effect alone —even if valid—it is not possible to determine the social system context *to which* people conform or refer; hence the demonstration effect is a valuable principle only when the structure of role expectations themselves has already been established.

We are not recommending that the economist desert his

[1] This is an incorporation of the inertia (pattern-maintenance) assumption in a reverse direction from the Keynesian case. I.e., as income falls, there is an attempt to maintain patterns, even though the decrease in facilities does not permit this maintenance.

[2] Merton, R. K., and Kitt, A., "Contributions to the Theory of Reference Group Behaviour," in Merton and Lazarsfeld (eds.), *Studies in the Scope and Method of "The American Soldier,"* 1950.

field to formulate consumption functions based on intensive sociological research; his job in this area is to formulate the economic *effects* of known sociological and psychological facts. The starting-point for the empirical operation of any psychological mechanism such as the demonstration effect, however, is a clear statement of the patterns of role expectation in the community. In the preliminary model above, we attempted to define a typical situation from which *any* theory of consumption must begin. Certain elements in the contractual definition of the consumers' market and certain characteristics of the family as a system can be translated directly into implications for the economic use of the consumption function. A simple view of "human propensities" or "psychological postulates" without reference to the social structure is unsatisfactory as a theoretical basis for this aspect of economic analysis.[1]

To derive a consumption function from sociological theory, however, is not to exclude psychological considerations from the analysis of the consumption function and its behaviour over time. Certainly reference group theory, as incorporated in the Duesenberry model and developed independently in the social sciences, is relevant. Further, the principles of deviance from the structured role expectations should provide aspects of the detailed psychological behaviour of the consumption function. Psychological theory, therefore, concerns the mechanisms of conformity to, alienation from, and elaboration of the system of role expectations, with special attention to the "kinks" and potential fluctuations of the consumption function. Psychological theory provides the processes operating *within* the structure of role expectations which define the situation. It cannot be reduced to a single law.[2]

[1] If economic theory is the theory of process in one type of social system, it articulates best with *cognate* levels of theory in other systems.

[2] The assumption of a sort of unidimensional variability in indeterminate "non-economic" areas is a common theme in several fields of economic inquiry. We noted its appearance in the discussion of imperfect competition and the structure of markets (cf. pp. 143–46) and in connection with the formulation of the profit motive (cf. pp. 179–84 ff.). Cf. also Chap. V, pp. 279–80.

THE INVESTMENT FUNCTION

We have repeatedly emphasized the principle that to provide a specific solution to a theoretical problem such as consumption or investment requires considerations from several system references. Thus, in discussing consumption, we referred to (1) the broadest boundary interchange between the economy and the pattern-maintenance system,[1] (2) the contractual regulation of the consumption market,[2] and (3) the specific exigencies facing the family as a consumption unit. No one of these three system references provides sufficient theoretical resources to construct a specific and useful consumption function. It is necessary to bring all three, and for some purposes even more, to bear on the problem on consumption, however.

Similarly, a multiplicity of system references constitute the conditions for determining an adequate theory of investment. Thus, the fact that the phenomena of lending and investment are involved in the polity[3] means that the role of investor is partially governed by certain non-economic exigencies or constraints. These limitations are specified even further at the level of the institutionalization of the market for liquid funds.[4] Neither of these system references provides, however, a complete theory of short-term investment. In what follows we will discuss, in a preliminary way, some of the determinants of investment behaviour which emerge from analysis at a more microscopic system level, but which are not independent of the higher system levels.

In discussing the contractual regulation of investment, we noted the great empirical variability of the adaptive situation of the investor. That is to say, *his* own membership collectivity (as distinguished from the borrower's) may be the family, the polity, some fiduciary body, etc. The adaptive exigencies of course, vary widely according to the investor-owner's collectivity. As the starting-point for further analysis, we will take the situation as it exists in the United States today, namely, that the investment function is divided among a number of

[1] Chap. II, pp. 53–56.
[2] Chap. III, pp. 156–61.
[3] Chap. II, pp. 56–64.
[4] Chap. III, pp. 123–37 and 161–69.

empirically isolable collectivities—fiduciary bodies, government authorities, sub-divisions of producing firms, etc.—but that the investment role is generally independent of membership in any diffuse collectivity, such as kinship, ethnic, religious, or political (in the sense of "party") groupings. Since the number of ascribed financial obligations is minimal, the range of extra-economic exigencies to which the investor-owner must adapt is relatively small. The investor's manœuvrability is thus enhanced relative to the manœuvrability of, say, either the consuming agent or the labourer, who is economically restricted by the intimate relation between his economic function and his family membership. In many countries other than the United States, the relative insulation of the investor is not carried nearly so far.[1] This insulation permits, at least, a wide range of responses to the investment market situation; on this basis, the range and flexibility of values of the investment function is much wider than those of the consumption function.

Above and beyond the minimization of involvement in diffuse collectivities, the structure of the investment situation implies even greater instability of the investment function. Let us recall the general role of investment ($A_{A_a} - A_{G_a}$) in the structure of the economy. Investment is the adaptive cross-tie within the economy which articulates the sets of decisions occurring at the $A_G - L_G$ and $A_A - G_A$ boundaries. In several senses investment rests at the core of the economy: it co-ordinates these two boundary interchanges between the economy and two other distinct societal sub-systems, yet it is internal to the economy in that it is not *directly* involved in either the $A_G - L_G$ or the $A_A - G_A$ boundary. It seems reasonable, therefore, that the investment process should be the locus of an elaborate system of signs concerning the condition and success of the economy's functioning. On grounds such as these we expect risk and uncertainty to be most extensively institutionalized in the investment market. It is the most

[1] In France, for instance, the family connections with the investment function are widely apparent. We would expect a diminished investor manœuvrability in such cases. Cf. Landes, D., "French Business and the Businessman: A Social and Cultural Analysis," in Earle, E. M. (ed.), *Modern France*, 1951.

sensitive indicator that the factors of production are or are not being combined in the most productive way.

An analogy clarifies the way in which risk and uncertainty are institutionalized at this market.[1] Suppose it were incumbent upon the labourer to offer his services to that firm which he predicted to be the most productive in the coming year or years. No wages would be forthcoming, however, until the firm proved productive after this period. At that time he would be differentially rewarded according to the degree of productivity; if the firm failed, he would receive nothing. In such a market situation we might properly speak of the institutionalization of labourer's risk. Of course a certain labourer's risk is empirically evident, but not in such extreme form. His risk is primarily *post hoc*, i.e., there is a risk of unemployment *at the time* the firm begins to fail to be productive, but current wage income is not contingent upon its past productivity.

The market for investments, however, is similar to this hypothetical labour market. The goal elements of the interchange are investment funds as balanced against investment returns; the exchange is a performance-sanction system in that there is mutual advantage in exchange; furthermore, there is presumably some supply-demand relation which governs the input and output balance between the two elements of the interchange. The unique characteristic of this market interchange is an uncertainty—*created by the market situation*—to which both the investor and the business executive (or borrower of investment funds) must adapt, i.e., the uncertainty of the consequences if the invested funds fail to yield returns. Also, the investor may lose his principal (for a worker to "lose his labour capacity" is a really extreme case). The business firm risks its place in the market if the investment programme should fail. This is the familiar "borrower's risk," which "arises out of doubts in the borrower's own mind as to the probability of his actually earning prospective yield for which

[1] Risk and uncertainty are often interpreted as being completely beyond the control of human endeavour and hence removed from institutionalization of any form; we hope to show, however, that risk, uncertainty and insecurity are in part a function of the performance-sanction norms governing the exchange process.

he hopes."[1] On the side of the investor, he faces the "lender's risk," which may be due "either to moral hazard, i.e., voluntary default or other means of escape, possibly lawful, from the fulfilment of the obligation, or to the possible insufficiency of the margin of security, i.e., involuntary default due to the disappointment of expectation."[2]

The institutionalization of these risks in the investment market of course serves both sociological and economic functions. It sensitizes the investment core of the economic process to minor fluctuations in the productivity of capital and quickly eliminates those who choose wrongly by overloading the $A_{A_a} - A_{G_a}$ boundary with a large uncertainty factor. Sociologically the institutionalization of risk relieves other boundaries from elements of this type of risk—especially at the $A_G - L_G$ boundary, where familial exigencies preclude such a high level of uncertainty.

In sociological and psychological analysis, any situation can be typed along the dimension of structured-unstructured. In a highly structured situation, there are a minimum of possible responses other than the ones required by the norms of the situation; adaptation is carefully defined: and usually the situation is not very confusing psychologically. The investment market fails to adhere to any of these characteristics of a structured situation: the range of adaptive responses (i.e., speculation) is not limited in a formal sense; there is a great deal of room to manœuvre, as the daily quotations on the stock market show; and the loose definition of the appropriate adaptations (i.e., moves all made on the basis of "hunches," "tips," "shrewdness," etc.) produces a great deal of psychological confusion and strain. The investment market is a prototype of the unstructured situation. It thereby allows for the wide and rapid fluctuation of the investment function.

What are some of the behavioural consequences resulting

[1] Keynes, *General Theory*, p. 144.

[2] *Ibid.*, p. 144. The "lender's risk" and "borrower's risk" stress the negative side of uncertainty and unpredictability in the investment market. We might note, in addition, a "Durkheimian" uncertainty regarding large accumulation of gains in short periods. While the consequences of such uncertainty obviously from those of the negative risks, the whole complex of psychological and style-of-life adjustments which accompany a rapidly rising income should not be ignored.

from such a highly unstructured situation? Without going into a full classification of responses[1] we will merely point out that sociologically and psychologically unstructured situations commonly produce two types of reactions: psychologically irrational mass phenomena,[2] and deviance of several types. Enough is known about these types of reaction to permit us to identify various phenomena on the investment market as special cases of well-known generalizations about deviant and mass behaviour in general. The phenomena of boom and panic on the stock market, for instance, can be accounted for by more definite and fruitful principles than "psychological waves of optimism and pessimism." The starting-point for analysing such behaviour is, of course, the situation in which it arises; we have pointed out the unstructured nature of the investment market and its implications for irrational reactions. Furthermore, we would expect that various types of mass reactions on the stock market could be identified as sub-types of the panic, and aggressive riot, etc., each with definite phases of development, leadership patterns, exaggerating and/or diminishing tendencies, and definite social and psychological concomitants such as the impression of universality of the behaviour of others, a sense of anonymity, heightened suggestibility, etc. It is interesting to note that in the consumption market, which is structured in all the above senses, irrational explosions arise only under near-catastrophic conditions such as war, threatened shortages, famines in primarily agricultural countries, etc.

Less severe than such explosions are certain tendencies to deviance, examples of which are found in Keynes' discussion of the stock exchange processes analogous to the games of Snap, or Old Maid, or Musical Chairs, which are deviant in so far as they disturb the equilibrium of the continuous functioning of the investment market. Such phenomena are by-products of the great possibilities of manœuvrability permitted by the special features of the investment market. These processes, as well as many others which are less well known and understood, undoubtedly tap a great many of the

[1] Cf. Parsons, *The Social System*, Chap. VII.

[2] These usually involve in special ways "regression" in the sense discussed in Chap. III, p. 116.

deeper drives to deviance in individuals, such as unbridled acquisitiveness, sadism, phantasied wish-fulfilment, etc.

Reactions such as irrational mass behaviour and deviance do not run free, however, without the appearance of certain mechanisms of social control. Situations of uncertainty and risk are the classical foci for magic and superstition. A very important non-economic example is the uncertainty of health and consequent measures of the control of disease which is a principal area of magic in non-literate societies and much superstition and faddism in our own. Where there can be no reliable prediction of some future state, there arise extremely important attempts to interpret the significance of some plausible and tangible "sign" of what is going to happen.[1] In the case of speculation this often takes the form of basing decisions not on the available facts of market developments, but on the indications of the *opinion* of these developments on the part of the "one who knows," the alleged insider, or the fellow with a reputation for shrewdness; or the speculator may rely on traditionalized "rules of thumb," which may or may not be "objective."

Keynes suggested two further explanations of how this uncertainty in the stock exchange situation is partially stabilized. The first is the "convention" or belief that the situation will remain in the near future about what it has been in the recent past (a case of rule of thumb). The second is a non-rational orientation which Keynes picturesquely characterized as depending on the "animal spirits" of the lusty entrepreneur.[2]

In this connection, one of the primary functions of the "business leaders" who occupy a certain monopolistic position is to stabilize attitudes by "keeping confident." In turn this confidence is presumably backed up by that of prestige-bearing elements in the non-economic "public."

Sociology has tools which can help explain these clearly

[1] For general reference on the problem of uncertainty and its control, cf., Homans, G. C., "Anxiety and Ritual: The Theories of Malinowski and Radcliffe-Brown," *American Anthropologist*, Vol. 43, No. 2 (1941), pp. 164–172; Kluckhohn, C., *Navaho Witchcraft*, Papers of the Peabody Museum, Harvard University, Vol. 22, No. 2, pp. 1–49, and Fortare, R. F., *Sorcerers of Dobu*, 1932.

[2] Keynes, *General Theory*, pp. 152–153, 161–162.

non-economic phenomena in an economic setting. Much study is needed to probe to deeper levels of understanding, but it is a very promising field.[1]

Before leaving the field of investment, let us examine two further implications of the instability of the investment function as conditioned by the market situation and the reactions and controls organized about this situation. The first implication is for the market for investment goods at $A_{A_g} - A_{L_g}$. In one sense this market is an aspect of the $A_G - L_G$ interchange, for the purchase and use of investment goods is indeed consumption of economic goods. From another perspective, however, the investment-goods market is an intra-economic interchange, reducible to a stage in the process of adding value. Furthermore, the selling and the buying organizations in this market are *both* characterized by economic primacy. This latter fact bears on the problem of imperfection in the market for investment goods. Certainly there are imperfections because of the asymmetry of interests on both sides of the intra-economic boundary. The history of anti-trust policy is evidence enough for the existence of monopolistic practices in capital goods industries. On the other hand, we suggest that the *types* of imperfections which we have isolated—springing primarily from discontinuities in the *A*-, *I*-, and *L*-components of the relevant contract—are minimized at the $A_{A_g} - A_{L_g}$ boundary relative to the $A_G - L_G$ and $A_A - G_A$ boundaries,[2] precisely because of the less sharp differentiation of interest on either side of the boundary.

Another characteristic of the investment goods market is that it depends upon fluctuations of the investment function at the $A_{A_a} - A_{G_a}$ boundary. That is to say, if the decision to float securities or loans for an investment project is made ($A_{A_a} - A_{G_a}$), an early commitment to sink funds into the appropriate land factors usually follows.[3] This dependence is closely related to

[1] Cf. Parsons, *The Social System*, Chap. VII, for discussion of the mechanisms of social control.

[2] Cf. Chap. III, pp. 146–61 and 161–73.

[3] Note that not all the funds created by such flotations are devoted to land factors, but may go to labour as well. Cf. the discussion of the empirical asymmetry between these two types of commitment, Chap. III, pp. 134–37.

the economic fact that certain investment-good prices fluctuate faster than consumption-good prices. This differential rate is in part a reflection of the unstructured situation in the market for investment securities and the more structured situation in the consumers' market. In so far as mounting decisions to invest are accompanied by the decisions to purchase investment goods, then fluctuations in the $A_{A_a} - A_{G_a}$ relation involve activation of the $A_{A_g} - A_{L_g}$ rates and hence an increased need to exact higher prices or stiffer terms for the greater performance on the part of the investment-goods industries. Contrariwise, the relative stability of consumption good prices is in part a reflection of slow fluctuations of the consumption function arising out of its market situation. Of course, these facts are not new to economists; but they have not, to our knowledge, been derived from the institutional structure of the market situation.

Secondly, the unstructured situation of the investment market is in part responsible for instabilities in the $A_A - G_A$ market for control of liquid funds. What is *internally* significant to the investment market as an increased risk or as a deficit of returns, is *externally* significant to the creator of liquid funds as an impingement on his rights to intervene. Thus, increased internal instability in the economy diminishes the corresponding input of capital funds. Such reasoning gives an institutional basis, for instance, for Keynes' proposition that fluctuations in the marginal efficiency of capital *precede* fluctuations in liquidity preference, as a rule.[1]

To summarize: we have brought substantive sociological theory to bear on some of the problems which economists

[1] Cf. *General Theory*, p. 316. If the situation of the market for investment *and* the market for liquid funds were sufficiently undefined and unstructured, it is possible that a genuine panic for liquidity could result from "inadequate" cues, i.e., under conditions when the marginal efficiency of capital schedule had not fallen. This would cause an "unemployment of capital" depression without the accompanying unemployment of labour depression since there would be no genuine short-term fall of productive capacity. This sort of sequence of events perhaps lay behind some of the frequent speculative panics of the 19th century, which occurred without anything approaching mass human employment. Nowadays, liquidity panics are carefully safeguarded against by government intervention in banking practices; hence "liquidity cycles" are more likely to be in tune with genuine fluctuations in the marginal efficiency of capital.

isolate as areas of admitted indeterminacy. Economists have been able to formulate a great many statements concerning the movement of economic values—*assuming given values* for the indeterminate elements—in the case of the trade cycle, the consumption function and the investment function. We have tried, on the basis of the best sociological theory we now have available, to narrow these areas of indeterminacy by introducing determinate propositions of a higher level of generality, propositions which are theoretically and empirically important for their own field *and which can be translated directly into values for the basic coefficients of economic theories.*

A NOTE ON TIME LAGS

Let us take Hicks' classification of lags into consumption, output, and earnings as our starting-point.[1] The general process involved in these lags (and any others in economic process) is as follows: a time-consuming "something" happens, within the relevant collectivity in a market situation, between a given input and the corresponding output. Thus, (*a*) in the consumption lag, some process intervenes between the receipt of income by the household and the output of this income back into the economy; (*b*) in the output lag, between the input of consumer spending and the corresponding increase in production; (*c*) for the earnings lag, between the input of goods or services (in their productive capacity as capital) and the corresponding monetary return.

The economists' interest in such lags is to establish an appropriate number of lags and appropriate durations for each to make any given fluctuation accord roughly with the empirical facts. But as we have pointed out repeatedly, the two operations —arbitrarily assuming numbers and lengths of time lags and filling in specific empirical values for the length of time lags— do not maximize both the generality and the determinacy of a theory of economic fluctuations. Is it possible to establish, on sociological grounds, more specific criteria for assigning values to these time lags?

[1] This corresponds to the classification in Metzler, L., "Three Lags in the Circular Flow of Income," *Income, Employment, and Public Policy: Essays in Honor of Alvin H. Hanson*, 1948.

In the first instance, the number and length of time lags are a function of the level of differentiation of, and types of, imperfection in a given market structure. Hence an adequate sociological theory of markets, including the structure of the interchanging collectivities, is a prerequisite for the construction of any theory of time lags. For it is in these collectivities that the time-consuming "something" happens. For instance, a collectivity fusing both family and business structure into the same organization[1] is subject to different time-consuming exigencies in the face of a changed demand for its product from those confronting a fully differentiated and highly bureaucratized business firm. An adequate theory of time lags awaits, therefore, an adequate typology of market structure.[2]

May we not pin-point the problem of the "time-consuming interval" within certain collectivities more precisely?

In general, the paradigm of the adaptive, integrative, goal-attainment and latent tension-management and pattern-maintenance functions has been applied in two areas: (1) The structural differentiation of roles and the institutionalization of these roles into interpenetrating sub-systems. This has been our focus of attention in this volume. (2) Specialization along the *A–G–I–L* dimensions *not* in terms of structure, but in terms of time-sequences of activities. Processes of this type are called phase-movements. A phase is defined as a "changing state of the system, when movement in a given dimension (e.g., adaptive) is maximized relative to its movement in the other three dimensions."[3] A phase movement is a typical sequence of phases in relation to the *A–G–I–L* dimensions in any system. Certain fairly typical phase-movements have been established. For instance, the sequence of relative predominance of adaptation, goal attainment, integration and tension management is typical for the task-adaptive solution of a problem by a small group.[4] In the case of socialization, as well as several types of

[1] As, for instance, a high proportion of business firms in France are organized. Cf. Landes, *op. cit.*, esp., pp. 335–339.

[2] We have suggested some bases for the formulation of such a typology, cf. Chap. III, pp. 173–75.

[3] Parsons, Bales and Shils, *Working Papers in the Theory of Action*, p. 181, and especially Bales, *op. cit.*, Chap. IV.

[4] Cf. Bales in Parsons, Bales and Shils, *Working Papers*, Chap. IV.

social control,[1] the typical sequence is precisely the opposite order.

The analysis of typical phase-movements is a promising theoretical approach to certain processes within the family, business firm, and other collectivities relating to the number and length of time lags. The input (e.g., income, demand, etc.) establishes or activates certain goal objects for the receiving collectivity. A time lag is the by-product, or time component of a typical exigency-meeting sequence through which the collectivity must proceed before the goal state can be attained.

For illustrative purposes, we will deal with the output lag between an increase in demand (either short-term or long-term) and the increase in production to meet this demand (i.e., goal attainment). Given this goal, the system problems the firm encounters in attaining it are adaptation, or the procurement of facilities; integration, or the maintenance of communication lines and satisfaction levels of the incumbents of the differentiated roles; and pattern maintenance and tension management, or the operation of drainoff mechanisms for mounting dissatisfaction, etc.[2] While empirical investigation of business firms is not sufficient for us to outline precise sequences of primacies of these exigencies over specific time periods, there is adequate evidence that these exigencies are the foci of the decision-making process.[3]

Let us posit, therefore, a typical task-adaptive sequence in a firm following an increased input of consumer demand. The most pressing exigency for meeting this demand (goal of production) is to acquire facilities for the payment of labour and the acquisition of capital plant.[4] According to the degree

1 *The Social System*, *op. cit.*, Chaps. VI and VII. See also *Family, Socialization and Interaction Process*, *op. cit.*, Chaps. II, IV.

2 This classification of exigencies corresponds to those of the production sub-system A_G in Figure 15, p. 199. This is not an assertion, however, that the typical business firm and the production sub-system are identical. The difference is in system level and extensive segmentation of the former.

3 The executive aspects of these problems have been analysed sensitively by Barnard, C. I., *Functions of the Executive*, 1948, and Simon, H., *Administrative Behaviour*, 1943. Cf. also, Gordon, R. A., *Business Leadership in the Large Corporation*, 1945, and Learned, E. P., Ulrich, O. N., and Booz, D. R., *Executive Action*, 1951.

4 Cf. Chap. III, pp. 134–37, for a brief analysis of the asymmetry between the two purposes for which capital funds are put. For an analysis of the

of intra-economic differentiation and the level of reserves of the firm, *three* separate boundaries may be activated in this phase: $A_{A_a} - A_{G_a}$, the input of investment funds into the organization; $A_A - G_A$, the input of liquid funds into the hands of investors, and $A_{A_g} - A_{L_g}$, the acquisition of concrete capital goods. Thus the adaptive phase of the business firm (or aggregate of business firms) may set off a series of market interactions all of which are subject to sub-lags within the relevant interacting collectivities.

The second phase in the task-adaptive sequence is goal attainment itself. This entails hiring labourers, assigning them to positions within the firm, and producing, distributing and selling the goods and services. This is the "consummation" of the goal stimulated by an increased demand. But it takes time, just as the acquisition of facilities takes time.[1]

These two phases "complete" the process in the sense that the stimulated demand has been met temporarily. They constitute the "engineering" aspect of the output lag and hence coincide roughly with Barnard's conception of "effectiveness," which is the appropriate meeting of situational exigencies to accomplish the organization purpose.

But in order to meet this goal of production continuously, a third phase of activity, far removed from any "engineering" elements of the A and G phases, is required. This activity—long investigated by industrial sociologists—is that implied by Barnard's term "efficiency," which like effectiveness is a major pre-requisite for long-run goal attainment in an organization. Efficiency deals with the creation and distribution of satisfactions among individuals to assure continuing cooperative effort; it corresponds to the I and L elements of our paradigm. Examples of these integrative and tension-management exigencies are disruptive effects of output restrictions, dissatisfactions among individuals and/or groups in the firm, strain on the executive, etc. Encountering these exigencies is a

structure of the investment market, cf. pp. 233–39; and for the structure of the market for investment goods, cf. p. 239.

[1] This, incidentally, is a definition of the phase movement itself; it is a specialization of labour *through time*, as opposed to its specialization *in structures*. We are, in the discussion of the typical time-lag sequence, holding the structure constant and concentrating on the time differentiation aspect.

third typical phase in the lag between demand and successful supply.[1]

With careful empirical and theoretical analysis, it should be possible better to establish typical phase-movements within both the firm and other collectivities involved in the market. Furthermore, phase analysis should provide a theoretical basis for a direct translation of values—in terms of number and length of time lags—into technical models of economic fluctuations.

[1] We do not mean, by labelling these phases "first," "second" and "third" to imply that a firm adapts, attains its immediate goal, then attends to its integrative sequences in rigid order. As has been demonstrated in the task-adaptive sequences of small groups, it is a matter of relative predominance of these sets of exigencies over time. Empirically, all exigencies are met in certain degree at all times; it is a matter of primacy.

For a statement of the theoretical relations between "effectiveness" and "efficiency" on the small group level, cf. Homans, G. C., and Riecken, H. W., "Psychological Aspects of Group Structure," in *Handbook of Social Psychology*, ed. G. Lindzey, 1954 and Homans, G. C., *The Human Group*, 1950. On the disruptive elements in the introduction of technological changes and engineering projects, cf. Merton, R., "The Machine, the Worker and The Engineer," in *Social Theory and Social Structure*, 1949. The classic study of the integrative and tension-management elements of the factory situation at the lower levels is Roethlisberger and Dickson, *Management and the Worker*, 1939. For an analysis of the disruptive influences of technical change on professionals within the firm, cf. the case study by Homans, *The Human Group*, *op. cit.*, Chaps. 14 and 15.

CHAPTER V

THE PROBLEMS OF GROWTH AND INSTITUTIONAL CHANGE IN THE ECONOMY

THE NATURE OF CHANGE

Early in the book we noted the gap between the respective interests of the analytical economist and the economic historian. The former has contributed the overwhelming bulk of work in recent economic theory.[1] But the problems of the latter remain of great theoretical and empirical significance. Though our discussion cannot be carried so far as in the preceding chapters, we will now approach the problem of growth and change in terms of the analysis used throughout this volume.

Our central proposition is that quantitative changes of a sufficient order of magnitude involve changes of *organization* in the system in question. Furthermore, a change of organization, unless it is confined to the level of segmentation, is a modification in *the structure of the system*. If, therefore, the economy is treated as a social system in the full sense, then the focus of the problem of structural change accompanying and resulting from quantitative growth lies in the system of institutions. But in the general theory of social systems the structure of the system of economic or any other institutions cannot be primarily a function of economic factors, though it is in part determined by them.[2] Institutional structure is in the first instance an aspect of the *integrative* system of the society and is thus largely

[1] In a sense the "Keynesian revolution" was particularly welcome in many circles because the short-run focus of empirical and practical interest made it possible to relegate to the background some of the problems of long-run change prominent in the work of the classicists, of Marshall and of Schumpeter.

[2] Cf. note, Chap. I, pp. 6–7.

determined by the general variables of social interaction in connection with the parameters of the integrative system.

The problem of structural change in the economy and every other sub-system of the society must, therefore, be treated primarily as a sociological problem. Positive theoretical analysis in this area cannot be confined to economic theory, but must involve the specific interdependence of economic and sociological theory. Because analytical economists have not only worked but remained within the framework of technical economic theory and because economic historians, while close to the facts of institutional change, have tended to proceed without any theory on comparable analytical levels, the two fields of inquiry have failed to complement each other. We hope that the kind of sociological theory we have presented can, with its specific articulation with economic theory, help to bridge this gap.

Let us first emphasize a crucial distinction between two meanings of the term "process" (often qualified by the adjective "dynamic"): first, process *within* a given structure of the system in question, and second, process which results in major *changes in* that structure.[1]

Both economic theory and the general theory of social interaction, like many other scientific theories, make important use of the concept of equilibrium or stable state. The first meaning of "process" has a given equilibrium state as a point of reference. The processes are those series of events by which such a state is maintained by interchanging inputs and outputs both over its boundaries and between the units or sub-systems which constitute the system in question. The rates of inputs and outputs are not assumed to be constant; indeed the "dynamics" at this level of theoretical analysis consist precisely of the effects of changes in these rates. But on this level such changes are in general relatively small in magnitude and short in duration. The "equilibrium" conception is that such relatively small changes tend to be "counteracted" by the effects of their repercussions on other parts of the system, in such a way that the original state tends to be restored.[2]

[1] Cf. *The Social System, op. cit.*, Chap. XI.

[2] Another possibility is an equilibrium maintaining the line of development on which the system was set. The concept of equilibrium need not

The second meaning of "process" focuses on major changes in the character of this equilibrium state itself and hence on changes in the structure of the system. The transition between two structurally different equilibrium states involves periods of disequilibrium and/or unstable equilibrium. The criterion of an unstable state is that even a small relevant departure from such a state leads not to tendencies to restore the original state, but to depart from it *further*. Such departure continues until a different state of relatively stable equilibrium is attained.

We define "organization" or "structure of a system" as the essential internal conditions of a relatively stable equilibrium, changes in which, beyond certain limits, result in unstable equilibrium and probably structural change.

We treat systems of social interaction as "boundary-maintaining systems." This term refers to a relatively distinctive set of conditions on which depends the maintenance of the boundaries in approximately their given form at a given time. These conditions link particularly closely with the integration of the system, i.e., with its institutions. By virtue of theoretical considerations such as these we feel it is possible to define the *problem* of structural change in the economy and other social systems as a problem of institutional change.

Institutional change is closely connected with two other important considerations. The first is the *order of magnitude* of the changes in the relevant input or output categories which are considered. The greater the magnitude of a change, the greater the likelihood that it will be associated with structural change in the system, even though the input-output change is not itself directly a structural change. This is a simple deduction from the primary defining characteristic of a system: the values of its variables are interdependent. There must be constraints on the range of compatibility of the values of different variables in the same system at the same time. A large change in *any* one, therefore, is likely to induce change in the others sufficient to produce a change of state of the system as a whole.

The second consideration is that major structural changes are unlikely to be completed in short time intervals. Of course there are no general theoretical reasons why systems cannot be

be entirely "static" in the sense of assuming *no* trend of secular change. Cf. L. J. Henderson, *Pareto's General Sociology*, 1935.

stable over very long-run periods, so a great time span does not necessarily mean a great change. But structural change is a very complex process which takes time. Other things equal, large structural changes generally are long-term phenomena.[1]

A MODEL OF ECONOMIC GROWTH

As a critical point of reference for structural change in the economy, we have chosen a model which occupies a sort of "middle ground" between the two senses of "dynamic." Formally, this model treats the problems of economic growth in the framework of *process dynamics*, i.e., a number of givens are held constant, and the operation of a determinate number of variables is traced without considering the possibility of systematic changes in the givens. Yet the magnitude of change of the variables and the long time span over which the model is meant to apply make it questionable to assume empirical constancy of these givens.

The illustrative model is an early version of that presented by Domar.[2] We do not choose this model on grounds of formal excellence; our aim is not to discuss the model critically from an economic standpoint but to illustrate the articulation of economic models of growth with institutional analysis of the social system. Hence we might have chosen any one of several theories of growth—those of the classicists, of Marx, of Schumpeter, of Harrod, etc.—for our purposes. The choice of the Domar model rests largely on its brevity, simplicity and clarity of presentation.

Domar makes several assumptions: (1) a constant general price level; (2) no time lags; (3) savings and investment refer to income of same periods; (4) both savings and investment are

[1] "Revolutionary" overthrow, particularly in political regimes, of course can and does occur very suddenly. Nevertheless structural change in our sense, which concerns the society as a whole or any of its major sub-systems, does not occur in short time spans, even in such cases. Extensive structural change in the Soviet economy, for instance, did not occur during the year 1917 but during a long period extending at least into the middle 1930's. The mere transfer of "top control" of existing structures from one group to another is not structural change.

[2] Domar, Evsey D., "Capital Expansion, Rate of Growth and Employment," *Econometrica*, April, 1946, pp. 137–147.

net, i.e., over and above depreciation; (5) depreciation is measured in terms of the cost of replacement of the depreciated asset by another one of *the same productive capacity*; (6) productive capacity of an asset or of the whole economy is a measurable concept. The last two, he holds, involve various psychological and institutional factors such as distribution of income, consumers' preferences, wage rates, structure of industry, etc. But for his purposes all these factors are held constant.

The bases of Domar's theory of growth are: (1) increase in labour productivity is not technological progress in itself, but is technological progress embodied in capital goods. The dichotomy between the $A_G - L_G$ and $A_A - G_A$ boundary-processes which we have discussed embodies this principle. (2) Employment is a function of the ratio of national income to productive capacity (as opposed to the short-term Keynesian version that employment is a function of national income). This allows for the long-run possibility of the unemployment of men and machines by virtue of the growth of productivity, or technological unemployment. (3) *Investment creates productive capacity as well as production.* This statement lies at the foundation of our characterization of the $A_A - G_A$ and $A_{A_a} - A_{G_a}$ boundary processes. This dual character of investment gives both sides of a long-term equation relating (*a*) the supply side, or capitalization of the economy and (*b*) the demand side, or the level of income necessary to allow full utilization of this supply.

How is the equation constructed? Let I = rate of investment per year and s = addition of productive capacity for the same period. Thus Is = net annual potential output of investment projects. Correcting for loss through transfer of labour, etc., Domar formulates the variable δ (usually less than s), or *potential social average investment productivity*. This coefficient δ depends upon technological progress and refers to *potential* productive capacity. The maximum δ of course equals s. On the demand side for productive capacity, Domar incorporates the marginal propensity to save α. The equation for growth is that r (some rate of investment) equal to $\delta\alpha$. This means that a constant compound interest rate of growth must be maintained for continuous full employment. If α is 12 per cent and δ 30 per cent, the equilibrium rate of growth is 3·6 per cent annually.

The long-run problem is that δ and α do not remain constant. When $r=\delta\alpha$, then full productive capacity is utilized. This assumes that the average propensity to save is equal to the marginal and that the ratio of productive capacity to capital for the whole economy is equal to that of new investment projects. Of course, when r falls below $\delta\alpha$, the failure of the economy to grow at the required rate creates unused capacity and unemployment. When $\delta<s$ (an imbalance caused by misdirection of investment, or by lack of the balance between propensity to save on the one hand and the growth of labour, discovery of natural resources and technological progress on the other) a certain amount of capital must be junked every year to maintain full employment. In so far as capitalists postpone this junking, unused capacity develops.

To summarize: the two crucial variables in this system are the propensity to save and the average potential productive capacity. The economist's task is to trace the consequences for the different values for the long-term supply and the long-term demand for productive capacity *if* there is a change in either one or the other or both (or in the relations between δ and s).[1]

Our point of departure is the word "if" in the last paragraph. Most economists and sociologists would agree that the problematical functions and coefficients change in value over time, since differing rates of growth, employment, etc., are apparent in history. If formal theories are to reach greater specificity the problem is to discern principles which govern the behaviour of these coefficients; only then is it possible to discuss not only the consequences *if* they change, but also the conditions determining *when* and *how* they behave in a given way.

This problem—to order theoretically the indeterminacy of the non-economic factors—is methodologically not unlike the problems of the classification of markets and the analysis of the trade cycle. The principles by which this non-economic order can be analysed for the long term involve the same theoretical elements; but they must be differently organized and applied

[1] There is an interesting parallel with the trade cycle theories as examined in Chap. IV. By holding certain conditions constant, it is possible to construct a model of high formal adequacy. The problem is to vary certain functions or coefficients and to trace the economic consequences of this variation.

in certain respects. In the cases of markets and of the trade cycle we investigated the implications of a *given* institutional structure for the behaviour of certain coefficients and functions. For changes of the magnitude envisaged by a full-growth model, however, the determinants of the values of the relevant coefficients and functions must be referred to a *theory of the structural change* of the economy as a social system. We will indicate lines along which it is possible to "translate" this theory into values applicable to the functions and coefficients of technical economic growth theories such as Domar's.

A STRUCTURAL CHANGE IN THE AMERICAN ECONOMY: THE SEPARATION OF OWNERSHIP AND CONTROL

To illustrate how an analysis of *institutional change* can fill some of the gaps left open by technical economic models of the type presented by Domar we will outline a sociological model of one type of process of institutional change. We think of this as a general model which in its outline applies to changes in the institutional structure of *any* social system; for present purposes, however, an economy is the system of reference. We will try to relate the model to the principal extra- and intra-economic factors as developed throughout the volume and represented in Figure 19, Chapter IV.[1]

We also will apply this model to one particular major change in the American economic structure which has been virtually completed within the last half-century, and illustrate it less thoroughly by referring to a few other processes familiar to economic historians. Before presenting the model itself, let us

[1] The model we will develop has not been so fully stated elsewhere. Its main reference-points are, however, formulated in Chapter V of *Working Papers*. In modified form it is involved in analyses of small-group process, particularly in Bales and Slater, *Role Differentiation in Small Groups*, in *Family, Socialization and Interaction Process*, Chap. V. A more generalized statement of certain aspects was attempted by Parsons and Bales in Chap. VII of the latter publication. As we will point out later, its logical structure is closely related to that of the levels of generalization of the factors of production which we analysed in Chap. III, pp. 118–122; 130–133.

sketch broadly in non-technical terms the main illustrative empirical example.

In 1932 appeared one of the most significant studies in the literature on American economic institutions, *The Modern Corporation and Private Property*, by A. A. Berle, Jr., and Gardner Means. It was an extensive analysis of the "government" of the type of large corporation which by that time already occupied the most strategic position in American business, and on the whole has increased in relative importance since then.[1]

Berle and Means' primary thesis was summed up in the phrase "the separation of ownership and control." At the time of the large-scale introduction of the corporate form of organization soon after the middle of the nineteenth century, and certainly before that, the control of the business firm lay overwhelmingly in the hands of the same "people" (e.g., household units) who legally owned all, or the preponderant share, of the property employed as capital in the enterprise. By a gradual process, however, control had come to be exercised by minority rather than majority stock ownership, via such channels as dispersing voting stock widely, raising a great deal of capital by bond issues rather than stock and finally "pyramiding" through the holding company device.

The most significant development, however, Berle and Means held, was the appearance of a situation in which *any* status of ownership tended to become more or less formal as far as control of the business policy of the firm was concerned. For the most part without formal legal changes, many large corporations had come under the effective control of career "managers" whose personal ownership of securities in the firm was only of nominal significance as an instrument of control. One condition of this development was the wide dispersion of voting stock ownership which had come to be held primarily as an investment (not as an instrument of control), a situation dependent on a ready market for such securities. The primary device for exercising minority or managerial control was through proxy machinery in elections to the board of directors. The locus of "real" control could,

[1] For the most recent general description of the structure and operation of the American economy, cf. Dewhurst, *et al.*, *America's Needs and Resources*, 1955.

of course, vary from a group of "insiders" on the board to career managers not on the board at all.[1]

These facts are generally familiar, and it is not necessary to dwell on them further. Suffice it to say that Standard Oil of New Jersey is now closer to the norm for big business in the United States than, for instance, the Ford Motor Company in the later years of Henry Ford, Sr.[2]

This structural change in business organization has been associated with changes in the stratification of the society. Around the 1890's, the most conspicuous group at the top were the great industrial magnates and their families, usually the founders and continuing controllers of the great enterprises: the Vanderbilts, Harrimans, Morgans, Carnegies, Rockefellers, etc. Fifth Avenue and Newport were the most prominent style-of-life symbols. But these families, who controlled through ownership most of the big business of the time, by and large failed to consolidate their position as the dominant *class* in the society.[3] The ensuing change in stratification was not effected by a "revolution." To be sure, it was probably substantially influenced by hostility to the great magnates of the "heroic age" of capitalism, as manifested in the "muckraking" literature, the "trustbusting," etc. High progressive taxation also contributed, but a policy so injurious to the interests of an alleged "ruling class" could not have been instituted had not other important forces been at work. The main processes in the failure of the older type of business leaders to consolidate their dominant position seem to have been less dramatic than

[1] In at least one large American corporation, Standard Oil of New Jersey, there has been a complete formal fusion between Board of Directors and appointed management. *All* members of the Board are full-time career men in the company; participation of "outside" interests, banking and otherwise, has been eliminated altogether.

[2] Of course this extreme separation of ownership and management does not apply in the same degree to the "small business" sector of the economy, but there can be little doubt of the strategic importance of big business for the economy as a whole.

[3] This group, not the "managers" of the 1940's and '50's, were the targets of Veblen's biting satire in *The Theory of the Leisure Class*. In general on this change in stratification, cf. Parsons, "A Revised Analytical Approach to the Theory of Social Stratification" in *Essays in Sociological Theory*, revised edition, 1954.

coercion by outraged public reaction; the explanation lies, we suggest, in the processes of interaction between the economy and the other sectors of the society through boundary relations.

A MODEL OF INSTITUTIONAL CHANGE

A. *The Impetus to Change*

There is no *one* source of a process of institutional change. Throughout this book we have emphasized the relevance of a plurality of variables and factors at every level. Forces inducing change may act on any one of the factors in a system; the analytical problem is to trace the system-wide repercussions of a change initiated at any given point.

At present, however, we are dealing with institutional change. As we have noted, institutional structure is relatively stable and relatively insulated from the immediate "play of economic forces" as usually analysed by economists; it serves functions of control. Since the control above all regulates boundary relations, for purposes of exposition, we will concentrate in the *first* instance on the boundaries of the economy itself which are most important in its interchange with the non-economic sub-sectors of the society, i.e., the goal-attainment and the adaptive boundaries.[1]

The *kind* of institutional change we will analyse is structural differentiation. Though such change is only one of a considerable variety of types, we consider this to be particularly significant in the general theory of action. We will make the following assumptions which cannot be fully discussed here. (1) A stage in a process of structural differentiation can be reduced to several steps whereby *one* unit or organization differentiates into *two* which differ from each other in structure and in function for the system, but which together are in

[1] The basis for these statements was developed in Chap. III. "Economic forces" operate through processes of exchange and hence within the framework of contract. But they centre on the G-factor and part of the A-factor of the exchange relation. These are less stable than the I- and L-factors, which are organized more directly about value-systems. This is thus a special case of the relatively greater stability of the elements of a social system most directly associated with its institutionalized value system.

certain respects "functionally equivalent" to the earlier less differentiated unit. In our illustrative example, since the "managerial revolution" the functions of "ownership" and of "control" have become differentiated in American big business in the sense that distinct units of organization usually perform these functions. But *taken together* these units perform economic functions equivalent to the performance of the earlier "ownership-controlled" *single* unit of organization. During such a step in differentiation, the *main value system* is assumed to remain stable. The change, that is, is not in the value-content of the pattern-maintenance cell of the system in question, but in the *number* of sub-systems and their structural and functional relations to each other.[1] (3) Differentiation is distinct from *segmentation*. Both processes involve an increase in the number of distinct units or sub-systems. But segmentation is the process by which one unit divides into two or more structurally and functionally equivalent smaller units. An example is the division of the original Standard Oil Company into several regional Standard Oil companies approximately the same as each other and the "parent" company. In the process of differentiation, on the other hand, the new units are neither structurally nor functionally equivalent, but each contributes different specialized ingredients to a more general function. The differentiation of retail outlets from transportation agencies, both of which have distinct functions but each of which contributes to "distribution," is an example. (4) We assume a principle of "inertia":[2] a system in a state of equilibrium, tends to remain in that state unless "disturbed" from outside.

As noted above, the most likely sources of disturbance are at the goal-attainment and the adaptive boundaries of the

[1] Empirically, a given institutional change may involve *both* structural differentiation and changes in value-pattern type, but theoretically it is essential to discriminate between the two. That they need not go together in a simple sense is evidenced by such facts as that American values, as described by de Tocqueville for the 1830's, seem remarkably like those of today; yet there certainly has been enormous structural change in the society in the interval. For the theoretical distinction, cf. *Family, Socialization and Interaction Process*, Chap. VII.

[2] On the concept of inertia applied to systems of action, cf. *The Social System*, *op. cit.*, Chap. VI and *Working Papers in the Theory of Action*, *op. cit.*, Chaps. III, V.

system. For the economy these boundaries involve inputs of labour service and consumers' spending from the household, and inputs of capital funds and "encouragement of enterprise" from the polity.

Let us look at the possibilities that variations in these input categories relative to a state of the economy might lead to kinds of disturbances eventuating in institutional change. Several variations are possible, according to the desired level of analytical refinement. The simplest would be to distinguish only increases and decreases of major input (i.e., factors of production) at each of the two boundaries. A step next would be to introduce the duality of interchanges at each boundary, e.g., considering both labour input and consumers' spending input at the *G*-boundary. Finally, it would be possible to break each of these latter inputs into the four components of a contractual orientation. To work systematically through every logical possibility of these three levels of analytic complication would be too burdensome to undertake here. Instead we will select certain possibilities at each level and compare the consequences for processes within the economy and at its boundaries with some broadly known facts.

Of the four logically possible variations of primary input change at the combined *G*- and *A*-boundaries, general theoretical considerations suggest that a simultaneous deficit at the *G*-boundary and increment at the *A*-boundary is a particularly significant combination for the initiation of positive structural changes in the system. The *G*-deficit is a stimulus to change because the system goal attainment is in some way blocked. According to the principle of inertia, a certain set of processes then develops tending to restore the previous level of goal attainment. But whether this restoration is achieved depends in part on the present and prospective availability of facilities at the *A*-boundary. If there is a positive increment of facilities, present or in prospect, then an opportunity to regain and increase goal attainment by some new method is created.[1]

[1] Though its immediate relevance may seem questionable to the economist, the best-authenticated cases of the importance of this combination lie in the analysis of learning processes in the individual. He must be "motivated" by depriving him of accustomed gratifications if he continues to act in the old ways, and he must be presented with an opportunity,

How does this general starting-point relate specifically to the economy? The primary *G*-input is, as we have maintained, *labour service*. The economy's goal attainment in a *performance* sense is of course production of goods and services, but this is an *output* not an input category.[1]

The conventional view is that the principal sanction or input for the production of goods and services is the money returns from their sale. This is true of immediate transactions; financial solvency is an essential condition of the firm's operation, and profit level is a primary success symbol. But the fact remains that the economy does not "use" money returns except in an intermediary and a symbolic sense. The more important sanction in the wider functional context is labour input, or the capacity of economic organizations to motivate people to "work" in the production process. Moreover, this sanction, seen in the same wider context, is contingent not simply upon wages, but upon the level of *production* received by households for the input of labour. The nature of the contingency in this respect and the mechanisms by which it operates are central to our problem. A deficit of input into the economy at the *G*-boundary is thus in the first instance a deficit input of *labour* as a factor of production. This deficit (relative to expectations of course) rather than a consumers' spending deficit is at the focus of institutional change, as distinguished from short-run fluctuation.

Each of the two *G*-deficits has several meanings. A deficit of consumers' spending might mean: (1) dissatisfaction with the kinds and qualities of consumers' goods produced and offered to consumers; (2) lack of purchasing power to buy these independent of any attitudes toward them, or (3) a decision that

i.e., realistic facilities, which can be adapted to new ways of behaving. If there is no goal-attainment deficit there is no motivation to change; if there is no *relative* facilities-improvement or prospect of it, there is no possibility of actually doing anything new. This paradigm has been generalized both to learning of new values in the individual and to processes of change in small-scale social systems. Cf. *Family, Socialization and Interaction Process*, Chaps. IV, VII. Also James Olds, *The Growth and Structure of Motives*, 1956.

[1] The deficit of the corresponding labour input may or may not be a *direct* consequence of the economy's output level; for present purposes we assume it is not.

part of the available purchasing power should be devoted to uses *other* than current consumption, i.e., saved. Withholding labour input relative to employers' demand might mean: (1) higher valuation of "leisure" than of "work," or (2) dissatisfaction with the *way* labour is employed and hence willingness to put "pressure" to have it employed "more effectively." We suggest that the combination of the second meaning of a labour deficit and the third of a consumers' spending deficit[1] gives maximum stimulation to economic growth and institutional change. What empirical meaning can we give to these processes of withholding labour input and consumers' spending?

Before attempting an answer, let us turn to the adaptive boundary. If a positive increase of input is important, then which of the two categories—the primary input of capital funds for investment through credit creation or the "encouragement of enterprise"—is more crucial for institutional change? We suggest that in the earlier stages of a "growth cycle" input of capital funds is not of primary importance; without any prospect for use, this might cause a glut on the capital market. The prospect that such funds *will* be available under the proper conditions is, however, very important. Such information defines a range of opportunity; furthermore, it is implicit in the *encouragement of enterprise*, which is the demand for productivity as distinguished from the demand for production.[2]

The relation of encouragement of enterprise to the input of new capital funds works out by well-known mechanisms. Demand for productivity from a section of the polity means a disposition to be dissatisfied with the *level* of economic productivity, not with the specific goods and services produced. Since this is a type of demand, there is also, in accord with economic doctrine, a disposition to "pay" for increased productivity by means of effective encouragements. The credit mechanisms supply the link with actual increases in capital funds, albeit with some possibilities of inflation; normally, however, we assume that real increase in productivity through processes of investment will follow an increased demand for productivity in due course.

[1] As we will see, the first has also probably been important in American economic development. Cf. below, p. 267.

[2] Cf. Chap. II, pp. 72 ff.

The combination of withdrawal of labour input in response to dissatisfaction with mode of employment and an increased demand for productivity is therefore the most favourable combination of input changes for initiating a process combining growth and institutional change.[1]

Are there empirical conditions which meet the specifications of the optimum combination of input changes? We do not believe that there is any *one* set of such conditions; but we wish to single out one important complex in the history of the Western economies, especially in Great Britain and the United States, which does fit the important theoretical conditions in cases where the simulus source was not primarily the activity of the state.

This is the complex of value attitudes which Marshall associated with his category of "activities" and Max Weber associated with the ethic of ascetic Protestantism and saw institutionalized in the attitude toward work as a "calling."[2] As characterized by both authors, this set of values is, in our terms, institutionalized in the pattern-maintenance system of the society and internalized in personalities. Above all, it concerns the *attitudes toward work which the individual brings to the contract of employment* from the household. It is thus part of the labour input.

But what part? Certainly it is not the *G*-component which is a direct function of wage payment. Rather it is the *I*-component, backed by the *L*, focused on the symbolization of responsibility for the effective fulfilment of the production goals of the firm and the economy.[3] Such attitudes thus involve the direct valuation of effectiveness in production. On institutional grounds,[4] they may be expected to be especially strong in the higher reaches of the status distribution of business management, but by no means confined to them.

[1] Withdrawal of labour without increased demand for productivity would result simply in a Keynesian depression.

[2] We have given a number of references to this complex before. For Weber, cf. *The Protestant Ethic and the Spirit of Capitalism*; for Marshall, *Principles*, esp. Bk. I, Chaps. I and II, Bk. III, Chap. II and elsewhere. For interpretation, cf. Parsons, *The Structure of Social Action*, Chap. IV and *passim*.

[3] Cf. Chap. III, pp. 114 ff.

[4] Cf. Chap. III, pp. 149–50.

How do these attitudes result in a *deficit* of labour input? They seem to imply the opposite—the tendency to excel in hard work. The problematical element of the value complex concerns the *conditions* under which this extra effort will be exerted and in what direction of activity. Like any system, a going economy tends to equilibrium. Given stable consumers' wants and stable capital resources, the tendency is to the traditionalization of the productive process. The "Puritan" attitude toward work, however, does not predispose people to perform given routine tasks faithfully, but to drive to increase productivity by improving methods and organization. In fact, the characteristic businessman (in this tradition) tends, if anything, to *neglect* the requirements of stable routine production; he restlessly changes and improves. Relative to the "expectations" of a steady state, therefore, he tends to *withdraw* labour services[1] from the routine productive process in order to re-introduce them with great intensity only if *his* conditions of a changed organization of production are met.

How does this value complex bear on consumption and spending? Weber emphasized how ascetic Protestantism encouraged a trusteeship attitude toward wealth, and a high level of saving for capital uses.[2] Marshall also described the corresponding ethical attitudes; his discussion of wants fits more specifically into our analysis. Marshall emphasized the distinction between "activities adjusted to wants" and "wants adjusted to activities." The first category characterizes a production equilibrium governed by a *given* state of consumers' wants and a corresponding input of labour. The second category refers to the pressure of attitudes manifested both in the motivation to work itself *and* in the structure of wants. An important element in this complex is a strong motivation to save and a belief in the development of productivity "for its own sake." Hence the specific conditions at both the goal-attainment and adaptive boundaries are implicit in the same extra-economic complex.[3]

[1] His own and those of others over whom he exercises control.

[2] Cf. Weber, *The Protestant Ethic and the Spirit of Capitalism, op. cit.*, pp. 170 ff.

[3] An interesting example is Marshall's assertion that low wheat prices in the late 19th century were accounted for by the fact that farmers in the

Marshall's empirical analysis of the motivations and processes of saving agrees with our own in Chapters II and IV. So far as saving originates in the household it is not an economic act at all; it is a manifestation of the values relative to the stability of the household and the society. So far as the household relinquishes control of savings and provides a base of reserves for credit creation, it is involved in a boundary interchange with the polity. Once such a base is established, of course, the level and channels of credit creation are subject primarily to political decisions. Much traditional economic theory, by assuming a direct feedback to the economy from the household, short-cuts this whole complex and thus implies that only "prudential" modifications of the household's consumption interests *could* enter into the motivation for saving. By prematurely closing the circuit, economic theory does not allow either for value attitudes transcending the "welfare" of the particular household or for various political considerations. Our analysis allows for the possible link between attitudes toward saving and encouragement of enterprise via a demand for productivity over and above short-term financial returns.[1]

In addition to this quantitative aspect of the attitude to consumption associated with the positive valuation of work there is a qualitative aspect which becomes important in connection with the factor of organization and the role of the entrepreneur. This is a relative lack of traditionalism in consumption, the consequence of which is a greater than average readiness to accept new products and new combinations

American West were engaged not so much in the production of wheat as of farms; the wheat was almost a by-product; their goal was productivity. Cf. *Industry and Trade*, 1921, p. 776.

[1] Of course, as we pointed out above (Chap. II, pp. 61–2), empirically in the lower levels of societal differentiation, the saving unit and the investing unit may be concretely the same, i.e.,the household. But even when this is true, the "motivation" of the saving-investment decision process *cannot* be primarily economic as postulated in the classical theory of saving. In terms of orientation there are two intermediate steps, the value-decision of L and the "political" decision of G, which are both necessarily non-economic. The role of credit-creation in G is particularly important. Willingness to create credit is a "vote of confidence" in the worthwhileness and realistic possibility of increasing productivity.

of the components in the standard of living, and a corresponding readiness to be dissatisfied with a traditional standard of living.

B. *The Propagation of the Impetus to Change*

Having established at least one set of conditions favourable to the initiation of institutional change in the economy, we will now turn to some subsequent repercussions of this initial impetus within the economy and at its boundaries.

By the principle of inertia there should arise a tendency to maintain the pre-existing equilibrium. Conditions making for institutional change are therefore likely to generate symptoms of disturbance independent of any "constructive" steps toward completing the change. This is a general concomitant of structural change in systems of action.

Such disturbances lead to the appearance of attitudes and action tendencies which do not help positively to solve the realistic problems of the situation. Disturbances are classed as negative and positive; psychologically, the negative ones are manifestations of anxiety and aggression; the positive are some kind of unrealistic phantasies of wish-fulfilment, some of which idealize symbols of the status quo or of the allegedly better "good old days," others of which, contain unrealistic Utopian phantasies about ideal states to be realized in the future.

Periods of rapid economic change are often characterized by conspicuous disturbances of this sort. Because of the institutionalized uncertainty prevalent there, manifestations of strain appear prominent in the capital markets,[1] especially waves of anxiety and of unrealistic optimism, the former tending to culminate in panic conditions, the latter in speculative "bubbles" where the participants manifest totally unrealistic expectations of profits.

The capital markets in a modern economy are associated with the activities of professionals. It is, therefore, significant that hostility and aggression tend to be manifested particularly in connection with the more visible markets for consumers' goods and for labour. Included in the former are the waves of public indignation about monopolies and trusts, especially

[1] Cf. Chap. IV, pp. 233–39 ff.

their alleged illegitimate perversion of the public interest,[1] e.g., the wave of hostility against the unethical practices of trusts in the first decade of the century, with Standard Oil as perhaps the most prominent target and to some extent a scapegoat. In the latter, waves of public indignation over firms' handling of labour and employment problems may be associated with the "pains" of certain phases of economic growth. As popular stereotypes against bankers and "Wall Street" indicate, the capital markets receive their share of hostility. We do not at all suggest that leaders in the processes of economic change have not been guilty of many ethical infractions. But *in addition* to indignation, justified in terms of institutionalized moral standards, this hostility often *also* expresses the disturbance generated by processes of change as such. It would appear to some extent no matter how exemplary the initiators of change, so long as they remained in their role as initiators.

How does the impetus we have described lead to actual differentiation in the structure of the economy? It proceeds by two channels. We have already described the first, which leads through the boundary between the household and the polity to the increase of capital funds available to the economy. This non-economic process provides the adaptive pre-requisites for increased productivity.

The other channel is also non-economic, but concerns the relation of the household in the pattern-maintenance system to the integrative system. Through this channel new patterns of economic organization are generated and then "fed into" the economy through its integrative boundary from the integrative sub-system of society. Let us develop this process of entrepreneurial innovation in some detail.[2]

Every human participant in an economic unit is to some degree both a "worker" and an "entrepreneur." Or, in our technical terms, there is both a *G*- and an *I*-component in his orientation to the contract of employment and hence to his occupational role. The *I*-component constitutes a mode of

[1] Cf. the Nye Committee of the 1930's with regard to the alleged role of the munitions makers in involving the U.S. in war.

[2] Cf. Chap. II, pp. 65–7, for the general analysis of the interchange at this boundary.

participation in the integrative sub-system of the economy; it is generally more prominent on executive than on "labour" levels. Whatever variation exists within limits is an empirically open question. Weber's and Marshall's emphases upon the need for a disciplined labour force suggest that the *I*-component is relevant to all levels.

Ego brings the *I*-component of the contract of employment *to* the economy from the household as part of the pattern-maintenance system. How does "dissatisfaction" with the mode of labour's employment in the economy result in motivation to innovate? Precisely by mobilizing the kinds of values described by Weber and Marshall relative to their participation in the economy.

In sociological terms it involves first a process internal to the pattern-maintenance system itself, second a set of boundary processes between it and the integrative system. The first depends upon technical psychological considerations which we will not develop here; suffice it to say that by "handling" the disturbances noted above, the pattern-maintenance sub-system mobilizes positive motivation to act in accord with institutionalized values. In this way, tendencies to discouragement and withdrawal, which always arise in connection with frustration, may be effectively counteracted.

The second set of processes which rewards this positive motivation and guides it into channels for developing new economic organization has at least three phases:

(1) The disposition to act in accord with the values to be institutionalized, receives diffuse support. This support comes from sources in the integrative system, i.e., some classes of people who manifest dissatisfaction with the economy's current operation are on the whole given encouragement and high "social standing." People with somewhat "visionary" ideas are tolerated, even lionized. The "folklore" of capitalism is full of illustrations, e.g., the virtual legend of young Henry Ford puttering over his "horseless carriage" and dreaming that every farmer might own one.

(2) In response to this tolerant and supportive attitude there is a positive trying out, in imagination, of new ideas. Such ideas, as they come to be more specific and circumstantial, come to deal with the actual reorganization of the economy

by means of recombining the factors of production. This may be manifested in technological innovation, as in the famous Ford-Edison pattern, or changing the firm's organization in some way, or in changing its relations to labour input (e.g., through positive valuation of high wages), or in its relations to consumers. This is the phase of "thinking up" new specific combinations which imply changes in the system of contractual relations.

(3) "New ideas" are actually applied to economic production. The great risk is whether they will work, i.e., be accepted in practice; the immediate measure of this outcome is financial survival of the introducing agency. When this stage is reached, the crucial reward factor is entrepreneurial profit in Schumpeter's sense. Willingness to pay profits constitutes the immediate demand for entrepreneurial services. We therefore accept the common economic view that at a certain stage in economic change profit is the dynamic incentive to productive innovation. But we would add one qualification: the prospect of profit does *not* account for the *genesis* of the motivation to innovate; to analyse this, one must turn to the society's value system, the mechanisms which control the effects of disturbance, and the mechanisms which provide encouragement to new ideas. Only at the point of specific practical trial of an idea does profit become the focal symbol of success and hence a reward factor.

At this third phase the "reorganization of motivation" which was initiated as a disturbance at the $A_G - L_G$ boundary impinges directly on the economy through $A_I - I_I$. The entire process thus increases the input of entrepreneurial service which results in new organization and higher productivity.

What is the connection between the two necessary conditions for economic growth and development—the processes leading to an increased input of entrepreneurial service and to the increased input of capital funds? Referring to the paradigm of the internal economic processes in Figure 19, Chapter IV, we are able to isolate points of connection. The more direct link is through $A_{I_l} - A_{A_l}$, at which are exchanged risk capital and long-term returns. In the proper atmosphere, some of an input of capital into the economy through A_A passes to A_I as risk capital and hence increases the "offer" of profit for entrepreneurial services. Or conversely, an input of entrepreneurial service into A_I generates purchasing power to act as effective demand for more risk capital.

The more indirect intra-economic channel leads first from A_{I_g} to A_{G_g}, then from A_{G_a} to A_{A_a}. That is, an input of entrepreneurial services results in new factor combinations which in turn influence the process of production in A_G. But this creates anew the demand for capital funds as facilities from the finance-investment sub-system. The two channels differ mainly in time reference. $A_{A_i} - A_{I_i}$ concerns the longer-run considerations in terms of economic structure, and the $A_{I_g} - A_{G_g}$ and $A_{G_a} - A_{A_a}$ sequence deals with shorter time references.

As in every other boundary process the output of entrepreneurial service which reaches its peak at this point in the process must be balanced by an output from the economy for which there must be an effective demand. As we have repeatedly said, the output in question is new output combinations, new products and combinations of the components of the standard of living. This is the point at which the relative flexibility and lack of traditionalism of the American consumer has been an important factor in economic development. The tendency to rationalize not only production but consumption (including shopping) has been a necessary condition of absorption of the products of entrepreneurial innovation.[1]

C. *The Process of Structural Differentiation*

How, then, do we conceive the actual process of structural differentiation to occur? In order to discriminate clearly between the elements of the general model and those specific to a particular case, we will outline the main developments in the case of the separation of ownership from control, then formulate the relevant parts of the general model.

We assume that in the larger owner-controlled enterprises there had been—in sufficient quantity, intensity, and distribution—certain types of dissatisfaction with the conduct of enterprise under that basis of organization. One important focus of probable dissatisfaction stemmed from the fact that the

[1] The importance of this factor has been particularly emphasized by Mr. J. R. Pitts. It stands out sharply when American and French attitudes are compared.

scale of enterprise had created a class of high-level "employees" with high-level responsibilities, but without the formal rights of control of "owners." This would be a case of the familiar instability which generally develops when responsibility is not balanced by adequate authority. We also assume a good deal of diffuse support for this dissatisfaction in the "business community" and related sectors of the society, e.g., among engineers, designers, etc. At least, there was sufficient support to prevent the "dissident" elements from merely being brought back into line.

What could be done positively? The essential problem was to try out ways of exercising managerial responsibility effectively outside the direct control of the owner-groups.

For this to be possible, three conditions besides direct motivation were necessary: (1) that in the direct context of productive organization such action could not be blocked, e.g., by the unchallengeable power and authority of owner-manager groups; (2) that new activities should not dry up the flow of investment; capital had to be available on terms independent of the direct owner-control of the productive process, e.g., through the securities market and bonds; (3) that the innovators could expect adequate rewards, mainly from the diffuse-symbolic component of success.

If these conditions were fulfilled, we would expect a differentiation between that complex of organization dealing with the input of capital into the economy, and that dealing with the input of the labour factor, particularly on the managerial level. We would expect the role of responsible manager to be organized more and more about the "occupational" component and less and less about the role of proprietor. The institutional complexes of the contract of employment and the contract of investment thus constitute the reference-points for this process of differentiation.

If the process of differentiation is not to result in *dis*-organization, however, the residual function from which the new one is differentiated must be provided for; furthermore, the two new ones must be integrated in a superordinate structure which co-ordinates them successfully. In the illustrative case the institution of ownership had to be restructured. It could not imply full right to control policy and to "hire" management as functionaries; yet there had to develop some co-operative relationship of joint responsibility. The typical Board of Directors of a large corporation probably approximates the result of restructuring, for it represents both sets of interest without any clear-cut primacy relation. Empirically, there is a wide spectrum of particular arrangements, near this central tendency we have described.

Connected with this is the tendency for investment to come into the hands of specialized organizations like banks and insurance companies which stand in a fiduciary relation to the ultimate owners of capital funds.[1] The corporation itself also develops into a more complex unit in a network of articulating organizations, such as the investing organizations, trade associations, other units of the "business community," and the labour union.[2] The modern corporation is the *economic* organization which stands at the centre of a complex of organizations mediating between it and the non-economic societal sub-systems.

One final step is necessary before the economy involved in such a process of institutional change returns to equilibrium. The relation between a *new* pattern of organization and the reward of entrepreneurial profit is essentially unstable. Only by institutionalizing the organizational innovation, i.e., linking it with the routine conditions of stable functioning of the economy, can this instability be overcome. Routinization involves shifting the primary relevant performance-output from "new product combinations" to "production of goods and services," and shifting the primary relevant input from entrepreneurial services to labour services. Concomitantly, "profits" must become "wages." In this respect we agree fundamentally with Schumpeter's position that entrepreneurial profit in the technical sense is a temporary phenomenon.

To put it another way, the innovation must be accepted as part of the normal expectation system. Those who produce it cease to be rewarded by a special type of profit for their daring and originality, and come to be rewarded in the usual way for carrying on routine functions. The new "organization" involved in its production becomes an institutionalized part of

[1] Cf. Chap. III, pp. 161 ff.

[2] Gordon, *Business Leadership in the Large Corporation*, *op. cit.*, Part II.

the economic structure, e.g., the expectation that management can take initiative and responsibility in capacities other than as agents of owners.[1]

This final transition occurs through the application of a *consistent organized pattern of sanctions* to the new product combination. The sanctioning agency shifts from I_I back to L_G, and the circle is closed. In so far as this happens, the motivation to save which grew out of the original dissatisfaction tension is deactivated, since the higher level of productivity has been attained. Of course, the value system may still have dynamic potentialities which in due course may generate still another cycle of change.

D. *A Summary of the Model and Its Application*

Let us summarize the model for institutional change as a series of logical steps in a cycle of change: (1) The process starts with a combination of "dissatisfaction" with the productive achievements of the economy or its relevant sectors and a sense of "opportunity" in terms of the potential availability of adequate resources to reach a higher level of productivity. (2) There appear symptoms of disturbance in the form of "unjustified" negative emotional reactions and "unrealistic" aspirations on the part of various elements in the population. (3) A covert process of handling these tensions and mobilizing motivational resources for new attempts to realize the implications of the existing value pattern takes place. (4) Supportive tolerance of the resulting proliferation of "new ideas," without imposing specific responsibility for their implementation and for "taking the consequences," is found in important quarters. (5) Positive attempts are made to reach specification of the new ideas which will become the objects of commitments by entrepreneurs. (6) "Responsible" implementation of innovations is carried out by persons or collectivi-

[1] An interesting example is the legal clarification of the status of corporate giving for educational and charitable purposes. For long it was held that each specific gift required formal permission of the stockholders, since "their property" was being given away. A recent New Jersey decision has, however, validated the right of "corporations," i.e., in effect their managements, to make such gifts where they feel it is in the "interest of the company."

ties assuming the role of entrepreneurs, either rewarded by entrepreneurial profit or punished by financial failure, depending on consumers' acceptance or rejection of the innovations. (7) The gains resulting from the innovation and consolidated by their acceptance as part of the standard of living and their incorporation into the routine functions of production. In this final phase the new "way of doing things" becomes institutionalized as part of the structure of the economy.[1]

We suggest the following "translation" into the terms of the separation of ownership and management in the corporate structure of the American economy: (1) There was diffuse dissatisfaction of responsible elements in the business world with the way the "owner-controlled" corporate system was working from the point of view of maximization of productivity, and an indirect feeling that the supply of capital was not wholly dependent on maintaining the status quo. (2) Symptoms of disturbance appeared; e.g., the "technological" view of the destructive consequences of business (owner-dominated Veblen) machinations as interfering with "efficiency"; utopian exaggerations of the results to be obtained from abandoning "business" altogether and becoming purely "technological". (3) Permissive-supportive attitudes toward the objections to the "captain of industry" system, and toward the opposite utopianism were found.[2] (4) The "new enterprise" of organizers of the corporate world, e.g., U.S. Steel after Carnegie-Morgan; General Motors after Durant and Standard Oil after

[1] The number and order of steps involved in this process corresponds with that postulated by Parsons and Bales in their paradigm of a cycle of internalization of a value pattern in the process of socialization (cf. *Family, Socialization, and Interaction Process*, Chap. VII). We feel that this correspondence is not fortuitous, but derives from certain general conditions and characteristics of the process of structural change in systems of action. But the proof of the particular "pudding" under present consideration does not lie in this correspondence but in the economic "eating," i.e., whether this paradigm in fact fits processes of structural change in the *economy* as a system.

[2] Anna Lee Hopson in a study of best-selling novels of the early 20th century found that the hero is unwilling to "knuckle under" to the "interests" and he is very generally rewarded by the idealistic love of the heroine who is regularly the daughter of one of these wicked men. Cf. Anna Lee Hopson, *Best Sellers, Media of Mass Expression*, unpublished Ph.D. dissertation, Radcliffe College, 1952.

Rockefeller, gains in relative prominence. (5) New financial practices appear, tending to "shake free" from the older family capitalistic control; e.g., free sale of securities to the general public; minority-control practices, the holding company, etc. At the same time, there is rapid technological and organizational development of the firm into a kind of "empire" in itself. (6) A new wave of profits follows, showing that the system can operate under the new conditions. For example, earnings of the post-Rockefeller Standard Oil Companies have been much greater than the Rockefeller fortune. (7) The new position is consolidated by its routinization, especially by the great output of new products to a high-wage consuming public; the "new economy" has become independent both of the previous "exploitation of labour" and the previous "capitalistic control."

There is thus in broad terms an encouragingly close fit between the outline of our theoretical model and the empirical facts[1] of one recent change in the structure of the American economy. Of course, this is a mere starting-point for more intensive exploration of this and other cases.

A set of very definite relations obtains between this sequence of change and the paradigm of the levels of generalization of labour and capital as factors of production.[2] In the case of labour, what we have termed "withdrawal of labour" initiates a process by which the labour factor is restructured. This process is not economic in the usual sense but occurs in the first instance within the patter-maintenance system of the society, which is most deeply involved in the motivational balances of the individual personality. Any substantial restructuring of motivation is closely connected with the products of earlier processes of socialization in the family and educational systems.

The new input into the economy occurs in the form of entrepreneurial service through the $A_I - I_I$ boundary. The "permissive-supportive" attitude toward the "dissident" elements in stage (3) of our model of change, therefore, is the integrative utilization of the previously unutilized emerging motivational elements. At stage (4) this becomes actual entrepreneurial service, i.e., proposals for direct and practical

[1] The best brief, non-technical account of these facts is in Frederick Lewis Allen, *The Big Change*, 1953.

[2] Cf. Chap. III, pp. 118–22 ; 130–33.

innovation. In terms of the levels of generality of labour, this means the addition of a new component to the available labour force. At stage (5) the new practices are incorporated as "organization" capable of implementing them; the new "labour" is "employed." Finally, stages (6) and (7) do not show such direct parallels since they are formulated from a different perspective; during and after the period of the new wave of profits, however, it is clear that the new labour has "found its place" in the organizational structure of the economy both in terms of the re-ordering of roles and the routinization of task-assignments.

The structure of the input of labour in the model for change is parallel with the structure of inputs in the series of levels of generality. The three major stages are: (1) the extra-economic genesis of the new input, (2) its availability in relatively fluid form as part of the labour force (or supply of entrepreneurial service), and (3) its commitment through successive stages to actual productive tasks.

With regard to the corresponding relation between the paradigm of institutional change and the levels of generality of capital as a factor, steps (1) to (3) of the change model are concerned with the technological basis of innovation. This involves (1) the combination of certain "dissatisfactions" concerning current methods with the beginnings of "new ideas"; (2) the crystallization of the technological aspect of possible innovations, and (3) the crystallization of practical plans and their tentative acceptance (the "permissive-supportive" attitude).

When this stage is reached, there is a basis for appealing for financial support to implement the emerging plans. Often the forthcoming credit means the diversion of purchasing power from other channels of use; but, if the proposal for innovation is at all general, the most likely source of finance is *new* credit creation. This stage (4) provides the decisive link, for example in Schumpeter's analysis, between the entrepreneur's plans and the capital support provided by the banking system.

Successful command of credit initiates the final sequence of stages. New credit is first made available to specific entrepreneurs (5), and then committed by them to capital goods and labour for specific production projects (6). Finally, through specific production and sales techniques, the projects are implemented (7). As a rule entrepreneurial profit is the measure of the success of these commitments.[1]

The inputs of labour and of capital as factors in *innovation* are both special cases of their inputs into an economy assumed to be stable. In both cases there must be a process of *extra-economic* organization or reorganization of the *basis* of the factor-input. Such reorganization is, in the present case, stimulated by some disturbance in the previous "traditional" equilibrium. Such extra-economic reorganization is essential in order to *increase* the supply of the relevant fluid factors. Once this increase is generated, of course, there must be an intra-economic incorporation of the factor, the stages of which follow a familiar sequence.

In the case of the labour input there is a shift from the pattern-maintenance system as a source of input to the economy to the integrative system as a source of input; this means that the new elements of input are not merely quantitative increases of effort or manpower but are inputs of *organization* of the labour factor. In the case of capital input this new element is discounted through the expected capital value of the innovation, since, through producing "new ideas," it forms the basis for new credit creation. The latter, however, can be realized only through an input of power—i.e., a decision to back the innovation—which involves the polity as well as the economy.

THE ECONOMIC GROWTH MODEL AND THE PROCESS OF INSTITUTIONAL CHANGE

Let us determine the extent of the potentialities of translation from our own model into the "open" elements of a technical growth theory of the Domar type. In general, the Domar model requires a necessary rate of investment in accordance with δ, the potential social average investment productivity and α, the average propensity to save.

One critical problem in the model is the relation between s (the addition of productive capacity of the total projects) and

[1] We cannot explore here the special time-lags and sequences in the relation between capital input and entrepreneurial profits, even though there are apparently special problems in this connection.

δ (an index of the "efficiency" of the amount added). The relation between δ and s, which determines the necessary rate of junking, etc., depends upon the degree of misdirection of investment, and the magnitude of the rate of investment relative to the growth of other factors, such as labour, natural resources, and technological progress.

The following elements, therefore, influence the equilibrium state:

(1) The propensity to save (α).
(2) The rate of investment (r).
(3) The labour function (growth of labour).
(4) "Technological" progress.
(5) Natural resources.

Changes in any element cause a change in the balance of all elements.

The question is: what are some of the principles governing the behaviour of each element, according to our paradigm of structural differentiation?

Since our model of structural change does not apply to changes in natural resources, we omit them, although they are of course empirically important for growth and institutional change. Let us consider the other four elements.

(1) The labour function. Domar treats the labour force in two different contexts. The first is labour's capacity to reduce the differences between s and δ. Growth of labour—though Domar is not explicit, we may interpret this to be strictly in terms of numbers—heightens the average potential social productivity relative to the addition of productive capacity. On the basis of the considerations above, we would include certain characteristics associated with Marshall's emphasis on activities and Weber's emphasis on the *calling* as manifesting an attitude toward work. Thus, growth in numbers of the labour force (or in amount of capital) is not the *only* problematical factor in the productivity of labour. The "calling" in its Puritan aspect implies a drive among workers at various levels to maximize productivity, to press for better conditions, to work hard to improve, and to offer services only on condition of a prospect of increased productivity. The growth of labour in population terms is certainly significant; but the level of

commitment to productive enterprise (primarily a "non-economic" commitment) may reduce differences between δ and s. This level of commitment is thus fully dependent upon neither population growth nor the going wage rate.

The second use of the category of "labour" is as a relatively passive element in the economy which is "employed" or "unemployed" according to the operation of the other variables, e.g., if the rate of investment is sufficiently low, a certain proportion of the labour force is forced into idleness. Again we would emphasize the positive pressures labour can exert on the economy by a disposition to withdraw from routine production, pressure for more alternative outlets for performance capacity, etc.

(2) The propensity to save also has potentialities for change on non-economic bases. We have emphasized the possibility of varying levels of the "ascetic" component of value systems (as analysed by Weber) and the "wants adjusted to activities" complex of Marshall as determinants of the level of saving in any given period.

(3) The rate of investment. Our analysis of the decision process whereby household savings are "processed" through the polity before "returning" to the economy introduces a range of "cultural" and political decisions. Commitment to productive activity in the economy is only one of several possible outcomes of these decisions, others being the implementation of political, integrative, and pattern-maintenance goals.

(4) The sequence leading to an increase in technological progress ties together the behaviour of Domar's other conditions of growth in the following way: The "dissatisfaction" of the first phase of our cycle of change involves both on the labour and the consumption (saving) side. An expression of some dissatisfaction with the current economic mode of activity. But as the process develops and support is given to bearers of "new ideas," the labour function and the savings function tend to stabilize at a point whereby willingness to devote services to the "new" projects and willingness to supply facilities are co-ordinated with the activities of the innovators. Furthermore, the actual "burst" of technological (and organizational) progress is located after the intial dissatisfaction and before the

stabilization period; it does not appear "randomly."[1] Certain decisions concerning the rate of investment are stabilized (via the $G_A - A_A$ input) in accordance with the success of the innovating entrepreneurial activity.[2] Finally, in the period of consolidation, labour "growth" (in all ways), savings function, and rate of investment are stabilized, and the "technological progress" (entrepreneurial input) becomes relatively quiescent.

This is a fragmentary but intelligible account of the *relations among* the elements which, according to the Domar model, produce an equilibrium rate of accumulation of capital. It is, however, a more determinate treatment of the conditions of equilibrium than merely to grant their importance but to leave their own operation indeterminate. Our preliminary paradigm of institutional growth modifies some of Domar's definitions and spells out certain determinate relations among the conditions of growth.

The sequence of steps in a process of institutional change which we have described represents an equilibrium system in process of adjustment to altered conditions. Furthermore, the equilibrium system in the process of institutional change concerns the balancing of forces outside as well as within the economy. Processes of adjustment outside the economy impinge directly upon those within; for instance, those balances between the pattern-maintenance sub-system and the integrative sub-system, respectively, which are primarily non-economic, articulate directly with the equilibrium balance of the economy in the sense in which Domar and other growth economists treat it.

Methodologically, therefore, economic growth of an economy cannot be strictly quantitative increase in the economic input and output categories governed only by the magnitude of the coefficients involved in the accumulation of capital. To introduce a higher level of determinacy into the conditions which govern the economic equilibrium, it is necessary to inquire into certain primarily non-economic relations among the coefficients.

1 Again we note that this is in accord with Schumpeter's view.

2 Of course the problem of allocating the funds as between the A_{A_a}–A_{G_a} boundary and the A_{A_i}–A_{I_i} boundary is a matter of *intra*-economic co-ordination. We are more concerned with the co-ordination of the behaviour of those *externally* determined functions and propensities by means of other than economic mechanisms.

In many respects, of course, technical economic models such as Domar's do not compete in the same methodological race as the model for a process of structural differentiation we have outlined; in fact they are designed in the first instance to attack separate ranges of problems. On the one hand, the Domar model is an outline of the conditions for the maintenance of a steady equilibrium rate of growth of national income. On the basis of such a model certain other economic consequences can be traced, e.g., the level of unemployed resources, the rate of capital accumulation, etc. On the other hand, the model we have presented deals with the conditions which produce a sequence leading to a particular type of economic innovations, namely, the re-formation of economic organization by means of a process of structural differentiation and reintegration.

There are, however, at least two ways in which the two types of models are related to each other, and two corresponding implications of our analysis for the construction of technical economic models: (1) As we have pointed out, quantitative changes over long periods of time, such as those produced by the Domar equilibrium rate of growth, do not occur without simultaneously producing and being maintained by changes of a distinctly qualitative or structural order. Structural differentiation is one major type of such qualitative change. Any theory of long-term economic development must therefore take account of changes introduced by such changes in the institutional framework. (2) More specifically, on the basis of the seven-step sequence of structural differentiation we have traced, it is possible to assign at least approximate values to those coefficients which are grounded in the boundary processes of the economy, e.g., labour, technology, investment, etc., and the direction in which the values of these coefficients will change during the sequence. In this way much more specific theoretical ties are established between the conditions of an equilibrium rate of growth and the process of structural differentiation. One implication of these two points is that technical economic models must be accommodated to the possibility of accounting for *systematic* changes in the coefficients during one or several processes of structural change. We will not, however, go into any of the formal alterations that such accommodation might imply.

Our analysis of this type of institutional change places us squarely on the "discontinuity" side of the controversy in the economics of growth between the theorists who view change as essentially a smooth process of accumulation and those who view changes in terms of discontinuous bursts or phases. The inputs generated by the sequence in the structural differentiation model are clearly discontinuous. Organizational innovation, for example, occurs in special temporal sequence relative to certain other inputs; furthermore, once a burst of innovation (i.e., structural differentiation) has been incorporated into the economy there is relative quiescence in the input of organization or entrepreneurial services until the necessary prior conditions for another wave have been established again at the *G*- and *A*-boundaries of the economy. Such considerations lead us into many problems, such as the role of such discontinuous inputs in the genesis and development of economic fluctuations; without pursuing such problems in detail here, we will merely point out that on general sociological grounds our model establishes a presumption in favour of the discontinuity school of economic development, in areas where institutional factors are involved.

By way of summary, let us merely indicate a few examples of attempts to deal with the indeterminacy (from the economist's point of view) of the non-economic factors impinging on long-term dynamic problems.

(1) The Domar model illustrates the common tendency to consider the relevant non-economic coefficients simply as "given data" for analytical purposes. The values of these coefficients may be varied arithmetically for purposes of tracing economic consequences, and may be filled in empirically for purposes of application. Such reasoning involves the theoretical dilemma we have outlined several times. To be sure, it is not only permissible but often necessary to hold constant certain conditions known to vary empirically in the interests of clarity of conceptualization and economy of variables. But the acceptance of such constants, without further theoretical analysis leaves no basis for assessing their precise ranges or patterns of variability, except to determine it empirically from case to case.

(2) Growth processes are sometimes treated as dependent

upon a series of long-term "propensities." Rostow's theory incorporates this methodological tool most completely.[1] In this theory the rate of output is a function of the size and productivity of the working force and of the level of stock of capital; the rate of growth in turn is a function of the rate of change in these stocks; these rates result from the interplay of certain yields and effective strengths of long-term propensities; and finally, the effective strengths of the propensities are a function of the prior operation of social, economic and political forces. Examples of the long-term dispositions are the propensity to seek material advance, the propensity to bear children, the propensity to apply resources to pure science, etc.

Rostow is careful to note the dependence of the propensities on the independent operation of non-economic forces. Primarily they are a function of the value system or value systems of the society in question. In this respect the formulation of the "propensities" argument takes account of the problematical nature of the boundaries between the economy and the other differentiated sub-systems. But, as we have pointed out repeatedly, characterizing the non-economic world in terms of "propensities" often leads directly to the assignment of linearity to these coefficients, and implicitly to the assumption of their determination by some simple law.[2] We consider the view of society as a plurality of cognate differentiated sub-systems, of which the economy is only one, less vulnerable to this methodological danger.

(3) Certain economic historians have considered change to be a problem of describing and analysing a qualitatively discreet historical process in terms of specific empirical sequences, but never in terms of an abstract analytic scheme either on the economic or the non-economic side.[3] This position is furthest from ours, since we consider its implication to be that

[1] Rostow, W. W., *The Process of Economic Growth*, 1952.

[2] Cf. Chap. IV, pp. 228–29.

[3] This view is closely associated with the name of J. H. Clapham. For a methodological statement of this position in the area of costs and returns, cf. "On Empty Economic Boxes," involving a controversy among Clapham, A. C. Pigou, and D. H. Robertson; reprinted in *Readings in Price Theory*, American Economic Association, 1952. For an application of this approach to a concrete historical process, cf. Clapham, J. H., *Economic History of Modern Britain*, 1926–51.

no positive abstract analytic statements can be made *at all* about the non-economic factors. The propensity logic is a step in the right direction, but we feel that a fuller use of the general theory of social systems can advance the theory of economic growth substantially.

Our limited programme in this chapter has been to formulate a model of one process of change in the institutional structure of an economy, namely, a step in structural differentiation, and to illustrate—and thus to test in a very limited way—this model by reference to the separation of ownership and managerial control in the American economy during the past half-century.

This model applies, we feel, very widely; above all it is not a specifically economic model designed to account for processes of change in our own or other economies. Its genesis lies, in the first instance, in the analysis of the decision-making process in small groups; it has been applied, furthermore, to processes of change in the family-personality field as well. Since its theoretical formulation and its application in the field of economics are new and tentative, much further analytical work and empirical testing are necessary before we can have confidence of the model's generalizability to other cases of interest to the theorist of economic growth and to the economic historian.

For these reasons and for reasons of space and our own immediate research capacities, we have limited the empirical discussion of the model to one historical case in the American economy. To what other ranges of empirical problems might such a model be fruitfully applied?

First, the separation of ownership and control is by no means the only structural change which has occurred in the American economy within the recent past. This illustrative case deals with those aspects of the structure of the economy most closely related to the input of capital goods and the control of productivity. An analogous set of changes seems to have been developing at the boundary dealing with labour input and the consumers' market. One aspect of this change is the acceptance throughout much of the business world that the policy of high wages is "good for business" rather than a necessary evil. Another is the extensions and consolidation of the labour union and a final aspect is the spread of the "human relations" idea with respect to the internal relations of the firm. These and other related phenomena seem to constitute a process of structural change parallel in many ways to the separation of ownership and control. Perhaps the most essential problem in analysing this process, and relating it to concurrent changes, is to define the appropriate systems and sub-systems clearly and consistently as points of reference.

Further, structural changes centring in the economy have been associated with similar changes focusing on the boundaries of the economy or in the non-economic sectors of the society. In the past fifty years, for instance, the level of urbanization developed to a unique historical point; only a little more than 10 per cent of the labour force in agricultural production produces almost unmanageable agricultural surpluses. Though this shift in urban-rural balance constitutes an economic change, it also involves a fundamental change in the structure of the local communities in the society, involving households, education, local government, churches and other institutions and collectivities. Related to these changes, but with even wider repercussions, is the process by which the American family has become a more specialized part of the social structure. Of course, this has been influenced by economic changes; but the family is neither primarily a part of the economy nor a simple "dependent variable." As we have pointed out, furthermore, the separation of ownership and control has been associated with changes in the American system of social stratification. The tendency for the emergence of a dominant class of owner-manager industrial and banking magnates and their families (a kind of *Patriziat* in the Hanseatic sense) has been checked; the American *élite* is less firmly structured, and several different elements compete for top positions. Finally, "big government" has emerged in the same period. This change is associated with the wars and political disturbances of the first half of the century and the emergence of the United States into a position of hitherto unknown power and responsibility in the international community, and with many internal problems, particularly the control of the consequences of an industrialized economy.

Hence a society, made up of many interrelated sub-systems, undergoes processes of change in each of these sub-systems similar to the structural change we have outlined for one part of the economy. These various processes are related in terms of timing, interdependence of inputs and outputs, etc.; they are all, furthermore, sub-phases of broad structural changes in the society as a whole. We can only indicate an awareness of the existence of these complex interrelations here. But, if our model of change is correct, it can prove very strategic in approaching such a complex of problems. Alone, however, it cannot solve such problems; an immense mobilization of empirical material and an immense amount of theoretical development of relations between systems and sub-systems are required before extensive empirical results can be obtained.

In the comparative context, the model we have presented is, we feel, applicable to social and economic structures other than those of the modern Western world. But, as we have pointed out, such applications require the introduction of certain parametric differences into the data of systems in question and the ways in which their sub-systems are interrelated. In particular, the level of differentiation of the social structure and the place of the economy in it are important considerations. In the "simplest" societies, for instance, there are seldom *any* collectivities or even processes of exchange which even approach economic primacy. Production is likely to be carried out mainly in household units or in more extended kinship groups. In such cases labour is not "employed" in the usual sense but ascribed in terms of kinship status. Access to land and capital is similarly based. Finally, there is no marketing problem since most goods and services are produced for immediate consumption by the producing groups or those bound to them by kinship or other non-economic ties.

In such cases the economy is "fused," especially with pattern-maintenance functions but also others, in a single multi-functional structural matrix. One of the major problems of economic development concerns the ways in which structures and processes with clear economic primacy become differentiated from this matrix. A first step is often the introduction of a market and with it the monetary mechanisms of exchange. While internal structural changes from this starting-point are different from those in an advanced industrial economy, the analysis in terms of our model seems feasible. The sequence beginning with an embryonic market structure would involve the differentiation of enterprises of production separate from consumption units, problems of labour input, etc. Once this market structure is apparent, then it is possible to follow the sequence of steps we have outlined in the appropriate empirical context.

What we have presented, therefore, is *not at all* a general "theory of institutional change of economies," but a first tentative attempt to formulate and illustrate a theoretical model. We have not been able, however, to extend its application over a wide range of empirical cases. Our main intention has been to attempt to clarify the nature of the *theoretical* problems involved in the analysis of the process of institutional change in economies. In particular our interest has been in the contributions and limitations of technical economic theory relative to other parts of the general theory of social systems.

SOME HISTORICAL AND THEORETICAL PERSPECTIVES

To conclude our substantive discussion of economy and society we will present a very tentative sketch of a few highlights of the development of modern Western society with special reference to the place of the economy in it. This sketch is not meant as a technical application of our theoretical model of institutional change but is on a much more diffuse and "intuitive" level. Toward the end of the chapter we will discuss, equally tentatively, certain theoretical problems of the direction and processes of social change.

Economic and ideological discussions of the nature of the modern Western economy on the whole revolve primarily about the antithesis between "capitalism" and "socialism," with emphasis on the problem of the locus of control of productive processes. The alternatives tend to be the role of the state (or its sub-divisions) *vs.* "private enterprise."

The point of reference for these alternatives is the consideration that private enterprise has usually meant control by *property* interests, i.e., by owners of capital resources. It is widely appreciated, of course, that the structure of ownership institutions and their relations to the control of enterprise in the United States, for instance, have changed greatly;

particularly since Berle and Means' publication, the empirical literature has contained an immense amount of information and a certain amount of interpretation on these points.[1] Nevertheless it seems to us that the opinion of most economists remains within the framework of the capitalism-socialism alternative, even though the relative stability of a "mixed system" is now fairly widely conceded.

Perhaps the most penetrating statement of the alternatives in recent literature, one which has scarcely been attacked on grounds of principle from this point of view, is that of Schumpeter,[2] who despaired of the future of free enterprise or capitalism, and posited the inevitability of socialism. To support this position he advanced the interesting sociological argument that the maintenance of capitalism depends on successful entrepreneurial foundation of a "family dynasty" which, through ownership and thus control of important productive enterprise, could establish and maintain an *élite* status in the society. In nineteenth-century Europe (including England), which was the classical locus of this pattern, the process worked out largely through an amalgamation between the rising bourgeois elements and the older aristocratic classes. Thus aristocratic or at least socially *élite* status for the *kinship unit* capable of being perpetuated from generation to generation (not the individual) was the ultimate reward of business success.

Schumpeter felt that in the United States the status of the corresponding business groups had always been precarious and had recently deteriorated, and in Europe the old aristocracies were rapidly being destroyed by socialization, progressive taxation and other measures. Schumpeter thus felt that socialism was the only remaining possibility for the fundamental organization of the economy.

We suggest that Schumpeter failed to appreciate the importance of a third possibility. Contrary to much previous opinion, we feel that "classical capitalism," characterized by the dominance of the role of ownership in the productive process, is not a case of full "emancipation" of the economy from "political" control, but rather a particular mode of such

1 Cf. T.N.E.C. report, National Resources Report, 20th Century Reports.

2 *Capitalism, Socialism and Democracy*, 1947.

control. This follows from our view that ownership is anchored essentially in the polity. Let us develop this by sketching a few highlights of institutional development in the Western world.

In certain "primitive" societies the primary locus of political function lies in a certain type of kinship units, technically called "lineages."[1] We suggest that European feudalism was a special fusion (involving a lineage organization) of political and kinship functions. Only in early modern times did parts of the polity and the kinship aspects of the pattern-maintenance system become differentiated. Indeed, where lineages by hereditary ascription enjoy political prerogatives and power, this differentiation is not yet complete.

In feudal conditions, not only was the political function, in the aspect most directly involved in the state, fused with kinship structure, but this was also true of the primary control of property through land ownership. Gradually, however, ownership of land in the property sense came to be differentiated from territorial jurisdiction in the more narrowly political sense. This complex of organization in which relatively large property holdings were fused with kinship units formed, in its relation to economic production, the matrix out of which modern "private enterprise," which became the structural focus of "capitalism," developed. In a strictly structural sense, however, this did *not* establish the primacy of economic goals and functions in the resulting type of firm, as this has occurred more recently. Early private enterprise developed by a differentiation between two complexes, both of which continued to be characterized by a combination of political and pattern-maintenance structures in terms of their primary goal and value patterns. These two complexes were (1) the state fused with politically privileged aristocratic lineages (including royal lines), and (2) lineages whose high position rested on land ownership, and later on capital and enterprise ownership. The latter positions were filled by lineages which had risen from below, probably more than the former, though mobility through political channels was by no means negligible.

In a structural sense, therefore, the capitalistic complex is a derivative by differentiation from the "feudal" structure

[1] Cf. Fortes, M., and Evans-Pritchard, E. E., eds., *African Political Systems*, 1950.

which still combined lineage and political (including property) elements. Traditionally, the division between the two derivatives has been characterized as "political" and "economic." Though correct as compared with the feudal background, we question this characterization, *if* the term "economic" is to be understood as meaning anchored primarily in the *economy* as a social sub-system.

In a later period a *further* process of differentiation has occurred in *both* complexes. On the one side the structure of the state has separated from the lineage structure of the upper class. The modern state, since the French Revolution particularly, has tended, on the one hand, to be progressively bureaucratized; on the other hand to be democratized. Political function has tended to be performed either in occupational roles by civil and military "servants" (bureaucratization), or in the role of associational leader and/or representative (democratization).

For reasons we cannot go into here, this process of differentiation between kinship and polity has tended on the whole to precede the corresponding process in the lineage-property complex; indeed, in a sense "capitalism" became the refuge of kinship-prerogative after its direct control of the state had weakened.[1] With increase of scale and other processes, however, economic organization also has been extensively bureaucratized and "rationalized" with respect to the market situation. Such developments have tended to loosen and even break the fusion between business enterprise and the older patterns of ownership.

Of course the primary *economic functions* of the society were performed for a long time in the context of capitalistic enterprise in the strict sense; in this respect such enterprise is "primarily economic." The organization of its control, however, was *not* on that basis in a technical sense, primarily economic. A primarily economic type of control has evolved, more conspicuously in the United States than anywhere else, only since the turn of the present century. It is the first case in economic history in which economic goals and values in a strict analytical sense have had clear primacy over a great range of the concrete social organization of economic processes;

[1] This much we will concede to the Marxist.

in this respect it is the highest level of functional differentiation yet reached in the course of social evolution. Clearly this is neither capitalism in the classical (and, we think, Marxist) sense nor socialism, in the sense that the state takes over economic functions.

Economic writings vacillate enormously over the problem of the role of government in an economically developed society. We have noted the tendency to hold that capitalistic free enterprise and socialism always add up to a given total—the more of the one that exists, the less of the other (and no third possibility exists). A related tendency is to think that as government develops, differentiated organization in the economy cannot, and vice versa. Indeed, there has been a disposition, seldom made perfectly clear, to think that as government grows "big" private enterprise must be proportionately restricted; this belief rests, we feel, on a misconception of the nature of social development.

The modern type of economy, developed by successive steps of *differentiation* from a less differentiated social structure. Feudalism involved all in one structural type: (1) a pattern-maintenance system, at least in its kinship aspect, (2) a polity including both governmental and property-holding aspects, and (3) an economy. These various functional aspects have differentiated progressively from each other. The modern state is *one* of these differentiated structures, and the modern economy (as business system) another; though they interpenetrate in complex ways they are, nevertheless, structurally distinct.

In a process which includes both large-scale quantitative growth and structural differentiation, it is to be expected that any two differentiated substructures which are organized about different functional areas of the total society should *both* undergo continuing growth; this is not incompatible with continuing, even increasing, differentiation from each other. The development of "big government," such a conspicuous phenomenon of modern society, is, therefore, by no means incompatible in principle with the continuing growth of a non-socialistic economy.[1]

[1] Contrary to much of the "economically" tinged thought of his time, Durkheim clearly understood this relationship. Cf. *The Division of Labour in Society*, *op. cit.*

The fact that the modern economy fits into a pattern of increasing differentiation of social structure *throughout* the society helps to explain why the fusion between the ownership-managership complex and *élite* kinship status has failed to survive from classical capitalism, particularly under American conditions.[1] The traditional European aristocracy is, from a sociological point of view, the prototype of a functionally *undifferentiated* structure in the higher reaches of the social scale. The essence of aristocratic status is its diffuse and *generalized* superiority. Membership in an aristocratic lineage cannot be treated only as a reward for specific, functionally differentiated types of achievement, mainly since this would undermine the basis of the generality of its superiority. In one aspect, the continuing insistence on the ascriptive basis of this superiority through lineage heredity rests on this lack of differentiation. It is not the individual who is superior by virtue of his specific, differentiated types of achievement; his superiority derives from his membership in the lineage. This basis of stratification *cuts directly across* that involved in a functionally differentiated social structure where performance is organized primarily about occupational roles.

We suggest, therefore, that the kinship-property combination typical of classical capitalism was, in the nature of the case, a temporary and unstable one. Both economic and political differentiation were destined, unless social development stopped altogether, to proceed toward "bureaucratization," toward differentiation between economy and polity and between ownership and control, finally toward further differentiation of kinship as part of the pattern maintenance system, i.e., no longer as a functionally undifferentiated status group.[2] When

[1] It has survived more widely in Europe, particularly, perhaps, in France (cf. Landes, in Earle, ed., *Modern France, op. cit.*). We are also indebted to Mr. J. R. Pitts for much information about and insight into the economic structure of France. It is possible that the difficulty of maintaining this structure under the pressures of modern scale, technological development, etc., is one of the primary sources of "unrest" in modern Europe and that structural change is already under way. That the change came early in the United States is probably in considerable measure due to the absence of an entrenched aristocracy with its traditional roots in feudal society here.

[2] For the case that the American family has in fact been becoming a more differentiated unit of the social structure, see *Family, Socialization and Interaction Process*, Chap. I.

this process goes far enough, it becomes untenable for the older type of aristocratic lineage to maintain the pretension of generalized lineage superiority independent of its members' current functional performance achievements.

Over the last century a grand-scale process of social change has undermined the position of this ancient bulwark of Western social structure. Economic development, through classical capitalism, but also going beyond it, has constituted one of the principal threads of the process by which this has come about. Ours is not an unstratified society, and shows no signs of becoming one; but it is definitely *not* aristocratic society in the traditional European sense. For a brief historical moment American capitalism appeared to be creating a new Schumpeterian "ruling class" of family dynasties founded by the "captains of industry." But this moment passed early in the present century, and the trend since then is clear—the *occupational* manager, not the lineage-based owner, is the key figure in the American economic structure.[1]

This kind of revision of commonly held historical views rests, of course, on our particular views about the sociological environment of the economy and its exigencies, as well as views of the "autonomous" trends of growth and development of the economy itself. We have argued that larger empirical generalizations must incorporate propositions and assumptions on both these levels. Does sociological theory provide any more generalized theoretical basis from which we may contribute to these larger problems of social change?

We would like to attempt merely to open up this question by developing two important conceptions originally put forward by Durkheim and Weber, respectively. Durkheim, in the *Division of Labour* and in *Suicide* held that "happiness" could not increase cumulatively in the long run, and that the desire for happiness could not be the primary dynamic factor in social change. His statements were couched in the utilitarian terminology of the 1890's. But in our terms he may be interpreted to have stated a denial that a "propensity" to increase the

[1] For a general sketch of the current American class structure, including this phase, cf. Parsons, "A Revised Analytical Approach to the Theory of Social Stratification," *Essays in Sociological Theory, op. cit.* See also F. L. Allen, *op. cit.*

standard of living can serve as the main dynamic force in economic development. As Durkheim clearly stated in his later work, this is because the primary wants of individuals are not independently *given* outside social interaction processes (including the economic), but are a *product* of that process. To argue that the pressure to better satisfy wants is the prime mover of economic development is to argue in a circle, since wants themselves are a part of the changing entity in question.[1]

Modern sociological and anthropological analysis of comparative consumption patterns and of comparative socialization processes confirms this proposition and provides a better empirical and theoretical base for it than Durkheim commanded. Its implications for economic theory are far-reaching. There has been a strong tendency in the study of economic change to incorporate the assumption of a continuing pressure of increasing wants as the dynamic factor in an indefinite process of economic growth. We wish radically to question the legitimacy of such an assumption; situations in which such pressures exist must be accounted for in terms of the specific sociological and psychological conditions of the particular case. It cannot be assumed as the result of the operation of any generalized propensity of human nature.

Negative as this conclusion is, we consider it a corner-stone of the theory of economic development. In our paradigm we assumed the opposite, that there often is a tendency to curtail otherwise feasible consumption wants in favour of saving and investment. While we do not wish to generalize such a tendency, we deny that it is "contrary to human nature" and traceable only to exceptional "repressive" circumstances.[2]

Weber's proposition is more positive. Very generally, Weber held that all social systems tend toward progressive rationalization relative to a given set of values; this has been called the "process of rationalization." This is not a "linear" theory of

[1] Both Weber and Marshall had insight into this problem. For Weber, "traditionalism" was the "normal" state of economic demand; only a value change could create a new level of wants, once physical subsistence is taken care of. Similarly, Marshall felt that only "activities" could create the new wants necessary for a higher "standard of life."

[2] The bearing of this problem of the increase of "happiness," as this problem has been treated in welfare economics, is clear.

social development because Weber recognized the development of a plurality of possible value systems under conditions at least partially independent of the process of rationalization.[1]

We would like to reformulate the process of rationalization as the tendency of social systems to develop progressively higher levels of structural differentiation under the pressure of adaptive exigencies. Adaptive exigencies are not, it will be remembered, given only in the external situation, but involve the *relation* between the system and the situation. One aspect of this adaptive relation in every social system is a certain pressure to actualize the value system which is institutionalized in the system.

Given tension between system and situation, however, economic production itself is a mechanism which helps to meet the adaptive exigencies of the system. This is the basis on which we have treated the economy as differentiated relative to the society's adaptive function.

Mobilization of societal resources for adaptive functions, however, occurs on more than one level, of which the process of economic production is the first. But at any level, adaptive mobilization takes place *within* the institutional framework of the society. Economic growth within such a framework can proceed only up to a point without having repercussions on the other elements of society, in particular its institutional structure. As this point is approached, tendencies focusing on processes of institutional change arise to adjust and change this structure. In this process the economy itself alters in both its internal structure and its structural relations to other societal sub-systems.

Economic growth in the quantitative sense constitutes *one* aspect of the rationalization process. Over the longer run, however, economic growth merges with change in institutional structure which can be neither purely economic nor purely quantitative change. We have discussed again and again why institutional change cannot be purely economic. It cannot be purely quantitative because differentiation must be balanced

[1] On the process of rationalization, cf. Weber, *Protestant Ethic*, Author's Introduction. Also cf. Parsons, *Structure of Social Action*, Chap. XVII, and *Social System*, Chap. XI, and Weber, *Theory of Social and Economic Organization*, pp. 363 ff.

by new processes of integration unless it is to disrupt the system. There must be specific non-economic processes of institutionalization of the new level of organization within the economy, in the other sub-systems of the society, and in the boundary relations between them.

Weber's concept of rationalization thus formulates one aspect of the generalized process of social change which is closely related to economic growth processes. But it extends beyond what economists usually mean by economic growth to include the process of institutional change.[1] We have tried to carry the analysis of institutional change a little farther than Weber did, particularly with respect to its direct articulation with economic theory.

In this exploratory chapter, we have presented a model of the process of institutional change in a modern economy which, we feel, fits the broad facts of an important empirical case and accords with the local exigencies of both economic theory and the general theory of action. Moreover, we think it promises to improve the level of determinacy relative to some of the variables used in current economic models of growth.

The main logical pattern of this mode originated, however, as we have noted in inquiries extremely remote from the facts of economic history. Of course, the fundamental origin lies in the logical and empirical structure of the general theory of action. More immediately, it lies in the concern with differentiation over time in the structural characteristics of systems of actions, especially the phase movements formulated (1) by Bales and his associates for task-adaptive processes in small laboratory groups, and (2) by Parsons and others for the process of psychotherapy, generalized to other processes of social control.[2]

[1] The other principal factor in social change according to Weber was that of "charismatic revolution" (not necessarily political) by which value systems are changed directly. Discussion of this would carry us too far afield for present purposes. Cf. Weber, *Theory of Social and Economic Organization*, translated by A. M. Henderson and Talcott Parsons, 1947, Chap. III.

[2] Cf. R. F. Bales, *Interaction Process Analysis*, Chap. V; Parsons, *The Social System*, Chap. VII. The two perspectives were first brought together in *Working Papers*, esp. Chap. V. For application of the phase-movement logic to the problem of time-lags, cf. Chap. IV, pp. 241 ff.

Bales refined and generalized his paradigm for small group task performance into a series of seven time-ordered steps.[1] This model possessed, with certain paradigmatic differences, a *logical* structure identical to that developed by Parsons and Olds for the changes of personality structure involved in a major phase of the child's socialization process.[2] These two models were systematically compared by Parsons and Bales.[3] It seemed to us that this model of change in a system of action, if it applied to two such different cases, might be applicable to the analysis of institutional change in social systems, in particular the economy.

As we have noted, the ultimate validation of this model as set forth in this chapter rests on the facts of economic dynamics and no other data. But if it survives this test, it will represent a significant case of the interplay of knowledge in fields usually considered so "disparate" that scholars in each usually see no direct reason to inquire into those outside their own.

We are deeply convinced, however, that the kind of theoretical analysis we have presented, in this chapter and in the entire volume, is one example of the possibilities of theoretical synthesis not only in economics and sociology, but over much wider ranges of theory in all the behavioural sciences. We feel and hope that the little case history of the antecedents of our model of economic change may repeat itself many times in the development of theory in the future.

[1] Cf. R. F. Bales, "How People Interact in Conferences," *Scientific American*, March, 1955.

[2] Cf. Parsons and Olds, "The Mechanisms of Personality Functioning with Special Reference to Socialization," Chap. IV, of *Family, Socialization and Interaction Process*, *op. cit.*

[3] *Ibid.*, Chap. VII.

CHAPTER VI

CONCLUSION: ECONOMIC THEORY AND THE GENERAL THEORY OF SOCIAL SYSTEMS

The purpose of this brief concluding chapter is to summarize our analysis by stages and to point up some implications for economic and sociological theory, respectively, and for the relations between them.

A SUMMARY OF THE ANALYSIS

Our central proposition is that economic theory is a special case of the general theory of social systems, which is in turn one of the main branches of the developing general theory of action. We have applied this proposition to the following fields of economic inquiry: the general frame of reference of economic theory; the conception of the economy as a special type of social system differentiated from other societal sub-systems; the place of the economic sub-system in the society and its relations to cognate sub-systems; the institutional structure of the economy; processes within the economy and across its external boundaries, and the problem of growth and institutional change in the economy.

By way of preliminary analysis, we tried to show that economic theory conceives economic processes as processes of *action* (in our technical sense) oriented to a goal of production as available means. In so far as this involves interaction, the supply-demand schema is a special case of the more general performance-sanction schema which underlies all social interaction. Furthermore, the classification of commodities as goods and services corresponds to the general distinction between physical and social objects on the one hand and between qualities and performances on the other.

Beyond these simple congruences of categories, we demonstrated certain congruences between economic theory and the general theory of action as theoretical systems. Any social system, it will be remembered, can be analysed in terms of four functional problems or exigencies—goal attainment, adaptation, integration and pattern maintenance—which are the foci of differentiation of types of action, of roles and of the preponderance of particular types of action at different points in time. They are thus the foci of the differentiation of types of input and output processes over the boundaries of the system. If an economy is treated as a social system, the four factors of production (land, labour, capital, and organization) and the four corresponding shares of income (rent, wages, interest, and profits) correspond exactly to the categories of input and output, respectively, of any social system. Furthermore, the concept of real cost relates to the society as a system reference in so far as it refers to the input of factors of production in terms of the "sacrifice" made by non-economic sub-systems. Money cost, on the other hand, is cost to the economy as a system, for it concerns cost in terms of shares of income to be distributed to controllers of the factors.

These points, as developed in the first chapter, established a presumption in favour of our thesis that economic theory is a special case of the general theory of social systems. This presumption rested on two grounds: (1) the point-for-point correspondence of the logical structures of the two conceptual schemes, and (2) the fact that the goal of the economy is *less general* than societal goals. Production makes sense *only* as a contribution to the functioning of some larger system. Economic theory cannot be the theory of processes in a total society, but only those of a differentiated sub-system of a society.

In connection with the latter point, we found ourselves in direct opposition to the widely-held view in economics that utility and welfare are to be defined in the first instance in terms of individual preference lists or, in terms of the interpersonal comparison of these lists, i.e., in terms of the satisfaction of the wants of individuals, independent of their social relationships. Since, according to our scheme, the categories of wealth, utility, income and welfare are states or properties of social systems and their units, they apply to the individual personality only through the social system. Hence the theoretical basis for taking individual wants as given and independent does not exist. We defined these concepts in terms of their significance as facilities for the adaptive problems of social systems.

We found it possible to test our major thesis beyond this purely logical congruence. To do this we applied the paradigm of the economy as a social system to external interchanges between the economy and its cognate systems, largely because of the evident impact of non-economic factors on these interchanges. If, as we maintained, the economy is the primary *adaptive* sub-system of the society, it should interchange with three other cognate sub-systems—a "polity," an integrative system, and a pattern-maintenance and tension-management system—each differentiated according to the appropriate system exigency. Such a classification is not identical with the concrete structure of roles and collectivities in the society, but is a classification of modes of relationship and bases of decision.

We then asked how, specifically, the boundaries of these four major societal sub-systems match in their interchanges. We argued that each of the four has one boundary which interchanges primarily with *one* of the other three cognate sub-systems. This yields a total of six boundaries among the primary sub-systems. In addition, each sub-system possesses a fourth, extraordinary boundary concerned with the value system of the society as a whole and the primary societal sub-systems.

Because of the special character of the land category in economic theory, the input of land factors and the corresponding output of rents is the relevant interchange at the exceptional boundary of the economy. This means that certain factors of production—physical facilities, cultural factors and certain elements of human motivation—are committed to economic production relatively independently of short-term economic sanctions. Such commitment is controlled through the institutionalization of values.

Reference to the concrete social structures in which economic processes take place is of course essential for the solution for a wide range of short-term empirical problems, for an exhaustive comparative economics and for an adequate theory of economic development; we barely touched upon these matters, however, and limited the greatest part of our analysis to the relationships among the analytical sub-systems of society.

The first "open" boundary of the economy we considered in terms of the interplay of performance and sanction is between the goal-attainment sub-system of the economy and household as units primarily of the pattern-maintenance sub-system of the society; the relevant inputs and outputs are labour services and consumers' goods, respectively. Consumers' goods are purchased and contingent labour services are provided by family members in representative roles on behalf of the household. Secondly, control of the creation of liquid funds through credit is the primary adaptive output from units of the polity; control of productivity is the primary output of the economy at this boundary. Finally, the third open boundary is the source of input of organization from the integrative sub-system of the society and the source of output of new combinations of the factors of production.

In a highly differentiated economy the exchange of primary inputs and outputs is largely, but not exclusively, mediated by intermediary mechanisms. In the case of the household, labour is balanced by payments of wages, which are in turn the source of consumers' purchases (though not usually to the same firms which supply wages to the particular household). At the adaptive boundary, the control of the creation of credit is balanced by certain "rights to intervene" in the supply and use of the resulting funds, and the control of productivity is balanced by certain "encouragements of enterprise." The common element of these two intermediate interchanges is a sort of political endorsement of the credit standing of the relevant economic unit in question. Credit standing is a form of political power (i.e., the power to command facilities); hence the interchanges at this boundary between the economy and the polity are not "markets" in the usual sense of the term. Thirdly, at the integrative boundary, the input of entrepreneurial services is balanced by profits and the output of new product combinations is balanced by a kind of demand for innovation.

Besides this systematic linking between the economy and

the other societal sub-systems, we barely indicated that the other three cognate systems undergo an equally systematic interchange among themselves. All four related sub-systems constitute a coherent system.

As a still further demonstration of our "special case" proposition, we submitted several well-known economic theories to an analysis in terms of the general theory paradigm. Schumpeter's "circular flow," for instance, can be interpreted as dealing with only one problematical "open" boundary, the *G*-boundary of the economy *vis-à-vis* the household. The economy—the structure of which is provided by the commitment of land factors—adjusts to essentially random fluctuations at this boundary.

The classical theories leave all three of the boundaries open, but assume definite and symmetrical supply and demand functions for all of them. The general assumption is of continuity of slope of schedule, so that there is always a price which will clear the market of inputs or outputs of the economy. Such an assumption is approximately the same as the assumption that all decisions on the non-economic sides of the respective markets are made primarily on economic grounds.

Keynes' modifications of classical theory focused at the *G*- and *A*-boundaries of the economy. At the former, he introduced two empirical modifications of the perfectly smooth classical functions. For the labour market his assumption is that labourers will withdraw employment completely at a certain low level of wage offerings; for the consumption functions Keynes posited the peculiar shape of the consumption-savings function by virtue of which the proportion saved rises as income rises, but not so rapidly. These two functions are the focus of mass unemployment of labour. Such imbalances at the *G*-boundary, operating in conjunction with monetary and capitalization mechanisms at the *A*-boundary—which has imbalances of its own through the operation of "attitudes to liquidity" and its relation to expectation of yield, confidence, etc.[1]—can combine into a vicious circle of depression. Such a vicious circle is not possible under the strict classical assumptions.

Schumpeter dealt primarily with the processes involved in

[1] Certain aspects of Keynes' treatment of the investment process are internal to the economy and hence were discussed in Chap. IV.

the input of organization and the entrepreneurial function. Indeed, he treated the *A*-boundary primarily as dependent on processes at the *I*-boundary. In a general way Schumpeter's analysis fitted our treatment of organization and its relation to the economy's integration. In sum, the *differences* between the classical, Keynesian, and Schumpeterian analyses are attributable primarily to differences at the external boundaries which each considered relevant and the assumptions each made about the non-economic sides of these boundaries.

The next stage of analysis dealt with the capacity of sociological theory to handle problems on the non-economic side of these boundary relations. As a starting-point we developed an extended analysis of the institutional structure of the economy and of its primary external boundaries. We began this analysis with the conception of the division of labour and its necessary concomitant, exchange. The latter is the primary process by means of which economic adjustments are carried out. The framework within which exchange processes are regulated and stabilized is the institution of contract. Hence the structure of the economy as a social system is a network of institutionalized patterns regulating contractual relationships.

Each contracting party in any relationship acts on behalf of a collectivity (e.g., the firm or the household), membership in which is of primary importance for the contractual relationship in question; by interacting, the relationship between the contracting parties or an indefinite plurality of such parties (a market) constitutes a social system. Hence the same four fundamental problems apply to the contractual relationship as to any social system. Any given contracting party, therefore, is concerned with (*g*) the specific goal object of the exchange transaction, i.e., to establish a relation between a "quid" (e.g., quantity) and a "quo" (e.g., price); (*a*) the organizational environment in which the settlement of terms takes place, especially power and facilities implications of the structure of the collectivities which both contracting parties represent; (*i*) the diffuse symbolic meaning of the terms of exchange as related to the welfare of the collectivity, its standing in the market, etc., and (*l*) the patterns of value by means of which a stable orientation for both parties is established. In general, *g* and *a* form the focus of the elements of "interest" in a contractual relationship *i* and *l*—Durkheim's "non-contractual element of contract"—the focus of social integration.

We then applied this paradigm (which is relevant to any exchange relationship) to the input of labour through the contract of employment and the input of capital through the contract of investment. These two contractual forms are the centres of the nexus which constitute the institutions of occupation and property, respectively. In the first placc, the *g*-component of these (and other) exchanges depends on the level of generality of the factor of production in question. For both labour and capital as factors we discriminated among a series of levels extending from the genesis of the factor in the processes of social interaction to its final utilization in the performance of productive tasks. The series involves seven steps for each factor. The first three are primarily extra-economic and determine the primary constraints on purely economic manipulation of the resources. The middle stage involves the "factor" itself in a fluid state; at this stage the "labour force" and "generalized purchasing power," respectively, constitute the direct factor inputs into the economy. The last three steps constitute successive stages of commitment within the economy (to a firm, a role, and a specific task, respectively) which are required actually to produce goods and services.

Given these *g*-considerations, contractual relations vary *also* as a function of the *a*, *i*, and *l* components. For instance, the role of the breadwinner in a household is different, in all these respects, from that of salesman for a firm. The *i* and *l* components are important in defining the responsibilities to the household in the contract of employment and the fiduciary "political responsibilities" in the contract of investment.

We next explored the relevance of these strictly sociological features of contract to the economic problem of the imperfection of market structure. Economic theory, while it provides an excellent analysis of certain consequences of imperfection, tends to treat the problem in terms of *degrees* of imperfection and underplays the qualitative variation of types. On the basis of our classification of contractual components, we isolated types of imperfection in the labour market, the market for consumers' goods, and the "market" for productivity, and the capital market. Thus the "one price" system in the consumers' market, collective bargaining in the labour market, and fiduciary organizations in the capital market are examples of institutional deviations from the ideal of a system of perfect markets, deviations based partly on factors *other* than size of firm, differentiation of product, or degree of concentration of power. Even further deviations are evident in the market for professional services, which is characterized by such economically irrational practices as the "sliding scale." In general, therefore, even an approximation to a perfect market is possible only in cases where both values and interests have clear economic primacy. The closest approximations are naturally in intra-economic markets. In boundary processes in which one of the contracting roles is anchored in another (non-economic) sub-system of the society, primary economic orientation is effectively impossible. The qualitative character of the non-economic anchorages and the specific contractual exigencies in each of the above categories are the tentative bases for a classification of sociological types of imperfection.

With this background we turned to the problem of economic motivation in general and the postulate of economic rationality and the doctrine of "self-interest" in particular. To assume any generalized propensity of human nature such as the "rational pursuit of self-interest" is precluded by our analysis; furthermore, such assumptions have not been borne out either by psychological or by sociological theory. Economic rationality we treated, not as a "psychological" generalization, but as a value system appropriate to the economy as a differentiated sub-system of the society; it is institutionalized in the economy and internalized in personalities in their roles as economic agents. Given the generalized commitment to such a value system, economic motivation is not different theoretically from that of any other behaviour in an institutionalized context. In order to analyse economic motivation, the relevant frame of reference is the generalized success goal as defined in the context of economic production. *Both* performance in the form of effort and achievement *and* direct monetary and other sanctions are components of the success goal. Further, money earnings are significant not only "in themselves," but as symbols (as formulated in the *i*-component of the contract of employment). Responsibility for the affairs of an organization is symbolically "recognized"; this recognition is a status symbol. Investment decisions were analysed on a similar basis.

In the fourth chapter we turned to some technical problems of economic dynamics, especially the operation of the multiplier and accelerator as mitigated by time lags. Since these processes involved both internal and external economic interchanges, we dissected the four primary sub-systems of the economy even further and examined the interchange among these sub-systems within the economy.

The major problem of dynamic economic analysis is the degree of determinacy of empirical solution of certain dynamic problems. We chose several models of the trade cycle—those of Samuelson, Kalecki, and Hicks—as illustrations to show that in economic theory as such there is no basis to choose among a range of different assumptions concerning the values of the multiplier and accelerator functions and the number and duration of time lags. At the same time, empirical results vary over an enormous range, depending upon the particular assumptions.

Economists most commonly handle such a difficulty by assuming "given" data for any particular empirical analysis. Such an operation is appropriate in so far as particular data are in fact decisive in the solution of any specific case. To limit the values of appropriate coefficients to one set of data, however, limits the empirical scope of the application of the model. The determinacy problem is, therefore, to arrive at a formulation of principles, on *other* than economic grounds, which govern the range of values of the functions relevant to the dynamic model in question.

Sometimes this formulation of principles takes the form of postulating "propensities" of behaviour; these may even be treated as general psychological laws as in Keynes' case. On empirical and theoretical grounds the generalizability of such propensities is questionable. The Keynesian consumption function, for instance, tends to limit the variability of the value of the consumption coefficient in an *ad hoc* and arbitrary way. In the first place, there is a strong temptation to postulate a linear function on the model of a supply or demand curve. Since there is no technical theoretical backing for such an assumption, it is easy to presume that this linear variation is a function of a simple law.

The "propensity" methodology ignores the possibility that there is theory available to deal with non-economic elements involved in consumption and other cognate problems. We attempted in a tentative way to analyse the household as a social system in its consumption aspect and hence derive a function which is, in our society at least, different from and more realistic than the Keynesian assumption. We feel that this sociologically derived function comes closer to maximizing both determinacy and generality than either the "givenness" or the "propensity" solution.

Similar reasoning applies to the capitalization processes in the economy. Investment itself is an intra-economic process, involving two main aspects: supplying capital funds to the producing firm (the $A_{A_a} - A_{G_a}$ boundary) and bringing land factors into active economic circulation ($A_{A_g} - A_{L_g}$). In the former process there is a high level of institutionalized uncertainty; many of the phenomena at this boundary are therefore best understood in terms of established sociological knowledge about the modes of adapting to situations of uncertainty. Keynes' empirical observations are pertinent in this respect. Little is gained, however, by assuming any "propensity to be confident" or a "propensity to follow the lead of insiders," for instance. This question of uncertainty and its control presents many difficult problems; nevertheless, we feel that the direct and careful articulation between economic theory and the relevant theories of other types of social systems is the most promising line of development.

Time lags present similar problems. Concrete processes of economic adjustment take time because of the exigencies facing each of the collectivities within which the processes occur. In particular, the time lag refers to what happens between the time of occurrence of an input and that of a relevant output. The number and duration of time lags is a function of specific exigencies of households, financial institutions, firms, etc. Analysis of these collectivities as systems is necessary to reduce the indeterminacy of economic generalizations about lags. As a starting-point we attempted to apply some sociological principles of phase movements to the case of a firm's response to an increased consumer demand.

Finally, we directed our attention to the problem of processes of change in the institutional structure itself. Subject to the above qualifications, processes *within* the economy and even over its boundaries may be primarily economic and hence subject to analysis in terms of economic theory within the appropriate parametric limitations. But institutional *change in* the economy, however—indeed in any social system—*cannot* be primarily an economic process, because institutional structure is a phenomenon of value patterns and social integration, not simply of the interplay of economic factors. Of course, pressure to adapt to changed conditions is one of the primary instigating sources of institutional change, but the change cannot be carried out primarily by adaptive mechanisms.

Our principal effort was to develop and illustrate a model for institutional change and to compare it with a typical economic model of continuous growth (that of Domar). To illustrate our model we chose the process by which the "separation of ownership and control" has appeared in the last fifty years in the American economy. The primary adaptive problem which set off this process rested on a deficit in labour input into the economy, a deficit motivated by valuation of productivity "for its own sake" (as described by Marshall and Weber). Combined with this was opportunity for capital expansion. Accompanying the process of change itself were a number of "irrational" symptoms of disturbance, e.g., utopianism with respect to the possibilities of technology and bitter hostility. Besides these, however, there had to be positive support for possible entrepreneurial activity and a response to this support by a new type of entrepreneur. The emerging type was the "professional" corporate manager, as opposed to the earlier "capitalist" captain of industry who was primarily an *owner*-manager. With one important modification, Schumpeter's account of the process of entrepreneurial innovation—including the special role of profits—fitted this case.

The formal development of the model of institutional change and its illustration are very sketchy; the model's empirical validity and generalizability must rest upon a great deal of further investigation though we believe it to be widely applicable. We presented it in order to demonstrate the *kind* of analysis which is most promising in the field of long-term change. Economic theory as such, it is safe to say, has been unable to cope with the problem of long-term institutional change. On the one hand, theory has been concentrated on rather *ad hoc* explanations of the sources of capital accumulation, which is one, but only one condition of institutional change or growth. Economic history, on the other hand, has tended toward theoretical nihilism in that it concentrates only on the study of particular empirical cases. This dilemma—between economic theory in the narrow technical sense and no theory at all—is a false dilemma in general, particularly in the area of institutional change. Despite its immaturity and other defects, sociological theory possesses resources from which points of departure for a more adequate theory of change can be derived.

CONCLUSIONS

To pull together some of the theoretical implications of our exposition for economic theory and its relation to the general theory of social systems, let us list a series of propositions which we feel have been demonstrated.

1. *Economic theory is a special case of the general theory of social systems and hence of the general theory of action.* On the most general level which defines economic theory, there are no specifically economic variables; the variables are those of the general theory of action. The economic element depends upon the parameters which define the particular class of system in question and its relation to its situation. These parameters, in combination with the values of the general variables, define "economic factors" which differ from various types of non-economic factors. (Developed in Chapter I and amplified throughout the book.)

2. *An economy, as the concept is usually formulated by economists, is a special type of social system.* It is a functional sub-system of the more inclusive society, differentiated from other sub-systems by specialization in the society's adaptive function. It is one of four sub-systems differentiated on a cognate basis and must be distinguished from each of the others. It must also

be distinguished from all concrete collectivities which, whatever their functional primacy, are *always* multifunctional. As a social system the economy has all the properties of such a system: a common value system; institutional structure; adaptive, goal-attainment, integrative and pattern-maintenance processes, etc. (Developed especially in Chapters I and II.)

3. *The economy, like any social system exchanges inputs and outputs over its boundaries with its situation.* The most important part of the situation for the economy consists of the other cognate functional sub-systems of the same society and the institutionalized value system of the society. The economy's relations to the non-social ("natural") environment and to motivation ("human nature") are mediated through this situation; they are not independent of it. (Developed in Chapters II and III.)

4. *Interchange between the economy and its situation is not randomly distributed, but particular input-output categories are concentrated* vis-à-vis *other specific cognate societal sub-systems.* At the "open" boundaries, the input of labour and the output of consumers' goods and services are concentrated at the boundary *vis-à-vis* the pattern-maintenance sub-system; the input of capital and the output of productivity *vis-à-vis* the polity; and the input of entrepreneurial service and the output of innovation *vis-à-vis* the integrative sub-system. The special "closed" boundary case of land factors derives from economic value commitments as limited and defined by their relations to the value systems of other sub-systems and of the society as a whole. The nature of the specific non-economic sub-system involved in each exchange imposes specific exigencies at each boundary. (Developed in Chapters II and III.)

5. *Concrete economic processes are always conditioned by non-economic factors which are most clearly apparent in the parametric characteristics of the non-economic sub-systems of the society.* This applies to processes at the boundaries *and* within the economy. At the very least, therefore, analysis of concrete economic processes always must rest on non-economic assumptions. In most cases, however, partially independent operation of non-economic processes is necessary. (Developed in Chapters II, III, and IV.)

6. *A theoretical scheme other than economic theory is the only possible way to analyse these non-economic factors in such a way as*

to articulate successfully with economic theory. If the factors involve other parts of human society or human personality or culture, at least initially such a scheme rests on one or more other branches of the theory of action; of course other factors are to be accounted for by other theories of modern science, e.g., mechanics or physiology. To treat these non-economic factors *merely* as given data is scientifically unsatisfactory. To treat them as resulting from "propensities" is, when empirically valid, a step in the right direction, but only one step; the tendency is for such explanations to degenerate into one-law explanations. (Developed in Chapters II, III, IV, and V.)

7. *The problem of institutional change in an economy is a particularly striking special case of Proposition* 6 *because the primary factors involved cannot be economic.* (Developed in Chapter V.)

8. *Economic theory need not remain an "island" of theoretical specificity totally alone in an uncharted "sea" of theoretical indeterminacy.* Economic theory must be regarded as an important member of a family of closely related theories. Even though the general theory of action which binds the branches together is unevenly developed, we have been able to place economic theory within the general theory of social systems with considerable accuracy.

We have approached economics not as professional economists, but as sociologists; for this reason, perhaps, we have stressed certain difficulties and unsolved problems, and the need for supplementation of economic theory. This does not imply that we believe that establishing closer connections between economics and its sister disciplines will benefit only the former. Economic theory is, in a technical theoretical sense, by far the most developed and sophisticated branch of the behavioural sciences; until recently it has been the only one working with a generalized theoretical scheme. We might mention two areas in particular in which economic theory should prove beneficial to the other social sciences: (1) If economic theory is a special case of a more general theoretical scheme and if other cognate special cases can be established, then neighbouring fields should be able to make use, with the appropriate modifications and adjustments, of many economic achievements. This is not to say that other social systems should be treated as if they were economies; they clearly are not. It is possible, however, to adapt the definitions of variables and the formulations of their logical relations to the special parametric givens of other types of social systems in order to establish formally cognate patterns of analysis. (2) Just as non-economic factors at the boundaries of the economy are relevant to the solution of empirical problems which have occupied economists, the economic factors at the same boundaries can illuminate difficult non-economic problems by establishing stable points of reference.

A mutually advantageous two-way flow of theory is endangered, however, by the powerful divisive factors which tend to isolate the sister disciplines from each other. Indeed, we feel—and deplore—that economics and sociology have, if anything, drifted farther apart since the turn of the century. From time to time, especially in the Preface, we have tried to point up features of recent intellectual history which have led to a bifurcation of interest—economic and sociological—in the work of great synthetic minds, like Marshall, Pareto, Weber, and Durkheim. Indeed, in wide circles on both sides, the interest has been lost altogether. Whatever the factors responsible for this drift, the unfortunate fact remains that at present few economists and sociologists have even a modicum of interest or competence in the other's subject-matter.

It is our conviction that the trend of divergence between the interests of the respective fields must be reversed. If economics is to retain and build on the theoretical achievements of its great tradition and at the same time achieve greater empirical determinacy, it must extend beyond its traditional range of theoretical interests and resources. Conversely, if sociology, social anthropology and social psychology are to develop sophisticated bodies of theory, they must take advantage of the model which has ordered an extremely important range of the determinants of human behaviour and which impinges directly on their work at many points. In short, neither the economist nor the "behavioural scientist" can afford to ignore what lies over the boundaries of his disciplines.

ECONOMICS BIBLIOGRAPHY

GENERAL

American Economic Association, *Readings in Price Theory* (Chicago: Irwin, 1952). Essays and articles on the mechanism of supply and demand, and the conditions for the operations of each.

Clemence, R. V. (ed.), *Readings in Economic Analysis* (Cambridge, Mass.: Addison-Wesley Press, 1950). Reprints of outstanding journal articles and essays extending over a wide range of economic topics.

Harris, S. E. (ed.), *The New Economics* (New York: A. A. Knopf, London: D. Dobson, 1947). Essays summarizing, criticizing, and evaluating the Keynesian contribution to economics.

Keynes, J. M., *General Theory of Employment, Interest, and Money* (New York: Harcourt, Brace and Company, London: Macmillan & Co., 1936). The classic of Keynesian theory.

Knight, F. H., *The Ethics of Competition* (London: George Allen & Unwin, Ltd., 1935). Essays touching many borderline problems of economic theory.

Marshall, A., *Principles of Economics* (Eighth Edition; London: Macmillan, 1925). The most extensive development of neo-classical theory.

Pigou, A. C., *Unemployment* (London: Williams & Norgate, 1913). A development of neo-classical theory in the field of employment.

Ricardo, D., *Principles of Political Economy and Taxation*, ed. E. C. G. Gonner (London: G. Bell and Sons, 1913). The theoretical masterpiece of the classical economics in the narrower technical sense.

Smith, A., *The Wealth of Nations*, ed. Cannon, E. (Fourth Edition; Methuen and Co., 1925). The earliest classic of traditional economics in the English-speaking world.

Taussig, F. W., *Principles of Economics* (New York: Macmillan, 1911). A comprehensive general survey which has been widely influential.

WELFARE ECONOMICS

Boulding, K. E., "Welfare Economics" in *A Survey of Contemporary Economics*, ed. B. F. Haley, Vol. II (Homewood, Ill.; Richard D. Irwin, Inc., 1952). A brief summary of the issues of welfare economics.

Lerner, A., *Economics of Control* (New York: Macmillan, 1944). A development of welfare economics, and its application to pricing and other problems.

Little, I. M. D., *A Critique of Welfare Economics* (Oxford: The Clarendon Press, 1950). A primarily methodological treatment of "classical" notions of welfare, of the new welfare economics, and the applications of welfare economics.

Pareto, V., *The Mind and Society* (New York: Harcourt, Brace and Company; London: J. Cape, 1935). Vol. IV, Ch. XIII, secs. 2111–2146. A sensitive analysis of types of welfare and the logical relations among these types.

Pigou, A. C., *The Economics of Welfare* (Fourth Edition; London: Macmillan, 1932). A neo-classical statement of the principles of welfare economics.

MARKET STRUCTURE

Chamberlin, E. N., *The Theory of Monopolistic Competition* (Sixth Edition; Cambridge, Mass.: Harvard University Press, 1948). An economic classification of types of imperfection and analysis of the economic consequences of these types.

Florence, P. S., *The Logic of British and American Industry* (London: Routledge & Kegan Paul; Chapel Hill: University of North Carolina Press, 1953). An inquiry into the determinants of market structure, with emphasis on size of firm, segmentation, and productive efficiency.

Marshall, A., *Industry and Trade* (London: Macmillan, 1923). A comprehensive survey of the empirical setting of economic processes.

National Resources Planning Board, *The Structure of the American Economy* (Washington, D.C., 1939–40). A primarily empirical treatment of economic organization in the United States before 1940.

Robinson, E. A. G., *Monopoly* (London: Nibset, 1941). Types, bases and effects of monopoly.

Robinson, J., *The Economics of Imperfect Competition* (London: Macmillan, 1948). A theoretical treatment of the resultant supply-demand equilibrium under various conditions of market imperfection.

Schumpeter, J. A., *Capitalism, Socialism, and Democracy* (New York: Harper & Bros., 1942; London: Allen & Unwin, 1949). An assessment of the larger social setting of the modern economy in Western countries.

Temporary National Economic Committee, *Concentration of Economic Power* (Washington: U.S. Government Printing Office, 1939–41). An empirical investigation of the clustering of industry and commerce in the American economy.

THE BUSINESS CYCLE AND RELATED PROBLEMS

American Economic Association, *Readings in Business Cycle Theory* (Philadelphia: Blakiston, 1946).

Duesenberry, J., *Income, Saving and the Theory of Consumer Behaviour* (Cambridge, Mass.: Harvard University Press, 1949). Critique of the Keynesian theory of consumption and development of an alternative theory.

Hansen, A. H., *Business Cycles and National Income* (New York: Norton; London: Allen & Unwin, 1951). Primarily Keynesian treatment of economic fluctuations.

Hicks, J. R., *The Trade Cycle* (Oxford: The Clarendon Press, 1950). A highly developed model of the trade cycle, superimposed on a steadily growing economy.

Kalecki, M., *Essays in the Theory of Economic Fluctuations* (New York: Farrar & Rinehart, Inc.; London: Allen & Unwin, 1939). Development of yet another model of the trade cycle.

Oxford University Institute of Statistics, *Economics of Full Employment* (Oxford: B. Blackwell, 1944). Essays in the conditions for fully-employed resources.

Samuelson, P. A., "Interaction between the Multiplier Analysis and the Principle of Acceleration," *Review of Economic Statistics*, 1939, pp. 75–78. The simple mathematics of income fluctuations.

Schumpeter, J. A., *Business Cycles* (New York: McGraw-Hill, 1939). The place of economic fluctuations in Schumpeter's theory of economic development.

ECONOMIC DEVELOPMENT AND RELATED PROBLEMS

Baumol, W. J., *Economic Dynamics* (New York: Macmillan, 1951), Part I. A comparison of the models of growth of the classical writers, Marx, Schumpeter, and Harrod.

Dewhurst, J. F., *et al., America's Needs and Resources* (New York: The Twentieth Century Fund, 1947. New Edition, 1955). Comprehensive empirical data on the American Economy and its trend of development.

Domar, E. V., "Capital Expansion, Rate of Growth and Employment," *Econometrica*, April, 1946. An example of a recent equilibrium theory of economic growth.

Harrod, R. F., *Towards a Dynamic Economics* (London: Macmillan, 1948). A model similar to that of Domar, but more fully developed.

Lowe, A., "The Classical Theory of Growth," *Social Research*, September, 1954. Comparative analysis of classical statements of the conditions for economic development.

Marx, K., *Capital* (New York: Modern Library; London: Allen & Unwin, 1906). The classic text of socialistic economic theory.

Rostow, W. W., *The Process of Economic Growth* (New York: Norton, 1952). A treatment of economic development as a resultant of the interplay of a certain range of human propensities.

Sawyer, J. E., "The Social Basis of the American System of Manufacturing," *Journal of Economic History*, 1954, pp. 361–379. A statement of the importance of value-patterns in an earlier period of American development.

Schumpeter, J. A., *Theory of Economic Development*, translated by Redvers Opie (Cambridge, Mass.: Harvard University Press, 1934). The earliest statement of Schumpeter's theory of economic development, with emphasis upon the importance of entrepreneurial activity in the process of growth.

SOCIOLOGY BIBLIOGRAPHY

Bales, R. F., *Interaction Process Analysis* (Cambridge, Mass.: Addison-Wesley Press, 1950). Cf. Chapter II for a statement of the nature of a social system.

Durkheim, E., *The Division of Labour in Society*, translated by George Simpson (Glencoe, Ill.: The Free Press, 1949). The classic sociological analysis of the division of labour and the institution of contract.

——, *Suicide*, translated by John A. Spaulding and George Simpson (Glencoe, Ill.: The Free Press; London: Routledge & Kegan Paul, 1951). A sociological classic important for Durkheim's general theory and indirectly for economics.

Firth, R., *Primitive Polynesian Economy* (London: G. Routledge & Sons, 1939) and *Primitive Economics of the New Zealand Maori* (New York: E. P. Dutton & Co.; London: Routledge & Kegan Paul, 1929). Two excellent studies of the economic systems of primitive societies.

Halevy, E., *The Growth of Philosophical Radicalism*, translated by Mary Morris (New York: Macmillan; London: E. Benn, 1928). A study of the intellectual background of the classical economics.

Henderson, L. J., *Pareto's General Sociology* (Cambridge: Harvard University Press, 1935). Important both for interpretation of Pareto and for discussion of the concept of equilibrium.

Levy, M., *The Structure of Society* (Princeton: Princeton University Press, 1952). Cf. particularly Chapter IX for a discussion of economic allocation.

Lindsay, A. D., *Karl Marx's Capital* (London: Oxford University Press, 1931). Perhaps the best broader-than-economic introduction to Marx.

Löwe, A., *Economics and Sociology* (London: Allen & Unwin, 1935). A primarily methodological treatment of the relations between economic theory and sociology.

Malinowski, B., *Coral Gardens and their Magic* (New York: American Book Company; London: Allen & Unwin, 1935). One of the best anthropological descriptions of the concrete productive activities of a primitive people.

Merton, R. K., *Social Theory and Social Structure* (Glencoe, Ill.: The Free Press, 1949). Good general orientation to theory and methodology in sociology.

Moore, W. E., *Industrialization and Labour* (Ithaca: Cornell University Press, 1951). A general discussion of the labour aspects of economic development, and a case study in Mexico.

——, *Economy and Society* (New York: Doubleday, 1955). A brief review of the relations of economic and sociological problems.

Pareto, V., *The Mind and Society* (New York: Harcourt, Brace and Company; London: J. Cape, 1935). A classic treatise of general sociological theory. Exploit relations to economics (esp. Chapter I and early part of Chapter XII) and especially subtle treatment of social and economic utility.

Parsons, T., *Structure of Social Action* (New York: McGraw-Hill, 1937). Study of the convergence of Marshall, Pareto, Durkheim, and Weber on a common conceptual scheme.

——, *The Social System* (Glencoe, Ill.: The Free Press; London: Tavistock Publications, 1951). A general statement of systematic sociological theory.

——, *Essays in Sociological Theory*, Revised Edition (Glencoe, Ill.: The Free Press, 1954). Diverse sociological subjects including motivation of economic activities, kinship, and occupational structure.

——, Bales, R. F., and Shils, E. A., *Working Papers in the Theory of Action* (Glencoe, Ill.: The Free Press, 1953). Chapter V the most immediate theoretical background of present volume.

Radcliffe-Brown, *Structure and Function in Primitive Society* (Glencoe, Ill.: The Free Press; London: Macmillan, 1952). Main theoretical statements of perhaps the leading living theorist in the field.

Troeltsch, E., *Der Historismus and seine Probleme* (Tübingen: J. C. B. Mohr, 1922). Includes perhaps the best general treatment of Marx as a social theorist.

Weber, M., *The Protestant Ethic and the Spirit of Capitalism*, translated by Talcott Parsons (New York: C. Scribner & Sons; London: Allen & Unwin, 1930). A keynote source for one major theme of this book.

——, *The Theory of Social and Economic Organization*, translated by A. M. Henderson and Talcott Parsons (New York: Oxford University Press; Edinburgh: W. Hodge, 1947). A sociological classic: Chapter II by far most comprehensive analysis of economic institutions.

Weber, M., *Gesammelte Aufsätze zur Religionssoziologie*, 3 Vols. (Tübingen: J. C. B. Mohr, 1922–23). A comprehensive comparative study of the relation between religious movements and social change. Three parts available in English translation: *The Protestant Ethic* (New York: C. Scribner & Sons, 1930); *The Religion of China* (Glencoe, Ill.: The Free Press, 1951); *Ancient Judaism* (Glencoe, Ill.: The Free Press, 1952).

INSTITUTIONS

Bakke, E. W., *The Unemployed Worker* (New Haven: Yale University Press, 1940). An analysis of the labour role at the lower levels.

Barnard, C. I., *The Functions of the Executive* (Cambridge, Mass.: Harvard University Press, 1948). An analysis of decision-making within an organizational context.

Bendix, R., and Lipset, S. M., *Class, Status and Power: A Reader in Social Stratification* (Glencoe, Ill.: The Free Press; London: Routledge & Kegan Paul, 1953). A comprehensive anthology on the institution of social stratification.

Dubin, R. (ed.), *Human Relations in Administration* (New York: Prentice-Hall, 1951). Useful collection of sociological materials on organization and administration.

Mauss, M., *The Gift* (translated by T. Cunnison, Glencoe, Ill.: The Free Press; London: Cohen & West, 1954). An analysis of exchange, with emphasis on comparisons with non-literate societies.

Merton, R. K., *et. al.*, *Reader in Bureaucracy* (Glencoe, Ill.: The Free Press, 1952).

Noyes, C. R., *The Institution of Property* (New York: Longmans, Green and Co., 1936). A broad legal and sociological analysis of a central economic institution.

Roethlisberger, F. J., and Dickson, W. J., *Management and the Worker* (Cambridge, Mass.: Harvard University Press, 1939). A classic in the field of industrial sociology.

Stouffer, S. A., *et al.*, *The American Soldier* (Princeton: Princeton University Press, 1949). Comprehensive study of many aspects of organization and bureaucracy.

Veblen, T., *The Theory of Business Enterprise* (New York: G. Scribner's & Sons, 1904) and *The Instinct of Workmanship* (New York: Macmillan; London: Allen & Unwin, 1914). Institutions as conceptualized in the institutionalist movement in American economics.

Vogt, E. Z., *Modern Homesteaders* (Cambridge Mass.: Harvard University Press, 1955). Recent study of economy and society in an isolated farming community.

FAMILY AND CONSUMPTION

Anshen, R. N. (ed.), *The Family: Its Function and Destiny* (New York: Harper, 1949). A general anthology on kinship structure.

Katona, G., *Psychological Analysis of Economic Behaviour* (New York: McGraw-Hill, 1951). Cf. Part II for an empirical analysis of consumption and saving patterns.

Lévi-Strauss, C., *Les structures elementaires de la parente* (Paris: Presses Universitaires de France, 1949). One of the most suggestive comparative studies of kinship.

Murdock, G. P., *Social Structure* (New York: Macmillan, 1949). A cross-cultural analysis of kinship structure.

Parsons, T., Bales, R. F., *et al., Family, Socialization and Interaction Process* (Glencoe, Ill.: The Free Press; London: Routledge & Kegan Paul, 1955). A basis in family sociology for analysis of consumption and occupational roles.

Radcliffe-Brown, *Introduction to African Systems of Kinship and Marriage* (London: for the International African Institute by the Oxford University Press, 1950). The classic comparative study of kinship.

Warner, W. L., and Lunt, P. S., *The Social Life of a Modern Community* (New Haven: Yale University Press, 1941). Cf. Chapters XV, XIX for analysis of class differentials in consumption.

Zimmerman, C. C., *Consumption and Standards of Living* (New York: D. Van Nostrand; London: Williams & Norgate, 1936). A broad survey of problems in the field of consumption.

SOCIAL CHANGE

Ogburn, W. F., *Social Change* (New York: Viking Press, 1950). An influential sociological view.

Sombart, W., *Der moderne Kapitalismus* (Leipzig: Duncker & Humblot, 1902). An attempt to trace and interpret the historical forms of capitalism.

Troeltsch, E., *Der Historismus und seine Probleme* (Tübingen: J. C. B. Mohr, 1922). A comprehensive survey of 19th Century theories of history.

Weber, M., *The Theory of Social and Economic Organization*, translated by A. M. Henderson and Talcott Parsons (New York: Oxford University Press; Edinburgh: W. Hodge, 1947), especially Chapter III: the theory of charisma and its routinization.

INDEX